1865

**THE GOLDEN AGE
OF MOUNTAINEERING**

Gilles Modica

1865
THE GOLDEN AGE
OF MOUNTAINEERING

—

Translated from the French
by Deke Dusinberre

First published in French in 2015 by Éditions Guérin under the title
1865, l'âge d'or de l'alpinisme by Gilles Modica.

This English edition first published in 2016 by Vertebrate Publishing and Éditions Paulsen.

www.editionspaulsen.com
www.v-publishing.co.uk

Gilles Modica has asserted his rights under the Copyright, Designs and Patents Act 1988
to be identified as author of this work.

ISBN: 978-1-910240-52-6

Design and production by Éditions Paulsen.
www.editionspaulsen.com

Cover illustration: The conquest of the Matterhorn and the protagonists of 14 July 1865:
E. Whymper, C. Hudson, M. Croz, Lord F. Douglas, D.R. Hadow, P. Taugwalder father and son.
© Gustave Doré (1832–1883). Paris, Musée d'Orsay, kept in the Louvre Museum.

Following his first ascent of the Matterhorn a famous mountaineer
was asked what he thought of the view from the summit.
'Beautiful,' he said. 'The only thing missing was the Matterhorn.'

Franz Schrader
À quoi tient la beauté des montagnes?
(Annuaire du Club Alpin Français, 1898)

CONTENTS I

A few pioneers of the golden age, including the two great guides who led the way on the Brenva spur, Melchior Anderegg and his cousin Jakob Anderegg. Standing (L–R): M. Anderegg, R.J.S. MacDonald, F.C. Grove, J. Anderegg and P. Taugwalder the younger. Seated (L–R): L. Stephen, W.S. Short, E.N. Buxton, R. Liveing and F.F. Tuckett.

THE YEAR 1865 CAPPED A DECADE of first ascents all across the Alps. From the Wetterhorn in 1854 to the Matterhorn in 1865, that decade laid the foundations of mountaineering — its techniques, equipment, clubs, scrambles and climbs, as well as its imagery, its nightmares and its literature.

The Alps thus became what Leslie Stephen called a 'playground'. Eugène Rambert described mountaineering as a noble game, and H.B. George viewed it as sporting entertainment. But it was the Reverend W.A.B. Coolidge (1850–1926) who coined the felicitous label for this period: 'the golden age of mountaineering'. After 1854, an ever-growing host of 'gentlemen' and their guides raced up ridges and summits in a movement that was, in fact, already over half a century old. So the 'golden age' basically corresponds to a change in mentality: science was no longer the only acknowledged justification for conquest. Climbing a peak, whether virgin or not, became a question of a game jointly played by a number of clubs. The first such association, the Alpine Club, was founded in London in 1857, bringing together a new breed of gentleman armed with an alpenstock and shod like the shaggy guides he hired at the foot of the peaks. According to Charles Hudson, 'We went abroad for recreation: it was pleasure that we sought; and we gave but little thought to useful discovery. True it is, that the pleasure was of a noble and an elevating character.'

In France itself, the game was first dubbed *alpinisme* in the 1876 annual report of the Club Alpin Français. The same *Annuaire* had already referred to *alpinistes* in 1874, but the term only slowly replaced previous favourites such as 'ascensionists', 'excursionists', and 'tourists', or expressions such as 'Alpine scrambler' or 'Alpine traveller'.

The founding of clubs created an alpine milieu and generated so-called 'mountaineering literature' comprised of personal, subjective accounts of adventures and impressions, with no scientific pretensions. At the heart of such literature was the tale of a climb. Edward Whymper published *Scrambles Amongst the Alps* in 1871, immediately translated into French by Adolphe Joanne (1813–1881), who travelled on foot, wrote tourist guides, and was one of the founding members of the Club Alpin Français in Grenoble in 1874. Whymper's book, illustrated with his own engravings, made a lasting impression on Western minds — and not just for its thrilling account of the 1865 Matterhorn disaster. It was a lively book full of refined wit, becoming a classic of mountaineering adventures, as well as Whymper's sole literary masterpiece.

Between 1786 and 1854, an earlier movement – *ascensionnisme* – had constituted a sixty-year prelude to the birth of mountaineering. Some ascensionists were alpinists unbeknown to themselves, savouring and ruminating over their avowed pleasure, becoming what Émile Javelle, that poet of the peaks, called 'useless members of the club' – useless to science, that is. Instead, they preferred the risks and thrills of the game so wonderfully recounted by Whymper. It was a game played by a few travellers and guides who formed a team or 'party', sometimes roping themselves together, sometimes not. They were a 'happy few' wandering among the virgin Alps.

The names of these lucky souls will crop up frequently in this book. They include, among others, the guides: from the Oberland came Christian Almer, Melchior Anderegg, Jakob Anderegg, Ulrich and Christian Lauener, Peter Bohren; from Valais, Johann Josef Bennen; from Valtournenche, Jean-Antoine Carrel; and from Chamonix, Auguste Balmat, Auguste Simond, and Michel Croz and his brother Jean-Baptiste. Then there were the English travellers: John Ball, Alfred Wills, William Mathews, Leslie Stephen, E.S. Kennedy, T.S. Kennedy, Francis Fox Tuckett, Charles Hudson, Douglas Freshfield, John Tyndall, A.W. Moore, and Edward Whymper.

Without the literature produced by these travellers, we would know little of those great guides, who had often been hardened chamois hunters before turning their sights on virgin peaks. Some of those summits, whether round or pyramidal, blunt or sharp, offered themselves up easily, while others held out, like the Matterhorn with its four defensive ridges. On 29 June 1865, just below the summit of the Aiguille Verte, certain of victory, Christian Almer cried, 'Ah, Aiguille Verte, now you are well and truly dead!'

A list of conquests was like a collection of trophies standing tall on the horizon. That inaccessible peak, the mountain of mountains, the Matterhorn – also known as the Cervin or Gran Becca – finally fell on 14 July 1865 after eighteen attempts spanning nine years. Yet this end was merely a beginning, because virgin routes up conquered summits already gleamed like future trophies in the eyes of certain mountaineers. On 15 July 1865, the Brenva spur on Mont Blanc was first climbed. Modern mountaineering was launched, well and truly launched, from peak to spur. No fewer than sixty-five first ascents were made in 1865 alone, forty-three of them on totally virgin summits. Such mastery already. But a mastery incomprehensible without an understanding of the ten-year-long golden age.

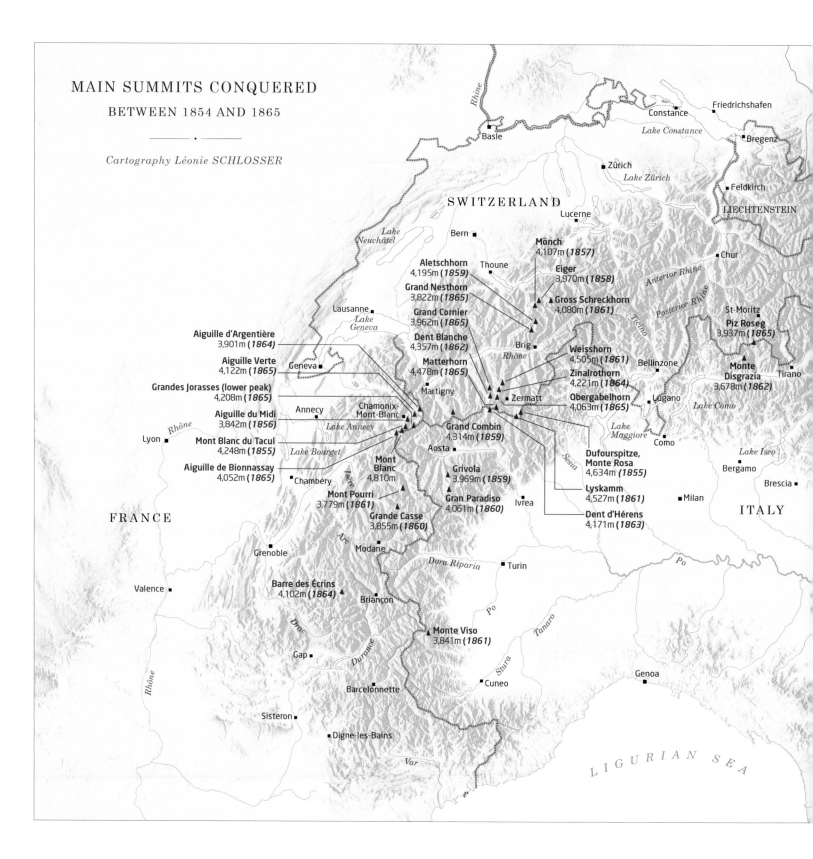

MAIN SUMMITS CONQUERED

BETWEEN 1854 AND 1865

—————— • ——————

Cartography Léonie SCHLOSSER

SWITZERLAND

LIECHTENSTEIN

FRANCE

ITALY

LIGURIAN SEA

Friedrichshafen

Constance

Lake Constance

Bregenz

Zürich

Lake Zürich

Feldkirch

Basle

Chur

Anterior Rhine

Rhine

Lucerne

Bern

Mönch
4,107m (*1857*)

Eiger
3,970m (*1858*)

Posterior Rhine

St-Moritz

Thoune

Aletschhorn
4,195m (*1859*)

Gross Schreckhorn
4,080m (*1861*)

Ticino

Piz Roseg
3,937m (*1865*)

Lake Neuchâtel

Grand Nesthorn
3,822m (*1865*)

Grand Cornier
3,962m (*1865*)

Brig

Weisshorn
4,505m (*1861*)

Bellinzone

Monte Disgrazia
3,678m (*1862*)

Tirano

Lausanne

Lake Geneva

Dent Blanche
4,357m (*1862*)

Rhône

Zinalrothorn
4,221m (*1864*)

Aiguille d'Argentière
3,901m (*1864*)

Matterhorn
4,478m (*1865*)

Zermatt

Obergabelhorn
4,063m (*1865*)

Lugano

Lake Como

Aiguille Verte
4,122m (*1865*)

Geneva

Martigny

Lake Maggiore

Como

Grandes Jorasses (lower peak)
4,208m (*1865*)

Annecy

Grand Combin
4,314m (*1859*)

Lake Iseo

Aiguille du Midi
3,842m (*1856*)

Chamonix-Mont-Blanc

Lake Annecy

Dufourspitze, Monte Rosa
4,634m (*1855*)

Bergamo

Lyon

Rhône

Mont Blanc du Tacul
4,248m (*1855*)

Lake Bourget

Aosta

Grivola
3,969m (*1859*)

Lyskamm
4,527m (*1861*)

Milan

Brescia

Aiguille de Bionnassay
4,052m (*1865*)

Chambéry

Mont Blanc
4,810m

Gran Paradiso
4,061m (*1860*)

Ivrea

Dent d'Hérens
4,171m (*1863*)

Mont Pourri
3,779m (*1861*)

Grande Casse
3,855m (*1860*)

Arc

Modane

Isère

Grenoble

Dora Riparia

Turin

Valence

Barre des Écrins
4,102m (*1864*)

Briançon

Drac

Po

Monte Viso
3,841m (*1861*)

Tanaro

Gap

Durance

Stura

Genoa

Barcelonnette

Cuneo

Sisteron

Digne-les-Bains

Var

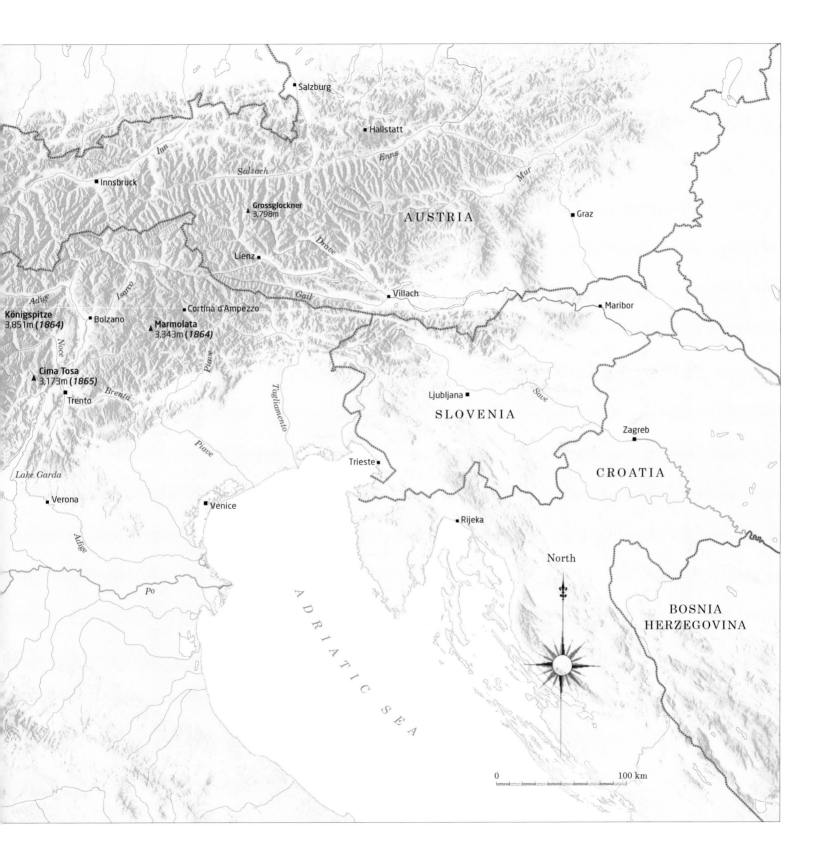

■ Salzburg

■ Hallstatt

Inn

■ Innsbruck

Salzach

Enns

Mur

▲ **Grossglockner**
3,798m

AUSTRIA

■ Graz

Drave

Isarco

■ Lienz

Gail

■ Villach

Adige

Königspitze
3,851m *(1864)*

■ Bolzano

■ Cortina d'Ampezzo

▲ **Marmolata**
3,343m *(1864)*

■ Maribor

Noce

Piave

Cima Tosa
3,173m *(1865)*

Brenta

■ Trento

Tagliamento

Save

■ Ljubljana

SLOVENIA

■ Zagreb

Piave

■ Trieste

CROATIA

Lake Garda

■ Verona

■ Venice

■ Rijeka

North

Adige

Po

**BOSNIA
HERZEGOVINA**

A D R I A T I C   S E A

0   100 km

EARLY ASCENTS

(1744-1854)

28 July 1800 was a red-letter day in the annals of the eastern Alps, as a party headed toward the summit of the Grossglockner. By Markus Pernhart, 1857.

THE FIRST ASCENT OF MONT BLANC was made in 1786. This escapade enjoyed the fate it deserved thanks to the efforts and fame of Genevan naturalist Horace-Bénédict de Saussure who, after making the third ascent in 1787, let it be known far and wide. After Mont Blanc (4,810 metres), the next great summit of the Alps to be conquered was the Jungfrau (4,158 metres) in Oberland, on 3 August 1811. Rodolphe and Jérôme Meyer, the sons of a rich merchant from Aarau, who also published maps, found a route up to the summit from the south-east, guided by two hunters from Lötschental.

The Meyers planted a flag on the summit. But their claim was challenged because the flag could not be seen from all the points it should have been visible. Accusations of error – or, more serious, of lying and imposture – are the rule in the history of the major victories of exploration. Accounts always lack accuracy when read with a jealous or disbelieving eye. Cairns may topple, winds may flatten or shred flags. A leading citizen or merchant said to be worthy of implicit trust may one day acquire the reputation of a deceiver or deceived: trust, everything rested on trust, from a marriage contract

The chalets of Grindelwald, below the Wetterhorn.

to a cairn on Jungfrau. And since everything rested on trust, there was all the more reason for wariness and suspicion.

Woe to the naïve! Anyone who made it to the top but failed to make it known in the right way would regret it. The people of Grindelwald refused to take anyone at their word, and doubted any ascent if a *flagge* did not fly clearly on the summit. When Alfred Wills climbed the Wetterhorn in 1854 – the third ascent, but passed off as a first by his guide – he shelled out for a metallic flag and was glad he did. On his return to Grindelwald he was greeted with suspicion despite the flag clearly visible to anyone of good faith. 'I never saw such a race of unbelievers as the people of Grindelwald,' wrote Wills, a judge by profession and therefore accustomed to doubting a witness.

The same wariness and doubt could be found at Chamonix. Impatient, angry disbelief greeted the first ascent of the Aiguille Verte by Whymper and his two Oberland guides, Christian Almer and Franz Biener, on 29 June 1865. On the second ascent a few days later, a group composed of G.C. Hodgkinson, Charles Hudson, and T.S. Kennedy guided by Michel Croz, Michel A. Ducroz, and Peter Perren, carefully planted two flags on the summit. A brief account of that ascent published in *L'Abeille du Chamonix* by Reverend Hudson, who had conquered Mont Blanc without guides in 1855, stated that, 'two flags were planted on the summit. Both can be seen from La Flégère and various other points in the valley'. The summit of the Aiguille Verte is capped with snow and ice – although Whymper had stuck a piece of rope in the snow, it was never seen again.

Being born and honourably known in Chamonix, not to mention being a good Catholic and a member of the Compagnie des Guides, was no protection against doubt or mute accusations. That is why Jean Charlet, a guide from Argentière near Chamonix, took

three implements on his solo attempt on the Petit Dru in 1876: an ice axe, a rope, and a flag. He needed the axe to get up, the rope to get back down, and the flag to serve as proof.

The younger member of the Meyer family, Gottlieb, had to repeat his brothers' ascent of the Jungfrau in 1812 with two hunters from Valais. The three men took a different route, Concordia Platz, which is now the normal route. Their solidly planted flag could be seen, beyond the shadow of a doubt, from the Strahlegg pass.

During that same expedition, the two hunters, Alois Volker and Joseph Bortis, may have made the first ascent of the Finsteraarhorn in the company of Arnold Abbuhl, a porter from Guttannen. Once again the reality of the claim was challenged. W.A.B. Coolidge, who knew the area like the back of his hand and who read the Meyer brothers' account through the lens of his experience, had no doubts about the success of their ascent of 1812. But the Finsteraarhorn (4,274 metres), that king of the Bernese Alps, only fell

The Finsteraarhorn, vanquished by chamois hunters from Valais. Early Swiss climbers. Illustration from F.J. Hugi's Voyages Scientifiques dans les Alpes, *1830.*

with complete certainty on 10 August 1829, to two guides accompanying a geologist from Soleure, Franz Josef Hugi, who himself gave up on the final slope. The two guides made sure to leave the usual traces of their passage, such as cairn and flag.

Männli: Little man

Steinmann means 'man of stone' in German. *Männli,* in Swiss German, means 'little man'. The word cairn, meanwhile, is Celtic, and is still used for the little pyramid of stones that grows on the summit with each ascent, provided that both time and stones are available. It is hard to imagine the moral and philosophical import that certain nineteenth-century mountaineering writers gave to the building of a *männli* or cairn on a great virgin summit.

Take Eugène Rambert (1830–1886), a writer from Lausanne who is forgotten today because he was Swiss. An article from 1864 has the contemporary-sounding title of 'The Pleasures of a Climber'.

The humble pyramids that now crown most of the high points in the Alps do not merely hoist proof of our nothingness aloft, they also bear witness to our perseverance in the eternal scheme of things, indicating that sentient beings have not given up just yet. These pyramids are simultaneously trophies and altars – they are *männli*, as we say in Swiss German, testifying to the fact that man has passed this way. Everyone who has had the good luck to build one with his own hands cannot fail to experience, on laying the first stone, a clearer feeling of what it means to be human, and to be privately moved by the witness he has been charged to bear. With labour as with play: most games contain some symbolism – chess simulates battle, ascents represent a conquest. And of all games an ascent is the only one that creates the illusion of what Columbus must have felt when claiming possession of a new world.

Early Swiss climbers.

Cairn, stick and flag – signs of mankind's pride in human accomplishment.

In 1842, when the Finsteraarhorn was climbed for the third time, rods of iron, rusty nails and scraps of fabrics testified to the two previous ascents. (Placing a bottle at the summit, or else a little tin box to hold the calling cards of travellers, were somewhat later traditions that became widespread during the golden age.) In 1839 brothers Pierre and Benoît Magnin from Saint-Jean-de-Maurienne left coins on the central peak of the Aiguilles d'Arves – irrefutable proof of a first ascent that had been doubted until the coins were found thirty-seven years later, in 1876, by Italian climbers who were unaware of that earlier climb.

Swiss forerunners

The Swiss – of every faith and station (naturalists, topographers, chamois hunters, inn-keepers, servants at a mountain hospice, roofers, foresters, priests and monks) – preceded the English in the conquest of the Alps. There was no particular connection between mountaineering and Protestantism, as one might be tempted to think due to Saussure and his Genevan friends and colleagues.

Placidus a Spescha (1752–1833), a Benedictine monk from the Disentis monastery in the canton of Grisons, explored the mountains of central Switzerland, including the Rheinwaldhorn (3,402 metres) in 1789, the Oberalpstock (3,328 metres, the highest point of the Disentis area) in 1792, Piz Urlaun (3,359 metres) in the Tödi chain in 1793, Piz Aul (3,121 metres) in 1801, and Piz Terri (3,149 metres) in 1802. W.A.B. Coolidge, the undisputed master of Alpine erudition, had great esteem for the Benedictine monk and ranked him, alongside Saussure, as a leading precursor: 'In early Alpine history the name of Spescha must always be bracketed with that of Saussure.'

Placidus a Spescha.

Spescha on the Rheinwaldhorn.

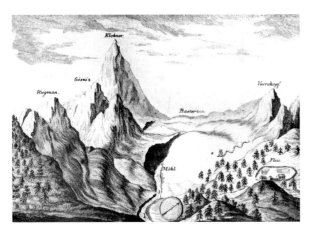

The earliest known drawing of the Glockner, by B. Hacquet, 1782.

The peak of Grossglockner seen from Kleinglockner.

Spescha was not an isolated case among clergy of the day. It is a little-known fact that ecclesiastics played a major role in the early conquest of the Alps from 1744 to 1854. It might be added that clergymen were rarely absent from accounts of the second period. Priests would receive travellers at their homes, advising or even hosting them, recommending this or that chamois hunter as reputable and trustworthy. In certain cases, such as in the parish of Saas, Father Johann Josef Imseng was the first real local explorer – a true hunter of summits and a team leader – as were certain Austrian priests in the eastern Alps at the turn of the century.

Higher than the Glockner

A red-letter day in the annals of the eastern Alps was 28 July 1800, when five men climbed to the top of Grossglockner (3,798 metres), the 'big bell-ringer' of Carinthia in the Hohe Tauern range. Franz von Salm, the prince-bishop (and later cardinal) of Carinthia, had long prepared the ascent of this double, bell-shaped mountain (hence its name), which towered over the valleys of his diocese. The lesser peak, Kleinglockner (3,770 metres), was reached in 1799 from the village of Heiligenblut to the south, but hardly satisfied the prince-bishop, who financed a climbing party of seventy-two people the very next year. Almost all gave up before reaching the Kleinglockner, and two more halted at the narrow ridge, broken by a gap, that separated the two summits. Five men nevertheless stubbornly made the short journey across the highly exposed ridge, reaching the summit of Grossglockner. All were carpenters and roofers, as though woodworking predisposed them to climbing and overcoming a fear of heights. All except one, that is: Abbé Horash, the priest of Doellach. Like Father Placidus a Spescha, he was a man of the church, although a member of the secular clergy.

A cross was erected on the summit the day following the ascent. That day Abbé Horash was replaced by a future priest, Valentin Stanig (1774–1847), who got into the spirit of things by climbing to the top of the pole planted near the cross. Stanig said he wanted to 'be higher than the Glockner or any one else who had climbed it'. This lover of lofty perches would go on to make many climbs in the eastern Alps in his cassock – including a few first ascents of major peaks, such as the Watzmann in 1801 – botanising as he went along. Coolidge, having read Stanig's accounts, was struck by his enthusiasm and said Stanig was 'deservedly reckoned as the earliest amateur mountaineer in the eastern Alps'.

Swiss priests

The Vélan (3,371 metres) is a major peak overlooking the valley of Entremont in the Swiss canton of Valais, protected by the Valsorey glacier. Its mountaineering history began with the keen enthusiasm of another man in a cassock, Abbé Murith. Originally from Sembrancher in Valais, the priest of Liddes was a naturalist in his spare time, and was in contact with all the naturalists and physicists in Geneva, including Saussure, whom he liked to receive as a guest. One day, while still young, Abbé Murith climbed Mont Vélan with two chamois hunters, encountering difficulties on an icy slope. The abbé himself attacked the ice.

As he wrote to Saussure:

> How happy I would have been to have had you alongside me. You would have enjoyed the finest spectacle imaginable for a lover of mountains and glaciers; you would have been able to gaze upon a vast circle of mountains with their different heights from Turin to Petit-Saint-Bernard, from Mont Blanc to Lake Geneva, from Vevey to Saint-Gothard, and from Saint-Gothard

The summit of the Glockner, by Markus Pernhart, 1857.

Abbé Laurent-Joseph Murith.

Horace-Bénédict de Saussure, after Jean-Pierre Saint-Ours.

to Turin. But I dare not go so far as to propose this ravishing sight to you, for I had far too much difficulty myself, despite my boldness, in reaching that icy colossus.

The bold young abbé later became prior of the Great Saint Bernard monastery. Yet another Swiss clergyman, the priest of Champéry in the Illiez valley, managed to arrive at the top of the Dents du Midi (3,257 metres) – or, at least, one of the peaks of that grandiose mountain high in the sky over Lake Geneva – during one aimless trek on 22 August 1788, thanks to the grace of God.

Over fifty virgin summits for the Swiss

Between 1744, when monks from the abbey of Engelberg made the first ascent of Titlis (3,238 metres) in central Switzerland, and 1865, the year the Matterhorn was conquered, Swiss travellers reached more than fifty summits taller than 3,000 metres. Titlis, Buet (3,096 metres) and Vélan were all conquered prior to Mont Blanc.

Swiss historian Charles Gros, a fount of Alpine scholarship, has justly stressed Swiss primacy and pre-eminence in exploration of the Alps. The most famous Swiss explorer was of course Horace-Bénédict de Saussure, the Genevan scholar who began travelling in the Alps prior to 1770. Although the goal of those expeditions was scientific, his passion for the mountains was the initial spur, the prime mover, as he acknowledged in the four-volume opus he completed in 1796, *Voyages dans les Alpes.* In it, Saussure described his early enthusiasm for the mountains. By the first half of the nineteenth century, every educated European was reading, quoting and honouring Saussure. He became a model for the scientists who followed, as well as standard reading for all travellers to Switzerland and its glaciers. But Saussure's fame masks the broader movement of exploration and conquest that extended beyond his personal tale. The Alpine voyages of the golden age were rooted in that earlier movement, and would be incomprehensible without that wave of exploration, which the English turned into a game to be played for fun, devoid of scientific purpose.

Noble game: Eugène Rambert

The idea of climbing for fun – a noble game with an element of chance – was already in the air. Swiss writer Eugène Rambert developed the theory as early as November 1864 in the first chapter of his book on the Swiss Alps. 'I have always found a strong analogy between the pleasure to be had from ascents and the pleasure of games.' Later in the same chapter on the fun of climbing he added, 'Ascents, or scrambles as they are called by a witty fellow who adores them and jokes about them, are perhaps of all games the one that best allows one to savour the pleasure of feeling alive'. Given this game-playing attitude, Rambert promoted the idea of climbing without a guide. Remaining behind a guide meant sacrificing half the pleasure of a game played unaided. 'Many climbers rely on their guides – they let themselves be led, they merely follow. Understood thus, the game is spoilt, losing half its appeal. Ascents made by oneself offer a far fuller pleasure. True enough, one must seek one's way, study the mountain, make multiple tries, redo all or part of the attempts already made by others, but therein lies the interest … those are the true stakes and great contests.'

Conceived as a kind of Alpine encyclopaedia complete with accounts and personal considerations, Rambert's five-volume *Les Alpes Suisses* never met the success in France that its author might have expected. Himself a charter member of the Club Alpin Suisse, he described and advocated mountaineering without guides as early as 1864, with all the sincerity and enthusiasm of a fair-minded player. Rambert even discussed, with the usual caution,

Eugène Rambert's Alpine encyclopaedia.

solitary climbs. 'A few tourists have reached the point where they attempt truly difficult passages alone. While this is not impossible for a Tyndall or a Weilenmann, it should not be recommended to anyone, for in most cases it would be extremely imprudent. Two or three experienced amateurs, however, could try it without risk, especially if they are accustomed to travelling together.'

Fancy English tourists
The golden age cast its shadow over the Swiss mountaineers of the earlier period, creating the illusion that the sporting challenge was only born with the gentlemen of the Alpine Club. Coolidge pointed out 'that before about 1840 very few Englishmen made any high ascents, a fact which is certainly curious'. The absence of the English in the saga of erecting the first cairns is all the more striking in that the English constituted the bulk of travellers who in summer occupied the fashionable inns – guaranteed free of fleas – and who visited the Swiss cantons. Parties of 'fancy' tourists hiked up Mont Rigi (1,789 metres), the most accessible of vantage points, armed with metal-tipped walking sticks and guides to handle the donkeys or mules.

It was not until the next generation of travellers – the likes of J.D. Forbes, Alfred Wills and John Ball – that the English abandoned the beaten paths, discarding the image of fancy tourists lounging on terraces, as mocked by Genevan wit Rodolphe Töpffer.

The same comment could be made of the Pyrenees, where the movement began by the late eighteenth century as a direct consequence of the conquest of Mont Blanc and Saussure's publications. The politician, author and naturalist Louis Ramond de Carbonnières (1755–1827) reached the summit of Monte Perdido (3,355 metres) on 10 August 1802, having been preceded a few days earlier by his guides, who paved the way. Ramond de

A chart of the relative altitudes of the main European mountains, 1828.

Archduke John of Austria's party heading for the summit of the Grossvenediger, 1828.

Carbonnières compared Monte Perdido – 'Mont Perdu' in French – to Mont Blanc, recommending both trips. 'From Mont Blanc itself one must come straight to Monte Perdido. When one has seen the first among granitic mountains, there remains the first among limestone mountains.'

Austrian explorers

Mountain exploration was a Europe-wide movement. By 1841, three great peaks in the Tyrol at the other end of the Alps had already been added to the list of conquests: Ortler (3,905 metres), Grossglockner (3,798 metres) and Grossvenediger (3,666 metres). In the case of the Grossvenediger, during one attempt none other than Archduke John of Austria (1782–1859), seventh son of a future emperor of Austria, hiked alongside the seventeen men of his party. The party retreated on 9 August 1828 after a salvo of fresh snow knocked one of his men, an imperial forester, into a crevasse. The man, who was rescued, was Paul Rohregger, the key player in the archduke's scheme. Rohregger remained convinced that the Grossvenediger was still feasible, which he demonstrated fourteen years later, on 3 September 1841, at the head of a party of twenty-six – but with no archduke – which reached the summit by the south-east face.

The Ortler, that citadel of the Tyrol, and the peak that geographers elevated to the highest point in the Austrian Empire, succumbed to a plan laid by Archduke John. During a trip to the upper valley of the Adige he was struck by the majesty of the mountain's glaciers and ridges, and entrusted the mission of climbing it to his liegeman, Gebhard. Following a series of failures with guides from Zillertal, Gerhard looked for new men. Three local hunters, whose progress Gebhard followed through a telescope, skirted the glaciers and attained victory on their first attempt, on 27 September

The Rigi and the old Habsburg castle near Lake Lucerne.

Archduke John of Austria.

A party on the slopes of the Ortler.

1804, via the rocks on the mountain's south-western flank. The next year Gebhard himself repeated the ascent, setting out from the town of Sulden and taking the mountain's south-east ridge, the Hintergrat. It was a much better route, identified by the guide of the first ascent, Josephe 'Josele' Pichler. A large bonfire burned for two hours on the summit of the Ortler before the party slowly snaked its way down by torchlight. This torchlit descent of the Ortler became a legend in the region, as did the treks, ideas and garments of Archduke John, often dressed as a Styrian hunter.

Thirty years later, during a fourth ascent, Josele, who had wielded the torches on Hintergrat, was hale enough at age seventy to lead a trip up the Ortler and deal with the rocks on the ridge. His travelling companion was a priest from Salzburg wearing round, thick spectacles, Peter Karl Thurwieser (1789–1865). The scholarly cleric had read his breviary and his barometer on numerous summits in Dachstein and the Austrian Alps, and is credited with the first tourist ascents – and sometimes the very first ascent of any kind – of peaks such as Strahlkogel (3,288 metres) and Schrambacher (3,416 metres). His enthusiasm for scrambling was such that Coolidge wondered whether the bespectacled priest might not have been a mountaineer despite himself. Thurwieser repeated ascents of other great peaks in the eastern Alps, including Watzmann (2,713 metres) in the Berchtesgaden region, Ankogel (3,252 metres) in the Hohe Tauern range in Carinthia, Grossglockner and Ortler – all well before the Alpine Club held its first dinner or the other alpine clubs were founded.

The siege of Monte Rosa

In the Zermatt chain, chronicles mention the ascent of the Breithorn (4,166 metres) in 1813 by a French traveller, Henri Maynard, who, like his guides, thought he had reached the summit of

Monte Rosa. The powerful Monte Rosa incorporates a number of peaks: In 1801 Pietro Giordani, an engineer from Alagna in Valsesia, reached the top of one of the spurs (now known as Punta Giordani, 4,046 metres), and immediately sat down to write an account of his 'voyage' in the style of Saussure on Mont Blanc and the Col du Géant. Engineer Giordani sought to 'elucidate the secrets of icy nature'.

Between 1813 and 1822, men from Gressoney – J.N. Vincent and Josef Zumstein, an inspector for the Gressoney forestry commission – climbed three major peaks on Monte Rosa: Vincent Pyramid (4,215 metres), Zumsteinspitze (4,563 metres) and, accompanied by an Austrian baron, Ludwig von Welden, Ludwigshöhe (4,341 metres).

In the neighbouring valley of Alagna, a young priest, Giovanni Gnifetti, was piqued by the iron cross planted on Zumsteinspitze, and made three attempts before reaching the summit of Signalkuppe (4,554 metres). The men around Monte Rosa and the rivalry among valleys for reaching the highest peak of the mountain strongly resembled the generation of the Matterhorn twenty years later – it was not so much a question of science as of adventure and honour.

The Hôtel des Neuchâtelois

At the same moment, in the Alps near Bern, scholars became emboldened by the sight of the grandiose summits ringing the low walls of their shelter. They dined before nightfall, and sought to understand why their cigars took on a different taste when they looked at the Schreckhorn.

Sometime later, candles flickered beneath simple roofing and dripped onto the stone. A rustic shelter, dubbed the Hôtel de Neuchâtelois, had been built at an altitude of 2,700 metres beneath

The east face of Monte Rosa.

The flag over the 'Hôtel des Neuchâtelois' greeted travellers.

Louis Agassiz.

A watercolour by John Ruskin of peaks flanking the Jungfrau.

an enormous, erratic boulder of schist from the Unteraar glacier, sixteen kilometres from the Grimsel inn (2,165 metres). It was marked by a flag flying at the top of a pole. One of the most frequent guests at the 'hotel' was Édouard Desor (1811–1882), a naturalist who had been a student and disciple of Louis Agassiz (1807–1873) before teaching natural history at the University of Neuchâtel. Between 1840 and 1845, Agassiz, Desor and geologist Daniel Dolfuss-Ausset (1797–1870) tested Agassiz's theories on the movement of glaciers and the existence of an ice age. During their long summer sojourns, fuelled by mutton and rice, the men – called glacialists – made notable ascents led by their guides.

Desor made the first ascents of Ewigschneehorn (3,239 metres), Gross Lauteraarhorn (4,042 metres, on 8 August 1842), Rosenhorn (3,688 metres) and Galenstock (3,586 metres) in the eastern Bernese range.

In 1842, Desor and two other scientists, Arnold Escher von der Linth and Christian Girard, contemplated climbing the Schreckhorn with five guides. According to Desor, 'The ambition to plant the first flag on the Schreckhorn, the only great Bernese summit that remained virgin, was too natural for us to resist it'. All of them, scientists and guides, mistook the Lauteraarhorn for the Schreckhorn. The previous year, Agassiz and Desor were moved to tears on the summit of Jungfrau (the fourth ascent). Each member of the party followed, one after another, to the top. Desor magnificently described the emotion of reaching a summit: 'I hurried to reach Agassiz, because I somewhat feared that I would lose my customary self-assurance under such strong impressions; and I wanted to shake the hand of a friend, and I dare say that my life never seemed so happy as when I sat next to him on the snow. I think both of us would have wept, had we dared, but the tears of men must have their modesty.'

An English colleague, John D. Forbes (1809–1868), accompanied the Swiss glacialists to the summit of Jungfrau. We will soon encounter Forbes again on the Col d'Hérens in Valais striding toward the snowy, virgin peak of Wandfluehorn with his gold chronometer. Forbes, in emulation of the Swiss scientists whose work and adventures he knew, was the first English traveller to adopt the flag-planting spirit. He would later be named an honorary member of the Alpine Club, unanimously hailed as a pioneer by his compatriots.

Topography as a factor of success: Gottlieb Studer

Gottlieb Samuel Studer (1804–1890) from Bern only gave up the pleasures of scrambling in 1883, after sixty years of practising it. With the accuracy typical of his profession, he claimed 643 distinct climbs in various regions from Valais to the Tyrol, from the Bernese Oberland and Pennines (his home turf) to the Dauphiné. As Coolidge commented, 'Everywhere he went he made new ascents or passes, or opened routes known previously only to the natives'.

As a topographer, Studer drew 710 views of vistas and summits from 1823 to 1881. His two maps of the southern valleys of Valais were published in 1840 and 1853, ten years before advancing age converted him into a historian of the conquest of the Swiss Alps. His four-volume history, published between 1869 and 1883, was titled *Über Eis und Schnee* (On Ice and Snow). It has never been translated into English or French despite the contribution it would make to any history of the pioneers.

Studer experienced and observed mountain exploration spanning both periods, before the English arrived and during the English campaigns. The Wildhorn (3,248 metres, 19 September 1843) and Diablerets (3,209 metres, 19 August 1850), two summits

Gottlieb Samuel Studer.

Johann Coaz.

Edward Shirley Kennedy.

in the western Bernese Alps, usually credited to Studer, are not the only trophies garnered by this typical, nineteenth-century bourgeois gentleman. He left his mark on the Alps of Valais, notably the Combin de Corbassière (3,716 metres, 17 August 1851) and Tête Blanche (3,710 metres, 15 August 1849), a broad snowy belvedere above the Col d'Hérens. In the eastern Bernese Alps he climbed the Sustenhorn (3,504 metres, 17 August 1841) and in the Bernese Oberland he scaled the Wannerhorn (3,905 metres, 6 August 1864) and Studerhorn (3,638 metres, 5 August 1864). In the Simplon range of the Lepontine Alps he bagged Monte Leone (3,553 metres, 1850), and in the Tarentaise itself he climbed the Testa del Rutor (3,486 metres, 16 August 1858).

Studer was often accompanied by a topographer and theologian from Zurich, Melchior Ulrich (1802–1893).

Engadin: Johann Coaz

Johann Coaz (1822–1918) was born in Belgium but spent his career as a forestry engineer and topographer in Switzerland. He was the primary explorer of the Alps of the Engadin district, which the federal government had commissioned him to map. His work prompted him to make numerous explorations in the area.

Piz Bernina (4,049 metres) is the highest point and sovereign peak of the Bernina range. It was Coaz's most difficult and most famous climb. Note the date: 13 September 1850, four years before the Wetterhorn. (The first English ascent of Piz Bernina, by E.S. Kennedy and J.F. Hardy in the summer of 1861, marked the launch of the Alpine Club's campaign into ranges where no one had had ever seen an Englishman on a summit of any significance.) Coaz, who lived to be nearly 100, was wittily described by Coolidge as 'the Nestor of living climbers'.

Beata solitudo: Johann Jakob Weilenmann

Among the six climbers cited by Coolidge in the next generation of explorers (one Swiss and five Austrians), it is worth mentioning Johann Jakob Weilenmann (1819–1896). A Swiss from Saint Gallen, Weilenmann was the first mountaineer to make major ascents entirely alone. His tally included 350 summits and passes in Switzerland and the Tyrol, including the second ascent of Monte Rosa.

Piz Tremoggia (3,441 metres) in Engadin is a peak that straddles Italy and the Swiss canton of Grisons. Its ascent begins from a famous hamlet called Sils Maria, which is mentioned in the philosopher Friedrich Nietzsche's prophecies and writings about his summers spent in the Engadin valley, where he used to compose whilst walking.

One summer day in 1859 Weilenmann made the first solo ascent of Piz Tremoggia in the lofty silence that relativises and effaces all history.

Johann Jakob Weilenmann.

The silence of the summits

So many deeds, so many cairns and so many key dates even before we arrive at a golden age of mountaineering itself rich in names, deeds, dates, human faces and mountain types: we should never forget, when dealing with the very particular field of the history of mountaineering, characterised as it is by an inflation in exploits and names, that the history of a game becomes a different story when played in the silence of the summits.

JAMES D. FORBES
AND ALBERT SMITH

James D. Forbes, who described the Matterhorn's proud pyramidal summit as 'unscaled and unscalable'.

The circuit of Mont Blanc or Monte Rosa …
is sufficiently great to afford to at least nine-tenths of travellers the most
majestic conceptions with which [the mountains] can inspire them.

James D. Forbes

J AMES D. FORBES DREW HIS WATCH from his thick cardigan. It was a gold chronometer: his most precious piece of equipment. None of his three guides – Tairraz from Chamonix, Pralong from Arolla (in the Valais) or Biona from Bionaz (Valpelline) – owned a watch. The party had to get up at 3 a.m. The guides asked to be awakened by the shepherds of Bricola, who then asked the Scottish scientist for his watch. Never would Forbes have handed over such a treasure to unknown men. But the place and shepherds inspired confidence. After the meal, the shepherds recited their evening prayer together. Pralong kneeled alongside them. All Victorian travellers noted the intense piety of villagers from Valais. This touching devotion could occasionally be bothersome when guides refused to leave the village on a Sunday before having heard mass. Some guides even refused to walk in the mountains on Sunday, for fear of offending the Lord. The offence would have to be paid for sooner or later – if not that very day – by one of those misfortunes or severe warnings the mountains know how to deliver. The Genevan writer Rodolphe Töpffer, who went up from the

Rhone Valley to the village of Evolène in September 1842, penned some wonderful passages on the men who lived there. On Sundays the peasants calmly observed the Ten Commandments and would sit on the walls of their tiny fields, legs dangling, conversing about the ways of the world.

Bricola, some 2,400 metres high, was a high pasture slope with a shepherd's hut at the top of the Val d'Hérens, often swept by a harsh little wind at the break of day. It was the last stop before the glacier of Ferpècle. '*Der Gletscher!* (The glacier!)' exclaimed the guides from Unteraar at the glaciologists' headquarters, dubbed Hôtel des Neuchâtelois. On that night, between 18 and 19 August 1842, Forbes slept fitfully.

The four men were sleeping in a low-ceilinged shed, four square metres in size and carpeted in straw, that they had carried from the village of Evolène, a three-hour hike away. For the past week, since he left Chamonix on a mule, Forbes had been going from pass to pass, undertaking this exploratory journey through the Valais with curiosity and growing pleasure. It became an expedition 'for which [he] felt more and more disposed as [he] got better acquainted with the scenery of this interesting chain'.

This professor of natural sciences from Edinburgh had been inspired by the life and work of Saussure. Having come from Orsières to the Great Saint Bernard monastery, Forbes headed back down to Orsières the same day with a Swiss naturalist, Bernhard Studer, whom he had met up there. The guide was Victor Tairraz. Forbes had hurt his feet in a fall, thus in company with Tairraz he had left Chamonix astride a mule, like some lazy, 'fancy' English tourist, and had comfortably crossed the Col de Baume to the scent of grass, droppings and dung. On 15 August, after following the Bagnes valley from one end to the other, the party crossed the pass known as Col de Fenêtre (2,803 metres). On the other side –

A chamois hunter among the erratic boulders on the Aar glacier.

Mont Collon and the Arolla glacier.

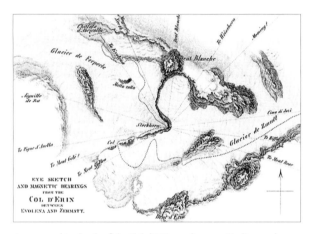

A topographic sketch of the Col d'Hérens, between Evolène and Zermatt, in Switzerland.

in Aosta – the valley of Ollomont was rife with goitre, an affliction as common as it was unexplained. On 16 August the party slept in the chalets of Prarayé (2,010 metres) after an interminable climb up from Valpelline, where they hired a guide from the village of Bionaz. The next day, after crossing Col Collon (3,074 metres), they were all stunned when they stumbled upon a corpse on the Swiss side of the Arolla glacier. The sun had exhumed the remains of a smuggler who had disappeared that winter. Forbes: 'We turned and surveyed, with a stronger sense of sublimity than before, the desolation by which we were surrounded, and became still more sensible of our isolation from human dwellings, human help and human sympathy – our loneliness with nature and, as it were, the more immediate presence of God.'

The party reached the hamlet of Arolla, where Pralong offered his services as guide for the Col d'Hérens. That evening they slept at Evolène (1,371 metres), minus a weary Studer who claimed he was disgusted from the smell of the hay in the barn and who therefore headed back down the Rhone Valley. Perhaps the real reasons for his departure were the shock of finding the smuggler's corpse on the glacier combined with the remoteness of Evolène.

Forbes was the first British traveller to visit Evolène. Coolidge: '[I]n the thirties and forties of the nineteenth century … it was thought quite a feat to visit Evolena [*sic*], or Arolla (no inn then), or Zinal: it was thought almost as necessary to write a book or article as to such a daring expedition as it was in the case of the ascent of Mont Blanc.' From the Rhone Valley, a trip to Zermatt was much more convenient.

The little shed on the high alpine pasture of Bricola released its four occupants the next morning. They were heading for the broad glacier pass called Col d'Hérens (3,459 metres), a well-known route long used by the people of Valais. Forbes, awakened by his excitement and the moonlight, had risen early. In the span of a quick wash, the moon set and left a sky of stars. The party headed down toward the Ferpècle glacier, an awkward descent hindered by a gushing torrent. Pralong and Biona splashed through the water without removing their shoes. Forbes, followed by Tairraz – 'the wary Savoyard' – sought a ford. Below the Col d'Hérens the snow was good, they made good time, and the sky was gentian-blue – Forbes wanted to scale a nearby summit presumed to be virgin (Stockhorn, 3,589 metres, now known as Wandfluehorn). The broad snowy hilltop presented no difficulty. Continuing their descent to the Col d'Hérens, the party had to take out a rope and belay Pralong across a difficult bergschrund.

Once in Zermatt, Forbes nursed his feet. The first inn in Zermatt, the Riffelberg, did not open until 1854. Prior to that date, travellers slept at the home of the priest or a local doctor called Lauber, who had a few rooms available. Agassiz and Desor spent time there in August 1839. As Desor later noted, 'In the visitors' book, begun just that year, we recognised some familiar names among the five or six travellers who had preceded us: they were Swiss zoologists and botanists. Clearly, tourists had not yet invaded the valley'.

Forbes made a lengthy examination of the Matterhorn before Studer rejoined him for their tour of Monte Rosa. The Matterhorn was yet another summit discovered, admired and described by Forbes' mentor, Saussure, on his way to the Theodulhorn. 'The finest object this place offers to the eye is the tall, proud summit of the Matterhorn, rising to an enormous height in the form of a triangular obelisk of sharp rock seemingly cut with a chisel.' In 1825, the peak made an even greater impact on William Brockedon (1787–1854), an English artist and traveller who arrived breathless at the Theodul pass from Breuil. 'More striking than any other object, the beautiful pyramid of the Mont Cervin [Matterhorn],

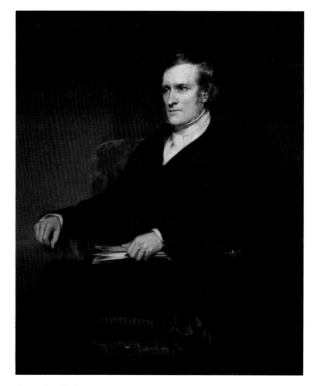

James D. Forbes.

The Matterhorn, a summit 'discovered' by Saussure.

Arrival at the summit:
Albert Smith's ascent of Mont Blanc.
Lithograph by J.J. MacGregor,
published in London, 1855.

springing 5,000 feet high from its bed of glaciers … burst upon the eye at once with unimaginable effect and grandeur.' Forbes called it 'unscaled and unscalable.' Meanwhile, in *Peaks, Passes and Glaciers,* John Ball called it 'an astounding peak … chief of them all … [a] stupendous obelisk whose form defies the boldest speculations of the geologist'.

The Theodul pass (3,301 metres), a little crevassed glacier passage between Zermatt and Valtournenche (Breuil), has been crossed by the residents of Valais since at least the fifteenth century. It is where Saussure had a hut built in 1792 in order to shelter with his guides during his long period of study. As Forbes crossed it, a thunderstorm growled. Peter Dammater, the guide he had engaged at Zermatt, shrugged and trudged on, as was the custom in the land, beneath a large umbrella with a metallic tip thumbing its nose at the sky. It was the guide's only piece of equipment – he had no alpenstock. Forbes, a physicist, ordered the guide to put away the huge umbrella.

In one of his letters, Forbes wrote of the unique sense of happiness he felt during those long weeks of hiking and exploring in Valais. It was the crowning event of his summer. In June 1842 he had studied the movement of the Mer de Glace glacier while holed up in the Montenvers hut with guide Auguste Balmat. He then headed to Courmayeur via the Col du Bonhomme (2,311 metres) and Col de la Seigne (2,513 metres) accompanied by Joseph-Marie Couttet, returning by the Col du Géant (3,365 metres), a large glacier pass par excellence which was a key site in the story of Forbes's mentor, Saussure, and often featured in 'mountainological' studies. It was a perfect trip. In 1844 Forbes published *Travels Through the Alps of Savoy,* a major tome on glaciology with a 1:25,000-scale map of the Mer de Glace, drawn up by Forbes during his explorations. The book was a hit and his tales of exploration – in particular his

James D. Forbes studying the Mer de Glace.

adventurous hikes over the glaciers and passes of Valais – spurred the curiosity of British gentlemen. A shorter, more anecdotal version was published in 1855 under the title of *The Tour of Mont Blanc and of Monte Rosa.*

Mont Blanc was fashionable at the time. In 1851, a witty journalist named Albert Smith (1816–1860) climbed Mont Blanc with three companions and sixteen guides. This ascent had been a goal ever since his childhood, when he was moved by a short book on the catastrophic Hamel party in 1820 (which resulted in three deaths). Smith had a jester's temperament – he was amused by the ascent itself, which included 300 bottles of wine on the porters' backs. Nine months after this escapade he put on a show at the Egyptian Hall in London, featuring his exploit depicted on a large screen incorporated into the façade of a cardboard chalet. All of London wanted to see this wildly popular show, which played night after night until Smith died in 1860.

Forbes's appeal to British readers cannot be understood without the popularity of Smith and his show, which occasionally included two chamois transported by one of his guides as well as dogs from the Grand-Saint-Bernard monastery. Smith even invented a board game with a fifty-step path from Piccadilly to the domed summit of Mont Blanc. Players crossed the English Channel, halted at the Vendôme Column and Notre-Dame Cathedral in Paris, boarded the train for Dijon, hopped a stagecoach, lounged in a hot bath in a hotel, strolled along the lakeside port of Geneva, meditated in the mortuary crypt of the monastery of Grand-Saint-Bernard, admired the Mer de Glace and suddenly sank up to their hips in soft snow – the ascent had begun.

Many travellers, including some of those who made the first ascent of Mont Blanc 'without guides' according to Whymper, dated their first cravings for the Alps to an evening at Smith's 'Mont

Albert Smith.

Albert Smith's illustrated show, London, 1852.

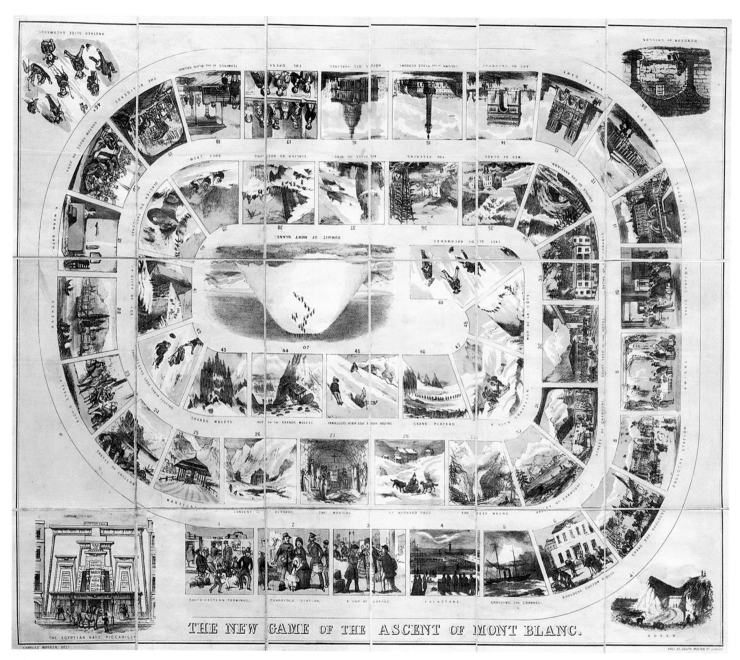

A board game devised by Albert Smith, leading from Piccadilly to the summit of Mont Blanc in fifty stages.

Blanc' show. Prior to 1851, certain years went by without a single ascent to the summit. The snowy dome was still draped in the black flag of the three deaths of the Hamel party. Again according to Whymper, 'Men commonly made wills before starting for it.' But after 1851, not a year passed without one or several parties bagging Mont Blanc.

Forbes himself never made it to the top of Mont Blanc. He had, so to speak, better things to see and do. Coolidge considered Forbes 'the first British explorer and mountain climber'. He was the first to climb a virgin peak, the first Briton who could reasonably be described as a 'mountain climber', and he had an exceptional list of ascents for the time – for a Briton, at least. By the age of thirty he had completed a tour of Monte Viso, and made an incursion into the poor, lice-ridden, flea-bitten Oisans region, taking a mule path from the Vénéon valley to the last village of La Bérarde with its thatched roofs. These long, slow, quiet valley treks to the sound of a stream, these endless preambles at a donkey's or mule's pace evoke a picturesqueness and sense of time that sparks nostalgia when one dully crosses the same places in an automobile. Heading on foot up a long Alpine valley offers an incomparable initiation into the secrets of its atmosphere and its architecture.

Forbes's first great year in the Alps was 1841: he crossed the Col du Says (3,122 metres) and Col du Sellar (3,038 metres) in Oisans; Col de Gauli in the Gauli circus (Bernese Alps); Ewigschneehorn (3,239 metres, Bernese Alps) and Oberaarjoch (3,212 metres), an icy pass between the Fiesch and Aar glaciers. Jungfrau (4,158 metres), his highest summit, behind Swiss glacialists Agassiz and Desor, was a first British ascent. After his exploratory journey in Valais in 1842, from Orsières to Zermatt – the account of which was enjoyed by all members of the Alpine Club upon reading his *Travels* – Forbes reached the summit of the Wasenhorn (3,246 metres)

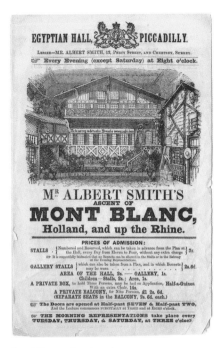

'A wildly popular show.'

in the Simplon chain in 1844, a first. The summer of 1850 was his last season of mountaineering. He climbed the Aiguille de la Glière (2,852 metres) in the Aiguilles Rouges opposite the glaciers of Mont Blanc, and on 20 July of that year he crossed Col Blanc (3,405 metres) and the Fenêtre de Saleina (3,261 metres) with Auguste Balmat (his usual guide) and Michel Charlet. These two glacier passes are part of the tour of Mont Blanc. A ridge on a nearby summit, the Aiguille du Chardonnet (3,824 metres), was later named after the Scottish glacialist – the splendid Forbes Ridge. That explorer with fragile health was a true forerunner of the golden age.

Seven years after Forbes, in August 1857, Alfred Wills followed in Forbes's footsteps with two compatriots, thus making a second crossing of the Fenêtre de Saleina. They bivouacked on the descent to Orsières, huddling with no blankets against a rock, near a fire of brambles and crackling rhodendrons. The guides were François Cachat, Auguste Balmat and, inevitably, the memory of Forbes. When Wills marvelled at the Aiguilles Dorées chain in the setting sun, Balmat reminded him that those 'golden needles' had been named by Professor Forbes. Their precursor had erected cairns and occasionally enjoyed the special privilege of giving a lasting name to a mountain, pass or ridge.

On the eve of World War I, in his guidebook *Chamonix and the Range of Mont Blanc,* Whymper recommended two books as essential reading to people staying in the hotel in Chamonix for a better understanding of their strolls on the glaciers: *Travels through the Alps of Savoy* by Forbes and *The Glaciers of the Alps* by John Tyndall.

Forbes, unanimously acknowledged as a pioneer by the founders of the Alpine Club, was the father of a movement whose beginning is conventionally dated to the ascent of the Wetterhorn in 1854. The British had joined the fray.

The middle of the Mer de Glace where the Talèfre and Leschaux glaciers converge — a glacial spike with clearly layered structure emerges. By Forbes.

THE WETTERHORN

17 September 1854

A winter view of the Wetterhorn – 'weather peak' – by Charles-Henri Contencin.

THE WETTERHORN (3,692 metres), also called the Hasle Jungfrau, served as a barometer for the village of Grindelwald (1,034 metres). Alexandre Dumas, in his *Travels in Switzerland,* described the view from the alpine pasture of Wengernalp: 'You are at the foot of the Jungfrau. To the right of it rises the Wetterhorn [Weather Peak], so-called because the weather can be forecast according to whether the peak is free from, or covered by, clouds.' Travellers to Wengernalp were offered the curiosity of witnessing a thundering avalanche. Dumas, armed with a rifle, fired a shot in the air. His guide explained how to distinguish the echoes of the shot from the rumble of a cascade of snow tumbling down the Jungfrau after he fired. Dumas found it hard to believe that an avalanche could make so much noise. At that very moment, a kind of mountain dwarf ran up to Dumas carrying a small cannon in his arms. The little man set the cannon in the grass, pointed it at the Jungfrau and bent over to blow energetically on a piece of tinder. The shot went off. The dwarf, whom Dumas termed 'a double cretin', was an avalanche-maker by trade. The generous

'The British join the fray.'

Dumas gave the fellow a few coins for an avalanche that his own rifle had triggered. Everyone had their role and usefulness in those little mountain regions. The double cretin created avalanches for 'fancy' tourists.

On 31 August 1844, twelve years after Dumas passed that way, two guides planted a flag of victory on the summit of the Wetterhorn: Hans Jaun and Melchior Bannholzer. The Wetterhorn proper is one of three peaks of the Wetterhörner group, the other two being the Rosenhorn and the Mittelhorn. Three days earlier (28 August) a party had scaled the Rosenhorn (3,689 metres). The party of ten mountaineers included the same two guides and the Swiss naturalist Édouard Desor. The highest peak, Mittelhorn (3,704 metres), was crowned with a *flagge* the following year, on 9 July 1845, by three guides and a Scottish tourist. During those same days a second ascent of the Wetterhorn was made, this time from the Grindelwald side, by guide Peter Bohren, known as the *Gletscherwolf* (glacier wolf).

In 1854 Bohren was hired by the Englishman Alfred Wills (1828–1912), but failed to mention that the Wetterhorn was no longer virgin – the ascent of a virgin peak cost the client a good deal more. The golden age of mountaineering began here at the Wetterhorn with the climb made by the twenty-six-year-old Wills, who went on to become a judge.

The golden age had begun, that is, as far as the British were concerned. But too often, given the fuss over either Saussure or the Alpine Club, over Mont Blanc or the Matterhorn, the work of the Swiss explorers and Austrian clergymen has been underestimated. Wills's ascent of the Wetterhorn was noticed only in England, where his account of *Wanderings Among the High Alps* found readers already steeped in Romantic culture for two generations, a readership liable to enjoy the sublime, picturesque aspects of travelling across glaciers in the virgin Alps.

C.D. Cunningham called Wills's account a 'fascinating book'.[1] The adventure of the Alps was described in a language of action – sober, detailed, lively – with a race to the summit by two parties that remained in every reader's memory. The first party carried a metallic flag (*flagge*), while the second, in guise of a standard, carried a young pine tree still strangely bearing all its branches and needles, like a Christmas tree. The man carrying the pine to the Wetterhorn was none other than Christian Almer, future guide to Edward Whymper.

Wills's Wetterhorn was neither a first ascent nor even a first ascent via Grindelwald, as Wills wanted to think, nor even the first ascent by a tourist. For this glacier expedition Wills had questioned his usual Chamonix guide, Auguste Balmat, who was with him during those late summer days. Following their planning session, Balmat left Wills's hotel in Interlaken and bumped into a lad from his home town of Argentière, Auguste Simond, who was on his way back to Savoy after a glacier voyage in the Bernese Alps.

In 1854, Interlaken – located between two lakes – was already a highly reputed and heavily frequented European tourist destination during the summer season. It offered a vista of three majestic summits – Jungfrau (4,158 metres), Mönch (4,107 metres) and Eiger (3,970 metres) – and boasted a broad avenue with carriages stationed in front of luxury hotels. It was a fashionable resort. According to Eugène Rambert, 'Interlaken is a place one has to have seen, like Naples and the banks of the Rhine, and it is said there is nothing finer in the world of the Alps.' Some passing tourists braved the majestic summits. They wielded long alpenstocks that rang out on stone-paved promenades; these fanciful sticks were decorated with a swirl of names: Chamonix, Staubbach, Tête

Le capitaine Lauener's party just beneath the cornice of the Wetterhorn, hauling a pine tree.

1. C.D. Cunningham and William de Wiveleslie Abney, *The Pioneers of the Alps* (Boston: Estes & Lauriat, 1888).

Noire, Reichenbach — all sites to be seen, sites to visit armed with a stick, frock coat, cigar and top hat, beneath a clutch of summits whose names no one recalled. So many summer tourists beneath so many virgin peaks — that was the reality and the paradox of fashionable Alpine and Pyrenean resorts in 1854. As he wandered through Interlaken, Rambert noted here and there, among the clusters of pretty ladies in long dresses, other women in sportier garments, wearing shorter, less flouncy dresses over fine gaiters with mother-of-pearl buttons which wrapped around and protected the instep.

Interlaken was what Zermatt would later become. Snobbery is inevitably a question of climbing. So behind the pioneers, in the wake of snobbery, came cohorts of curious admirers, compelled by their irresistible desire to see what there was to see as well as to 'be seen' in the places everyone was talking about.

Meanwhile, Balmat introduced his friend Simond to Mr Wills. Simond's air of self-reliance, tall stature and obvious strength spoke in his favour. Wills wrote that 'Balmat said he had seen [Simond] hold out a man at the end of his arm' — an exploit that was apparently popular in the valley of Chamonix, for the same thing was said of Michel Croz, the unlucky guide on the Matterhorn.

Wills hired Simond, whom he soon dubbed Samson [*sic*], after the biblical legend who slayed the Philistines. Shortly afterwards, Wills met Ulrich 'Ulch' Lauener, a guide from Lauterbrunnen. Leslie Stephen described Lauener as the most picturesque, gigantic of guides. This opinion is worth taking seriously in so far as Stephen himself towered over most of his friends and compatriots. How tall might Lauener have been? According to Stephen, 'Tall, spare, blue-eyed, long-limbed and squared-shouldered, with a jovial laugh and a not ungraceful swagger, his is the very model of

The Jungfrau and the valley of Lauterbrunnen near Interlaken.

Ulrich Lauener, dubbed le capitaine by Balmat.

'Interlaken turned its eyes toward the Jungfrau.'

a true mountaineer; and, except that his rule is apt to be rather autocratic, I would not wish for a pleasanter companion.' Balmat soon came up with a nickname for Lauener – *le capitaine*. 'Captain' Lauener had everything it took to be the captain of a voyage, including a long meerschaum pipe. His brother, Christian Lauener, was another highly respected guide of the day.

The summer was coming to an end. It had been dry and snowless, making ascents easier. But it was too late, repeated the giant Lauener, for such a difficult ascent as the Jungfrau. On fine evenings Interlaken turned its eyes toward the Jungfrau, the last summit to catch the light at sunset. According to Rambert, 'A deep silence would suddenly fall. The gravel pavements no longer crunched beneath the feet of strollers; everyone held his breath, as though afraid of disturbing this great, silent scene.'

This summit, whose conquest had been so strongly resisted, was one of the temptations of Interlaken. Wills asked:

'And the Finsteraarhorn, Mr. Lauener?'

'*Nein, nein, Herr!*'

'The Schreckhorn?'

'*Nein, nein, Herr!*'

'And the Wetterhorn?'

'*Ja, ja, Herr,*' replied Lauener, adding that no one had yet succeeded in ascending it. But he was sure it would be possible.

The history of mountaineering contains more foxes than lions.

When they gathered in Grindelwald on 16 September, *le capitaine* urged Wills to hire Peter Bohren – Peterli, the 'Little Peter' known as the 'glacier wolf'. But he was a stocky, sturdy wolf. Lauener also said they had to take a *flagge,* to be planted at the top once they trod the virgin peak.

'A flag? Do you have one?'

'We'll order it from the blacksmith!'

The *flagge* turned out to be 'a sheet of iron three feet long and two feet wide, with two rings strongly welded to one of the shorter edges.' It was accompanied by a pole 'of the same metal, ten or twelve feet long, and as thick as a man's thumb.'

'A confounded piece of nonsense,' sighed Sampson on weighing the thing, some twenty or thirty pounds.

But as they set off carrying this piece of nonsense, 'Captain' Lauener let off a terrific war cry. That evening in September, around the fire of their camp beneath a rocky cave, Lauener, Bohren and the porter who had carried the party's wood, sang a hymn to the Oberland.

The cave was low-ceilinged. Wills slept poorly, hampered by the ceiling and the sound of avalanches crashing down the slopes of the Wetterhorn.

The next day, after a passage on the rocks in which Wills had to be roped tight, the party reach the snow of the glacier and halted to eat and equip themselves.

It was 9 a.m. The Swiss guides put on crampons that Balmat the Savoyard thought were pointless – the Chamonix men and Wills would manage with their nailed boots and alpenstocks. They carried no packs, having left all their baggage – except a flask of brandy – there on the scree.

At a bend in the final slope, the party spotted two men below, incredibly agile and swift.

'*Gemsjäger!* (chamois hunters),' cried Lauener.

The two chamois hunters advanced at lightning pace, soon challenging the party's pretensions by seeking to overtake it. One of the two, Christian Almer, was carrying a fir tree, branches and all, on his shoulder.

'Where are you headed?'

'To the summit!'

Christian Lauener, Ulrich's brother.

'An axe to get up, a rope to get back down, and a flag to serve as proof.'

Faces hardened. The Savoyards swore, and even the pacific Balmat wanted to give a drubbing to the insolent men who were trying to pip them at the post. Following discussion, it was agreed that Almer would walk behind the party, tree on shoulder, with his companion and brother-in-law, Ulrich Kauffmann.

At the top of the slope, *le capitaine* had to cut through an overhanging cornice of ice. He worked very carefully – chunks of ice plunged into the void. Then came a shout:

'*Ich schaue den blauen Himmel* (I see blue sky)!'

The huge Lauener clambered through the rest of the cornice and stood against the sky; then, with another stride, he headed to the top. It would be the first and last time in the history of mountaineering that an iron flag and pine tree were planted on the same summit on the same day: 17 September 1854.

CHAMONIX GUIDES

Auguste Balmat and François Devouassoud

The office of the Compagnie des Guides in Chamonix, photographed by Edward Whymper.

ALFRED WILLS RETURNED TO ENGLAND pleased with himself and his guides, delighted to be told by Auguste Balmat that the Wetterhorn ranked higher than Mont Blanc on the scale of difficulty. Although he died in 1862, Balmat was a key figure of the golden age of mountaineering. He had been Forbes's guide on Montenvers for weeks in June of 1842, assisting the professor in his research on glaciers. Forbes was surprised at the pleasure and interest his guide took in their 'scientific' excursions on the Mer de Glace. Balmat liked to learn and to understand. The biblical maxim 'Knowledge puffeth up, but charity edifieth' was often central to nineteenth-century lives, but Balmat-the-Knowledgeable was an exception, and never became puffed up like a pedant. At one time head guide of the Compagnie des Guides in Chamonix, Balmat was credited by everyone who came in contact with him with one cardinal virtue often simulated but in fact as rare as hen's teeth: modesty. In his *Voyage en Zigzag autour du Mont Blanc* (1842), Rodolphe Töpffer sketched a purported portrait of Balmat. Add the modesty and you will have a complete picture of a man who was by all accounts

Jacques Balmat.

a loyal companion and a model of serene strength. 'The guides of Chamonix, among whom all the traditions of Saussure still survive, and who are mainly indebted to the scholars of Geneva, with whom they notably had contact, for their spirit of education and good-manner tact, are in fact pleasant travelling companions as well as excellent guides. One must be either totally devoid of curiosity or inappropriately disdainful if one finds oneself bored in their company. Knowledgeable in everything that concerns the mountains, and conversing sensibly and well, as all Savoyards do, with ample adventures to recount, they are, incidentally, fine observers by trade; there are all kinds of interesting things to be drawn from them, and we are among those who find their conversation alone to be cheap at the cost of six francs per day.'

Balmat was a common, indeed famous, name in the valley of Chamonix. Auguste was the great nephew of Jacques Balmat, who had been the first person to conquer Mont Blanc, then died in 1834 in the mountains near Sixt. The young Auguste had himself lowered on a rope into the gulf where his great uncle reportedly fell. Auguste was often hired by English travellers, who valued and recommended him, and he learned English on his own through contact with these gentlemen, who even hosted him in England on several occasions. Along with Jacques Balmat and Marie Couttet (known as Moutelet, or 'weasel' in local parlance), Auguste was one of the three guides immortalised in 1878 by Stephen d'Arve in his *Histoire du Mont-Blanc.* D'Arve labelled him 'a famous guide'.

Born in Chamonix during the Napoleonic Empire in 1808, Balmat was nearly forty-six years old when he scaled the Wetterhorn. He was a drinker of milk, like Tyndall, for whom he worked in 1858 and 1859 during two memorable ascents of Mont Blanc. In September 1858 Tyndall wanted to bury a thermometer that would record maximum and minimum temperatures in the ice on the summit, then recover it at the end of winter, having marked the spot with an iron bar. At stake was measurement of the differences in temperature between the ambient air and core of the ice, which Tyndall felt was one of the factors in the movement of the glaciers. On the day of their ascent, wind and icy mist chilled the summit of Mont Blanc. Whipped by needles of ice, the men used pickaxes and iron bars to make a hole in the ice that they had to clear by hand, having forgotten their shovel back at the Grand Mulets.

Balmat pitched in, bare handed, to help his men with the task. After an hour's labour, the thermograph was buried at a depth of four feet. Drained, Balmat turned to Tyndall and said, in a toneless voice:

'I think my hands are frostbitten.'

After heading back down in the mist for fifteen minutes, Balmat pulled off his gloves and had his friends rub snow on his hands and strike them.

'Hit – hit harder! Never fear, harder! Strike harder!'

Balmat lost a few nails from his swollen fingers, which remained painful for weeks.

The next summer, when he returned to the summit of Mont Blanc with Dr Pitschner, a physicist from Berlin, Balmat was unable to find either the iron bar or the thermograph.

On 22 August of that same year, Balmat stood once again on the summit, accompanied by two other guides, six porters, Tyndall and another British scientist, Edward Frankland. After making observations, hindered by a mist and wind that stirred unhappy memories for Balmat, the party hastened into a tent erected below the summit on the south slope overlooking Courmayeur, sheltered from the wind. It was the first time men had spent a whole night at the top of Mont Blanc. The tent was just ten feet in diameter. One can imagine how crowded it was for eleven strapping men.

Auguste Balmat.

Crevasse on Mont Blanc, photo by the Bisson brothers.

According to d'Arve, 'Balmat drank wine only for the pleasure of offering it to tourists who did what he innocently called the honour of wishing him to be their guide.' Balmat took a lively interest in new ascents, whether or not he took part himself. 'I like nothing so much as new ascents,' he told William Mathews when his advice was asked in 1856 about scaling the Grand Combin, a peak in Valais about which little was known.

In 1861 Balmat led the first photographic ascent of Mont Blanc alongside the Bisson brothers, even though he had been complaining of head pains for some time. It was the twelfth and last ascent of Mont Blanc for the fifty-three-year-old guide, who strangely remained a bachelor all his life. He was highly trusted and respected by the likes of Alfred Wills, who was indebted to him for services other than a guide's usual fare. It was through Balmat, for example, that Wills acquired the plot of land in Sixt, in the Giffre valley, where he built his own house, Eagle's Nest. Wills later took in the ailing Balmat at Eagle's Nest. There Balmat died impoverished, which startled everyone who had been unfamiliar with the man's ways.

'All wages humiliated him,' asserted d'Arve. Balmat preferred to be paid for his services in gifts and books. The friendship between Balmat and Wills was the first of several that sprang up in the following years between guides and travellers. Often cited is the comradeship between the young Edward Whymper and Michel Croz, the guide from the village of Le Tour who, like Sampson of the Wetterhorn, could lift a man at arm's length. Croz's death on the Matterhorn in 1865 only perpetuated the lasting memory of that friendship. The same might be said of the relationship between Johann Josef Bennen, the guide from Valais who died in an avalanche, and the scientist Tyndall: Bennen, that most capable of guides who led the way up the Weisshorn in 1861 and made bold attempts on the Matterhorn, was dubbed 'the Garibaldi of guides' by Tyndall (reflecting the popularity of Garibaldi at the time).

The friendship between two long-lived men, François Devouassoud (1831–1905) from the hamlet of Barats in the valley of Chamonix, who became a guide at eighteen, and Douglas W. Freshfield (1845–1934), lasted until Devouassoud drew his last breath. 'Monsieur François', as he was called, also worked as a schoolteacher in the Chamonix valley for fourteen years and had the same lively intelligence as the somewhat older Balmat (whom Wills hired for weeks at a time in the Swiss Alps.) Freshfield was more an explorer than a climber, according to his compatriot T.G. Longstaff, and he took his friend François on many trips to destinations such as the Italian Alps, Norway, Corsica, and Asia Minor (where they made an attempt on Mount Ararat in the Caucasus). 'Monsieur François' was the only guide on an 1868 expedition to the Caucasus by three gentlemen of the Alpine Club, namely Freshfield, A.W. Moore, and C.C. Tucker. Usually the ratio was the opposite – two or three guides per gentleman. This was proof of the trust and esteem they had for Devouassoud. True enough, Moore was a veteran of the Barre des Écrins (1864) and the Brenva slope of Mont Blanc (1865), equal to the best Chamonix guides in terms of finding a route and keeping his nerve.

Like all children in Chamonix in those days when the glaciers went right up to the stable doors, Devouassoud was born on a glacier, and he had a reputation for being top-notch on all kinds of snow and ice. The extinct volcanoes of the Caucasus – those white giants of ice and snow which become dreadful when a blizzard blows up, such as the eastern summit (5,595 metres) of Mount Elbrus, mistaken for the highest peak due to fog, and Kazbek (5,047 metres) – fell to these skilled mountaineers more easily than a major

Eagle's Nest, Alfred Wills' chalet in the Giffre valley.

F. Devouassoud (in black) and D.W. Freshfield (seated, centre).

François Devouassoud from Chamonix.

western Alpine summit such as the Aiguille Verte. 'Monsieur François' also bagged some of his fifty firsts in the Italian Alps: Punta San Matteo (1865, with Tuckett and Freshfield), Piz Badile (1867, with the young Coolidge), Cima Brenta (1871, with Tuckett and Freshfield), Rosengartenspitze (1874, with C.C. Tucker) and Sass Maor (1875, with Tucker). He was not, however, in the 1867 party that climbed the Tour Ronde in the Mont Blanc chain, an easy first ascent by Freshfield.

Devouassoud was Balmat's direct heir, maintaining the tradition of friendship between guide and traveller, as immortalised by a funeral stele at Devouassoud's death. This stele, erected by his British friends and engraved with an epitaph in Latin, is now placed at the entrance to the church in Chamonix. In a sign of the times – and of a stark generational break among people from the same culture – perhaps less than one in every 100,000 tourists lounging on the esplanade in front of the church is now able to decipher the Latin epitaph, which might be translated as follows:

> To the honest man,
> to the friend and companion,
> a delightful, beloved, lamented
> guide, wise and indomitable,
> whom for 40 years we beheld;
> Lest such merit
> and example be forgot,
> this stone
> is erected with care
> by friends whom he often led
> across Alpine passes
> and Caucasian snows.

Auguste Balmat and François Devouassoud were two guides, already spanning two generations (born in 1808 and 1831, respectively) of a profession that involved sharing the nourishing mountain environment with men of all stations. Since epitaphs of the day were still written in Latin, it might be pointed out that 'companion' etymologically means someone with whom you share bread (*panis*).

More of a guide at heart – and above all, more disinterested – than his great-uncle Jacques, Auguste Balmat died of a brain tumour at the height of the golden age. He is one of those mysterious figures who seems to escape the determinism of their environment. According to Whymper, Balmat passed for a doctor, lawyer or diplomat if his true profession was unknown. His refined, educated conversation and comments reflected the intelligence written on his face. Whymper published a portrait of Balmat in his guide to Chamonix, showering him with praise: 'An exceptional man all round – a good mountaineer, an excellent guide, and a man of admirable character, who endeared himself to all. He was equally efficient in escorting the Empress Eugénie across the Mer de Glace, or in scaling the highest Alps. From his appearance no one would have suspected him to be an Alpine peasant.'

Nor would he be mistaken for a chamois hunter with that wild, sometimes haggard look when hunting became an obsession, as recorded by Friedrich von Tschudi, a Swiss scholar and naturalist whose *Sketches of Nature in the Alps* will serve as our guide to the very particular, harsh and virile world of chamois hunters. With their thick skins, those amazing rough-hewn men of the Alpine valleys were extraordinary hunters. They were thus well-trained and well-tempered to become great guides: Jacques Carrel, Jean-Antoine Carrel ('the Bersagliere' from Breuil), 'Captain' Lauener and his brothers Christian and Hans, Johann Josef Bennen, and Christian Almer. Without such men, there would have been no golden age. Yet they were every bit as shaggy as Canadian woodsmen who spend the winters in the forests of the far north.

Jean-Antoine Carrel from Breuil.

CHAPTER V

CHAMOIS HUNTERS

Chamois hunters lying in wait in the Mont Blanc range, by Grenier (nineteenth century).

CHRISTIAN ALMER (1826–1898), aged twenty-eight when he reached the summit of the Wetterhorn, thirty-one at the top of the Mönch, thirty-two at the summit of the Aiguille Verte, and a solid fifty-two on the southern needle of Arves, was one of the great guides of the golden age. Coolidge, one of loyal Almer's unconditional fans, felt he was the greatest guide of all times. Coolidge did not merely hire Almer on an occasional basis, but engaged him for seventeen summers straight, from 1868 to 1884, for highly mobile, offensive, Coolidge-style campaigns from passes to peaks. They wasted no time on long sieges.

These two baggers of heights sometimes had the pleasure of erecting a *männli*, that cairn of rough stones signifying conquest, on some peak or pass assumed to be virginal. They thereby left a touching, fragile testimony of their efforts. In a significant turn of phrase, Coolidge 'worked' with Almer from one end of the Alps to the other, even hiring his services during three winters. Almer thus led the first winter ascents of the Wetterhorn and Jungfrau with Coolidge in January 1874. These feats of endurance were proof

Christian Almer.

of curiosity extended to a season that was normally dreaded. Winter alpine climbing began to take shape, whether done in boots or snowshoes. In January 1876 the crack Coolidge–Almer team made the first serious winter attempt on Mont Blanc, the highest summit in the Alps, before being whipped back by the wind on the Grand Plateau. Coolidge – who knew his dear Almer well, and who lived in Grindelwald and understood the local Swiss-German dialect – said that only two accidents had occurred during the guide's long career, begun back in 1851, three years before the Wetterhorn. Almer died in his bed in 1898, aged seventy-one.

Almer guided Whymper in his ascent of the Barre des Écrins in 1864 and the Grand Cornier, Dent Blanche, Grandes Jorasses (Pointe Whymper), Col Dolent and Aiguille Verte in 1865 – but was absent from the Matterhorn, where he might have prevented the catastrophe. Sometimes it takes good advice at just the right moment – an opinion delivered with conviction – to alter a decision that could lead to a plunge of death. Or else it takes a rope that is better maintained, monitored and kept tauter – as it should be in that kind of terrain. Almer had the maturity (and prudence that went with it) as well as great patience and a mountain instinct sharpened by vigilant hunting expeditions on the slopes of the Jungfrau. For he had been a *gemsjäger,* a chamois hunter, and one of the best shots in Grindelwald until he signed up for the campaigns that made him the talk of the golden age.

Widely practised in the Alps in the nineteenth century, but increasingly difficult as game decreased in number, chamois hunting forged generations of mountain guides up to World War I. Patient, hardy, confident and highly alert to every possible danger, these hunters were probably unmatched in the art of moving across every type of terrain in the mid and high mountains. When done alone, chamois hunting was the toughest and most dangerous of all forms of stalking. For a long time the scaling of peaks, whether virgin or not, caused far fewer deaths in the Alps than did chamois hunting, done in the autumn.

Hans Lauener, a hunter from Lauterbrunnen and the best climber in the Oberland, died in October 1852 while chamois hunting on the slopes of the Jungfrau. A snowslide swept him to a fatal fall of some 700 metres. The sound of an avalanche would give his brother Christian goose bumps for many years following the accident. As Christian told Tyndall in 1858, when a rumble alarmed the two men as they descended Monte Rosa during a snowfall, 'I can never hear those things without a shudder; the memory of my brother comes back to me at the same time.'

Johann Josef Bennen (1819–1864), during an attempt on the Matterhorn in 1860 in the company of Tyndall and F. Vaughn Hawkins, admitted that '*nur der Schnee furcht mich* (only snow frightens me).' Chamois hunting was the favourite pastime of Bennen and his friend Bortas, from the same village of Lax in upper Valais. The two men hunted together. Bennen, from the Germanic part of Valais, was one of the Swiss guides most highly appreciated by British travellers, along with Christian Almer.

Bennen died in an avalanche on 28 February 1864 at Haut de Cry (2,969 metres). That peak on the right bank of the Rhone overlooking Sion in Valais presented no difficulty in summer, with its slopes of pastureland and stones, but was impressive in winter. A party of six set out – two travellers, Bennen, and three local guides from the village of Ardon. On a thirty-degree slope where the snow was a good metre deep, Bennen hesitated and took out his rope even though the local guides were reassuring.

'We've never seen an avalanche here!'

They had no snowshoes, just boots. A dull crack sounded: a few metres above them the entire snowfield split apart. The chamois

Chamois on the rocky heights, by Ridinger.

hunter knew the power and danger of an avalanche, even on a broad, cliff-less slope. Bennen had just enough time to say, slowly and calmly, '*Wir sind alle verloren*' (We are all lost).' Then the hillside began to move. 'It was shortly after noon,' wrote Philip Gosset, one of the travellers, in a detailed report for the *Alpine Journal.* Two men died – Bennen and the other traveller, Louis Boissonnet.

Winter in the Alps increasingly piqued the curiosity of certain English travellers, spurring them into this kind of eccentric adventure. Winter at high altitude was a different winter, offering fabulous sunshine to anyone arriving from the mists and marshes of the Rhone Valley – a winter of light and glory. Bennen, whom Tyndall styled the Garibaldi of guides, died in the prime of his life, aged forty-five, during an assault in winter, that season of snow and snowslides justly dreaded by all *gemsjägers.*

Hunting accidents were often the product of avalanches, given that the season ran through October, November and December, before the early snows had been consolidated. In 1839, a few days before Christmas, Valais resounded to a hunting tragedy in the gorges not far from the Schwarzhorn. Six robust hunters died from the thrust of a snowslide that pushed them into the gorge. The sole survivor, halted by a bump in the terrain, was buried but managed to free himself. All chamois hunters could have echoed Bennen's comment: the only thing that frightened them was snow.

Some of the bolder ones, confident of their skill, seem to have banished the very idea of ever falling from the rocks. A hunter took a big risk by stalking chamois alone, with no companion, with no one in the village knowing where he had headed. Sometimes he found himself cornered. A chamois hunt might last anywhere from several hours to several days. It was said to be extremely hard to follow a chamois once it had taken flight from a hunter. But a stubborn, shaggy old native wouldn't abandon his prey so easily,

Hunting chamois in the Alps (nineteenth century).

A Swiss chamois
hunter in the canton
of Graubünden,
by R. Taner.

and would follow it into the wilderness. Should a fall or serious wound occur, the solitary man underwent the ordeal of weakness or blackout hours away from the nearest highland pasture, and therefore faced a more or less slow death.

David Zwicky, from Mollis in the canton of Glarus (the Tödi chain), hunted all kinds of game, but died on a lone hunt at the age of fifty-seven. His body was unexpectedly found by a stroller on a hill in the Auernalp, not far from the valley, after Zwicky had been missing for thirty-six weeks. Having apparently sprained a leg in a fall, he managed to crawl as far as that hill, and was within view of his village as he went through his death throes. The village, at the end of valley, did not hear his gunshots of distress. According to Swiss pastor and naturalist Friedrich von Tschudi (1820–1886), 'By his side was his double-barrelled gun, his money, hunting-pouch and watch. His handkerchief was bound round one of his feet; the bone was not broken, but the limb seemed to have been sprained. He was resting his head on his hand, as though asleep; but the birds of prey and the foxes had gnawed a portion of his body to a skeleton.'

Zwicky had bagged 1,300 chamois in his career, and hunted smaller game with the same zeal and efficiency. He targeted marmots, badgers, foxes, white hares, ptarmigan and rock partridge. This thorough-going killer was the only hunter in the region who, born poor, made so much money from hunting that he was 'comfortably off' when he died – an ironic turn of phrase considering how he died. Extremely frugal – 'his penuriousness increased with his riches,' wrote Tschudi – Zwicky drank water (sipping wine only on special occasions) and ate bread and thin cheese, yet owned a collection of twelve hunting rifles.

Around 1850, the most commonly used weapon was a rifle-bored gun with a slender stock of light wood, called a chamois

'A passion – a pressing need – passed from father to son.'

carbine by the hunters. Luckily for the 'antelopes of the Alps', it could only fire two rounds, because the animals' survival was threatened by a much more lethal weapon, the repeating rifle. Once the latter gained in accuracy, wrote Tschudi, the chamois herds would come under serious threat. A hunter's equipment also included a good spyglass (*Spiegel*). This item, extremely expensive for a poor hunter, was almost indispensable for scouring the slopes to discover the presence of 'antelopes', and was equally useful for glacier expeditions. A hunter would put his spyglass in a shoulder bag with powder, bullets, a snack (bread, cheese, butter) and some roasted, salted flour plus an iron ladle. A tiny flask of cherry brandy was the touch of luxury for these long days of hunting, fuelled morning and evening by a soupy mixture of water and flour heated in the ladle over a fire in a hut or bivouac. Hunters dressed in garments of grey wool, wore a soft hat or cap, and carried a long stick, the famous alpenstock that long survived in certain valleys in Switzerland and Austria. Its use – now as rare as the wearing of lederhosen – was still observed in regions of Austria, Swabia and Bavaria after World War II.

Zwicky remained obsessed by hunting till his dying day, and never worked as a guide for foreign travellers. Great hunters had a hard time giving up their passion. One hunter, whose leg was amputated after an accident, sent half a chamois to the surgeon in Zurich who had performed the operation, expressing his gratitude while remarking that 'the chase did not get on so well with a wooden leg, but that he hoped to kill many a chamois yet.' The man was seventy-one when he lost his leg.

We are more or less familiar with all the exploits of mountaineering, for we can assess the places and passages, comparing them thanks to a system of grading. But we will never know the feats accomplished by those chamois hunters, their acrobatic turns on the slippery moss, damp stone and rubble of some shadowy mountain corridor in the month of November. We will never know the levels of boldness and madness to which they were driven by the nature of the terrain and the demands of pursuit.

Hunting divides attention between the animal on the move – whether espied from far or stalked from near – and the irregularities of terrain that demands caution and agility. This split attention is the first pitfall to be avoided: the hunter must be able to think of more than just the conditions and potential efficiency of his angle of fire. The second pitfall is the excitement, fever and thrill of the chase. A hunter can suddenly find himself in desperate straits on a rock face that is unfamiliar or whose difficulty he hadn't assessed, because the fleeing animal had monopolised that part of his attention normally allocated to the lay of the land when one ventures into the mountains. Certain passages, and certain leaps, are one-way only. In driving his prey into a gorge with no exit, where he can get a good shot, the hunter may find himself hopelessly stuck – impossible to go further, impossible to go back.

Tschudi described the case of a hunter in the Bernese Oberland who leapt on to a shelf of loose slate barely a foot wide, which then began to crumble beneath his feet. He lay on his stomach, one leg dangling in the void, the better to distribute his weight and cling to the rock. He crawled for three hours before finding an exit from this extremely exposed ledge of crumbling slate. At one point he even had to roll over, prop his head on a shelf of slate and bend one knee in defence as he loaded his rifle to ward off a threatening eagle that was wheeling above him. The eagle might have knocked him off the ledge with one blow of its wing.

The value of a chamois had not been worth the difficulties and dangers of the hunt in the eighteenth century, as Saussure pointed out, any more than it was in the days of Bennen and Almer. Even

Chamois: the 'antelope' of the Alps.

'Chamois hunting forged generations of mountain guides.'

Returning from the chamois hunt.

though every part of a chamois could be sold – the meat, the hide (which yielded a very fine leather) and the horns – no one could make a living from chamois hunting alone. 'It takes nine hunters to feed one,' went an old Freiburger saying. Chamois hunting was not a question of filling the stomach. It was a passion, a pressing need passed from father to son in Alpine regions, an adventure whose risks were accepted with a kind of resignation and fatalism that struck Saussure.

A famous passage in Saussure's *Voyages dans les Alpes* recounts a comment by a young chamois hunter from the parish of Sixt. The handsome fellow said, 'My grandfather was killed in the chase of the chamois; my father was killed also; and I am so certain that I shall be killed myself, that I call this bag, which I always carry when hunting, my winding-sheet; I am sure that I shall have no other; and yet, if you were to offer to make my fortune upon the condition that I should renounce the chase of the chamois, I should refuse your kindness.'

Two years later, Saussure learned that the young man had died like his father and grandfather – just as he had promised, so to speak.

In 1832 Alexandre Dumas did not want to miss the picturesque and highly literary scene of chamois hunting. So a hunter from Glarus took him into the Glärnisch chain, one of the most beautiful ranges in Switzerland according to the Baedeker guidebook of 1901, with four peaks above 2,900 metres. Dumas suffered from dizziness, the perfect affliction for creating a memorable scene. The best remedy for dizziness, explained his guide, Prosper Lehmann, while slitting the carotid artery of the animal he had just slain, is to drink chamois blood. The animal was not quite dead at that point. Lehmann filled a cup with blood and handed it to Dumas.

'That's right, chamois blood. The surest cure you could find.'

'No thank you, I'm not that worried, I'd rather stay dizzy.'

Lehmann had killed two chamois, which he carried on his back to a nearby hut. Slitting one open, he removed the pluck and immediately set it to boil on a fire lit by Dumas, seasoning it with butter, wine, salt and pepper.

In 1832 the part of the Alps that rose above the highest pasturelands was a wilderness in the heart of Europe – there were no roads, no good maps, no reliable names. It was a virgin, sterile-peak version of the American prairie, an empty expanse of glaciers and escarpments suited only to independent temperaments. Dumas, nostrils tickled by the aroma of the pluck, recalled a succulent haunch of bison shared by trappers in one of James Fenimore Cooper's novels. Lehmann was his 'Leatherstocking' of the prairie, a prodigy of strength and agility able to track chamois following a rainstorm. Lehmann was a model of simplicity, frugality and candour while sharing meat won by courage – and by a bare-footed climb.

In 1878, finding himself blocked by the sheer face known as the Mauvais Pas on the southernmost needle of the Aiguilles d'Arves, Christian Almer removed his shoes as Coolidge watched. In ten years of climbing together, Coolidge had never seen Almer resort to bare feet. That is exactly what Lehmann had done before the slack-jawed Dumas in 1832. Rifle slung over his back, feet bare, Lehmann reached the rocks via the branches of a pine lying across a gorge. As Tschudi also recounted, hunters in the canton of Schwyz often preferred to climb barefoot on the rocks. The method had its advantages, especially when long habit had trained the feet to grasp the terrain firmly, each toe clutching its support independently, they way the fingers can. But since a bare foot was not as solid as a heavily nailed boot, the hunters made it more adhesive by carefully rubbing it with resin, a piece of which they always kept handy in a pocket.

'Lehmann killed two chamois, which he carried on his back.'

CCLXXIX.

Antilope Rupicapra Pall.

I. E. Thle pinx.   I. Nußbiegel sc.

Antelope rupicapra *(Peter Simon Pallas)*.

In this same passage, Tschudi shot down an old myth. The assertion that Swiss hunters made bloody gashes in their feet, the better to hold on, was just an old wives' tale. At the same time, Tschudi made a delightful comparison between the foot of the hunter and the foot of the chamois. He pointed out that a bare foot with resin has an advantage over the shod foot in that it can widen and narrow on an inclined, slippery surface, as does a chamois foot; on the other hand, the human foot is less sure and much more likely to be wounded by harsh rocks – and a stab of pain might hurl the hunter in to the void at any moment. Finally, Tschudi noted that long excursions on glaciers would be impractical in bare feet.

When listing the qualities required of a chamois hunter, Tschudi effectively sketched the portrait of the great guides of the golden age of mountaineering, the men who spearheaded ascents often less complicated and dangerous than a day of hunting: the ascents were made without the burden of a rifle, without the need to avoid being heard or smelt, without the need to stalk, take position, fire and to pursue, not to mention the task of recovering the game and carrying it back. 'The hunter needs a sharp eye,' wrote Tschudi, 'a steady head, a strong, well-seasoned frame, a spirit resolute, calm, ready and circumspect; and, besides all this, good lungs and untiring energy. He must be not only a first-rate shot, but a first-rate climber also. For the chamois hunter often finds himself in singular predicaments; in places where he must exert every limb to the utmost, support himself by his elbow, his teeth, his back, his chin, his shoulders and use every muscle of his body as a lever or cramping-iron, in order to support or push himself forward.' In that last sentence Tschudi described an athletic sport that people would soon be trying to name.

Like a mountaineer, a chamois hunter never forgot to take along a length of rope, which had multiple uses. In the valley of Glarus, apparently a paradise for hunters, Gaspard Blümer would sometimes slide down his rope in order to reach ledges no wider than a hand on the rock faces of Vorder Glärnisch. He was a miner by profession, and one of the boldest hunters in Glarus. One day he disappeared; a year later, his shattered body was found at the foot of a high cliff.

There were also miraculous survivors among the chamois hunters. One Bernese hunter fell deep into a crevasse on the Grindelwald glacier. Finding himself unhurt, he crawled along a dark trough in which water flowed. This endless channel finally opened on to a cliff, down which the stream cascaded. The rocks were damp and worn smooth, but he managed to climb down with an energy and sangfroid born of desperation.

As a peaceful form of hunting, mountaineering naturally spread among such resourceful men.

ONE GUIDE OR ANOTHER

La Compagnie des Guides de Chamonix

Guide Joseph-Marie Couttet wielding hatchet and alpenstock at the head of a party beneath the outcrop known as the Grands Mulets.

AT THE DAWN OF THE NINETEENTH CENTURY, the profession of mountain guide did not exist. By the end of that century – La Belle Époque – it had become a legendary one: shades of the great guides do eternal battle against clouds and lion-shaped rocks. The golden age was a turning point – the profession was embodied by figures and scenes that swiftly became famous following the disaster on the Matterhorn in 1865, thanks to inexpensive reproductions similar to the images of the conquest of Mont Blanc in 1786.

The march to the summits continued apace, with differences between one guide and another that shocked travellers from Britain. Not all guides in Chamonix resembled Joseph-Marie Couttet – the 'Captain of Mont Blanc' – who reached the top of that 'great molehill' thirteen times in eighteen attempts, a very decent rate which he vaunted in a tourist brochure that he published in Geneva in 1851.

Couttet was born in 1792, the son of Marie Couttet, who had been one of Saussure's guides during the latter's historic ascent of

Joseph-Marie Couttet, by Weibel.

Mont Blanc. At age twenty, Joseph-Marie served as a cavalryman in Napoleon's Grande Armée. He was probably the first guide from Chamonix to make notable ascents outside the local chain – he was hired twice to climb the Zermatt Breithorn (4,164 metres), the first time in 1821 by the great English astronomer, John Herschel, and a second time in 1830 by the Earl of Minto. Closer to home, in 1844 Couttet guided John Ruskin to the Mer de Glace and Mont Buet.

Couttet was a lucky survivor of the Hamel party disaster on Mont Blanc in 1820. He was pulled half-dead from a crevasse after the avalanche, his face blue. Another guide, Payot, questioned about the accident by Alexandre Dumas in 1832, said that Couttet became as skittish as a marmot following that headlong dive. The 'Captain of Mont Blanc' recounted his own version to Dumas before a bottle of the finest white Montmeillan wine. Three guides died that day, thrown into a crevasse by an avalanche above the Rochers Rouges at around 4,350 metres, never to be seen again. Most surprisingly, however, at the height of the golden age in 1861, their remains resurfaced at the lower edge of the Bossons glacier, some six kilometres in a straight line from the crevasse into which they had fallen. Couttet, still alive at the time, made a comment of unwittingly dark humour when the remains were found: 'Ah, who would ever have believed it! Who would ever have believed that I could once again shake the hand of my great friend, poor Balmat?'

The victims of the Hamel disaster were all guides. As Payot told Dumas in 1832, 'Thank the Lord, only guides were killed. God has always protected travellers.'

But forty years after the Hamel party, an accident at the Col du Géant during a descent on the Italian side of Mont Blanc resulted in the death of a guide, Frédéric Tairraz, and three travellers – all English. God no longer protected travellers.

*A sketch by John Ruskin
of Joseph-Marie Couttet,
'the Captain of Mont Blanc',
climbing a rock face.*

John Tyndall carried out an investigation on the site of the accident in order to explain how the four men slipped and died. The accident looked bad for the guides' guild, La Compagnie des Guides de Chamonix, already under fire in recent years by British voyagers who complained about the way it operated, citing a few unfortunate incidents. Some Chamonix guides seemed to be as incompetent as they were impertinent.

The unequal quality of guides was well known to all, and would not have had much impact had it not been for the guild's egalitarian method of operation. The guild was a municipal institution with its own rules and a head guide to enforce those rules. It was absolute master – after God and the king of Sardinia-Piedmont – of the entire territory of Chamonix. Theoretically a praiseworthy institution, La Compagnie imposed a strict rota and thereby prevented English travellers from choosing their own guide.

Alfred Wills ridiculed and complained of this system in 1853 during a trip to the Col du Géant with Auguste Balmat, whom he met at Sallanches and hired first to go to another pass, Col de Voza (1,653 metres), between Saint-Gervais and Les Houches. When a guide was hired outside the Chamonix city limits, it was not possible to retain him once the territory of Chamonix was entered by carriage. The only way to dodge the rule was to reach Chamonix via a pass such as the Col de Voza, on foot. Some British gentlemen became most annoyed, and so they sought a direct access to Mont Blanc without setting foot in Chamonix.

Unable to find men in either Courmayeur or Saint-Gervais who were able to take them to the summit by a new route, they made the ascent on their own. These gentlemen represented the avant-garde of mountaineering, for they launched the practice of 'climbing without guides' at the very moment the reputation of guides began to grow.

On the Col de Voza, between Saint-Gervais and Les Houches.

On 14 August 1855 there were five such gentlemen: Charles Hudson (1828–1865), Edward Shirley Kennedy (1817–1898), brothers Christopher and Grenville Smyth, and Charles Ainslie. Their successful ascent was all the more resounding because Hudson published his account the following year in a tale spiced with a certain insolence. 'We have ourselves found guides to be an encumbrance rather than an assistance, and in a long walk even the best would generally be distanced by English mountaineers.'

Hudson triggered a running battle between the Chamonix guild and British travellers. After several skirmishes, war broke out following a series of accidents on the glaciers of Mont Blanc (in 1870 and 1873), which were directly blamed on La Compagnie des Guides.

The success of Hudson's party raised another question, one extensively discussed within the Alpine Club and mountaineering circles: can an amateur be as good as a guide? Some members of the Alpine Club, such as Leslie Stephen and W.A.B. Coolidge, spent their entire careers between two guides. At the same time, mountaineering without guides was growing among English and Austro-German climbers.

The first ascent of the Matterhorn without guides took place in 1876, accomplished by Messrs Cust, Cawood and Colgrove from England. The first guide-less ascent of the Meije was done by Messrs Gardiner, Pilkington and Pilkington (brothers Charles and Lawrence), also from England. Whereas it took sixty-nine years before Mont Blanc was ascended without guides, the Matterhorn only required eleven, and a mere two for the Meije – nicknamed 'La Grande Difficile' for its great wall. Each of these ascents was an affirmative reply to the question, 'Can an amateur be as good as a guide?' They would have posed a serious threat to the future of the profession of guide if all men had the same youth, drive and taste

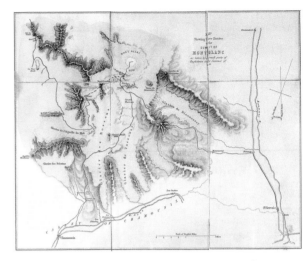

A map of Hudson's route up Mont Blanc without guides.

The 'gentlemen' reach the summit of Mont Blanc, 14 August 1855.

Reverend Charles Hudson.

The Compagnie des Guides was founded in Chamonix on 24 July 1821.

for adventure as Hudson. Or if they shared Hudson's will – the will to find a new way. In this particular case, the will went further and threatened the monopoly of a guild that defended its turf and income with the vigilance and fierceness of a poor peasant.

The mountain guide – the man in front, that epic figure throughout the Alps – was not born with the Compagnie des Guides, but it was the valley of Chamonix that first organised the profession into a guild in 1821, before any other valley in the Alps. The Oberland guides only organised themselves in 1856 and those in Pontresina, Engadin, in 1861.

On 24 July 1821, the agenda of Chamonix's municipal council meeting included the question of regulating the business of local guides for travellers. Thirty-four guides and twelve substitutes were authorised to practise the trade in a valley that, it should be recalled, still belonged to the kingdom of Sardinia-Piedmont. The door was open to any inhabitant of the Chamonix valley aged between eighteen and sixty. No exam was required – place of birth conferred competence.

Two years later, the royal administration adopted new regulations that were much more explicit and detailed, running to fifty-eight articles. This represented the true dawn of the profession of mountain guide and of an institution – La Compagnie des Guides de Chamonix.

The forty members of the guild were divided into two groups, based on experience. A head guide ran the guild, which operated on the principle of a strict rota. The guide was obliged to accept the traveller and the destination that resulted from this rota. There were two categories of excursion: ordinary and extraordinary, as per Article 15 of the royal regulations. Mont Blanc enjoyed its rank of monarch, above all the other extraordinary excursions in the chain.

Article 15: There will be two kinds of excursion, extraordinary and ordinary. Extraordinary excursions include those:

1. To the summit of Mont Blanc

2. To Le Jardin

3. On glaciers (except those that descend into the valley of Chamonix, but also those on which the traveller wishes to go above the line where vegetation ceases)

4. On the Buet glaciers.

The ordinary kind includes all other excursions to places not mentioned in the four items above.

'Le Jardin' (the garden) referred to the Jardin de Talèfre (2,787 metres), a pocket of rocks and grass in the middle of one of the tributary glaciers to the Mer de Glace at the foot of the Aiguille du Moine (3,412 metres) and the Aiguille Verte (4,122 metres), in a cirque that looked west and south toward the Grandes Jorasses, the Dent du Géant and the huge mass of Mont Blanc.

Compared to the summit of Mont Blanc, the Jardin de Talèfre was a mere stroll – but a stroll over a glacier, which meant crevasses, holes, blocks and blades of ice, and moraines that blocked the path. Travellers had to be sure of foot and equipped with a metal-tipped staff; the guide had to rope them up and monitor their progress. In short, an excursion was labelled extraordinary once the route left the beaten track, abandoning dry land for the ice of a glacier. What could be more extraordinary than a glacier?

Article 16 stipulated that the ascent of Mont Blanc required a minimum of four guides for every traveller. Each guide on a serious ascent was paid forty *livres*. To this initial expense of 160 *livres* was added the cost of provisions and porters. A party setting out for Mont Blanc – dubbed a 'caravan' in French – was a major event of the season, an important date and ceremony. After 1820,

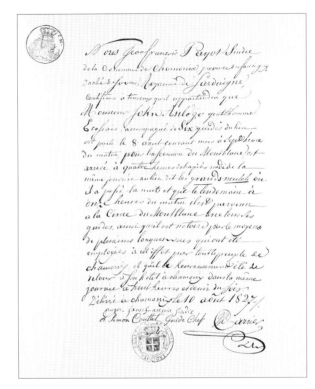

A traveller's certificate of ascent of Mont Blanc.

RÈGLEMENT

Art. 1ᵉʳ. — Il est institué dans la commune de Chamonix une Compagnie de Guides destinés à diriger les voyageurs et les touristes sur le Mont-Blanc, dans la vallée et dans les régions circonvoisines.

Art. 2. — Les habitants de Chamonix ayant leur domicile dans cette commune, et citoyens français, peuvent seuls faire partie de la Compagnie des Guides dits de Chamonix.

Art. 3. — Nul ne peut être admis Guide s'il a moins de vingt-trois ans et plus de quarante ans.

Les Guides cesseront leur service à l'âge de cinquante-cinq ans accomplis ; néanmoins, ils pourront le continuer jusqu'à soixante ans inclusivement si, par la production d'un certificat délivré par un médecin désigné par le Sous-Préfet, et d'une délibération du Conseil d'administration dûment approuvée par le même fonctionnaire, ils justifient d'une aptitude physique exceptionnelle.

Art. 4. — Tout candidat aux fonctions de Guide devra se faire inscrire au bureau du Guide-Chef sur un registre à ce destiné. Cette inscription qui donnera lieu au versement d'une somme de *cinq francs* au profit de la Caisse des

— 16 —

3° Sur les glaciers, excepté sur ceux qui descendent dans la vallée de Chamonix ; toutefois, les courses sur ces derniers glaciers sont considérées comme extraordinaires, lorsqu'on dépasse la limite de la végétation.

4° Sur les glaciers de la vallée de *Montjoie* ;

5° Et toutes les courses que les voyageurs voudraient faire dans les Alpes suisses et italiennes.

Toutes les autres courses sont comprises dans la catégorie des courses ordinaires.

Art. 33. — Pour l'ascension au *Mont-Blanc* et pour un voyageur le Guide-Chef fournira trois Guides au moins ou deux Guides et un Porteur ; pour deux voyageurs, quatre Guides ou bien trois Guides et deux Porteurs, en augmentant d'un Guide par chaque voyageur en sus.

Pour les courses aux grands cols, soit ceux du *Tour, d'Argentières, Triolet, Pierre-Joseph, Géant, Miage, Trélatéte et Tondu,* le Guide-Chef fournira, pour un voyageur, deux Guides ; pour deux voyageurs, trois Guides ou deux Guides et un Porteur ; au-dessus de deux voyageurs, un nombre de Guides égal à celui des voyageurs.

Pour les courses de sommets ou aiguilles, le nombre de Guides sera le même que pour les grands cols.

Pour la course des Grands-Mulets, il sera fourni, indépendamment des Porteurs, deux Guides au moins, s'il y a plus de deux voyageurs, et trois s'il y en a plus de quatre.

Pour la course du Jardin, il sera fourni deux Guides s'il y a plus de trois voyageurs.

Pour les autres courses ordinaires, un seul

The guides' regulations as revised in 1852.

the death of three guides in the Hamel party, buried in an avalanche, weighed on the departure of subsequent caravans. It was the first of the disasters that would occur on the slopes of Mont Blanc. Fifty years later, in 1869, as the golden age was coming to a close, the valley's annals recorded the 102nd ascent since Balmat first reached the summit in 1786.

In 1852, under King Victor Emmanuel II, new regulations containing ninety-four articles were introduced. They restricted the age of admission to the guild but abolished the limit of forty members. Henceforth any resident of Chamonix and villages in the upper valley (Argentière, Le Tour) could join the guild provided he was aged between twenty-five and forty, had obtained three certificates (certifying good morals, health and knowledge) and had 'profitably performed, in the company of an approved guide, the following excursions at least once: 1. The tour of Mont Blanc; 2. An excursion to Le Jardin; 3. Outings on the Buet glaciers and other excursions that foreigners to the valley of Chamonix commonly make.'

Guides were no longer divided into two classes. By 1824 it had been noted that this distinction had the drawback of 'making travellers think that second-class guides were less able to lead them.'

In 1823, an extraordinary excursion to Mont Blanc was six times more expensive than the cost of an ordinary guide for a day. In 1852, Mont Blanc cost fourteen times more than the ordinary day rate. The only route that led to the summit of Mont Blanc left from Chamonix. The Compagnie des Guides enjoyed a monopoly and would not brook any discussion of the price of an ascent of Mont Blanc nor of its rota system.

The principle was based on equality: each one in turn, whatever his capacities; to each guide the payment and the provisions he was due. There were no exceptions to the rule. Travellers had to

The Landscape of Susten, Switzerland by Auguste-Xavier Leprince, shows tourists and their guide on an excursion near the Aar Valley, 1824.

Crossing a crevasse near the Grands Mulets, by W. Pitschner, 1860.

accept as guides whomever came up on the rota, a rota significantly enlarged in 1851 and 1852 with the admission, in two phases, of over 150 candidates. As validated in April 1852, the rota numbered 265 individuals.

According to Article 25, a guide had to wear on his left arm a bracelet with a silver plaque inscribed 'Guides de Chamonix'.

Charles Hudson, in his famous account of his ascent of Mont Blanc without guides – published in 1856 as *Where There's a Will, There's a Way* – mocked these braceleted guides who were paid cash on the barrelhead for carrying a lady's shawl, or leading a caravan to the Flégère, or boldly slaying the Montenvers, or conducting an 'extraordinary' excursion to the Jardin de Talèfre.

The rota assigned the same task to a lap poodle as to a Pyrenean mountain dog. Hudson did not mince his words when describing the stupidity and greed behind the system's uniformity, a paradox in a land of irregular contrasts and terrific gaps between two peaks. The guild's egalitarianism was detrimental to the best guides, such as Victor Tairraz, an excellent mountaineer who went so far as to study and speak the travellers' language.

As Hudson put it:

> The traveller bent upon exploring the more difficult region of this Alpine chain is often compelled to accept as guides men competent only to escort the dilettante tourist to the giddy heights of the Montanvert, or to carry a lady's shawl to the dangerous pinnacle of the Flegère. It is not long since a friend of ours ascended Mont Blanc from Chamonix with two other gentlemen, when six of their guides, to each of whom they were obliged to give 100 francs, had never been up the mountain; while upon another occasion, two or three of the number forced upon the travellers were unable to proceed further than

the Grand Plateau, and our friend reached the summit without receiving the assistance for which he had paid so high a sum. There are, however, at Chamonix fine sturdy fellows whose intrepidity and skill have justly been the theme of admiration, and it is upon those men that the arbitrary laws press with severity and injustice. Victor Tairraz, a guide, who has taught himself English, and is a first-rate mountaineer, complains bitterly that he derives no advantage from his perseverance and superior education. At Chamonix he who is at home among the snow and glaciers, and he who is unable to pass the threshold of difficulty, are placed alike on the same level. In a country where the face of nature presents an irregularity at once so grand and so attractive, the folly or cupidity of man have attempted to establish the law of perfect equality.

At the summit of Mont Blanc, by William Beverley.

The very title of Hudson's account, *Where There's a Will, There's a Way,* speaks volumes, followed by its nose-thumbing subtitle: *An Ascent of Mont Blanc by a New Route and Without Guides.*

In 1852 Mont Blanc was indeed becoming an increasingly extraordinary excursion, if measured by total cost. Even independently wealthy gentlemen complained of the expense. The regulations required four guides for each traveller. A group of porters, more or less large depending on the guides' demands, was then needed to take the party as high as the hut known as Grand Mulets (3,051 metres), and was sometimes wanted even higher.

But in 1859, just before Savoy came under French administrative control, the number of guides per traveller to Mont Blanc was reduced to two. Hudson was perhaps right to think that his exploit would have a felicitous impact on the rates and the haughtiness of the honourable Compagnie des Guides.

CHARLES HUDSON

or Mont Blanc without Guides

The Romantic twenty-five year-old Englishman ... headed up toward the Aiguille du Goûter (3,863 metres) on his own.

CHARLES HUDSON WAS BORN IN LONDON IN 1828, the same year as Alfred Wills. His death on 14 July 1865 in the Matterhorn disaster, aged thirty-seven, was directly linked to an ascent of Mont Blanc he had completed a few days earlier. Mont Blanc was Hudson's favourite summit, his successful 1855 attempt without guides having been his finest victory. Climbing it – merely among friends, enlightened amateur gentlemen – represented a fine, forward-looking chapter in the history of mountaineering. Little by the little that history began to sparkle with bold, original feats by amateurs, given guides whose behaviour was shaped by the principle of maximum income for least effort.

Everyone in London – indeed in all Britain – dreamed of Mont Blanc, that snowy dome 4,810 metres high, ever since the journalist and conjurer Albert Smith put on his show in the Egyptian Hall. The man Whymper described as a 'genial showman' was a champion at generating publicity from his ascent of Mont Blanc, and he was partly responsible for the desire and imperious courage of the five gentlemen who reached the summit in 1855 without guides.

The Aiguille du Goûter seen from Bionnassay.

Hudson came from a good family and was a student at St John's College, Cambridge. He was an excellent oarsman, as was his future companion on Mont Blanc du Tacul and Mont Blanc itself, Edward Shirley Kennedy. Hudson was described as 'an accomplished sportsman' by a childhood friend, Reverend Joseph McCormick, who was among the party that went to seek Hudson's lifeless body at the foot of the Matterhorn in July 1865.

In the winter of 1853, Hudson had taken advantage of his studies in Geneva to make an ascent of the Dôle in January, to bivouac on the Col d'Anterne (2,264 metres) in February, and then in March to attack a summit whose steps descended toward Geneva: Mont Blanc.

In his first original move, Hudson approached the summit via the Aiguille du Goûter (3,863 metres); with unprecedented boldness, he attacked it in winter (March 1853).

Finally, in an unheard-of move, the romantic twenty-five-year-old Englishman refused to be discouraged by everyone else's dismay and headed up toward the Aiguille du Goûter on his own, for an hour and half, after his three chamois hunters defected.

The wind and whirling snow that paralysed the veterans awakened a wild enthusiasm in Hudson:

> He who from the deck of the tempest-tossed ship would revel in the approach of the angry foaming billows – he who would rejoice with a thrilling pleasure in the proximity of the resistless thundering avalanche – or he who on the rugged mountain, and while the lightning played about him, would feel an additional flow of spirits in battling with the furious elements; – this man, and perhaps he alone, could fully sympathise in the feelings of delight with which I now contemplated the scene around.

aus freier Hand gezeichnet.

Panoramic view of the peaks of the Monte Rosa chain.

Hudson, axe in hand, halted beneath the summit of the Aiguille du Goûter, fifteen minutes away from the broad, easy slopes that head toward the Arête des Bosses, the ridge that culminates at the summit of Mont Blanc. A few drops of alcohol on a piece of sugar, a last glance at the summit, then Hudson had to begin the tricky descent, sometimes wielding the axe and sometimes setting it down to grasp the rock with both hands. Two later attempts, in April, stalled on the same slopes. In 1854 Hudson served as a chaplain during the Crimean War, and travelled to Armenia. The historian Jacques Perret, in his foreword to a French edition of Hudson's famous account of Mont Blanc, referred to a probable ascent of Mount Ararat by Hudson. The English mountaineer had indeed planned it, but renounced the idea.[2]

2. Charles Gos, *Le Cervin: Vol. I, L'Époque héroïque* and *Vol. II, Faces, grandes arêtes* (Paris: Attinger, 1948).

'We reached the ice shelf ...'

Hudson did not pick up his ice axe again until August 1855. He warmed up on the Zermatt Breithorn, and made the first ascent of the highest peak on Monte Rosa, the Dufourspitze (4,638 metres), on 1 August 1855, in the company of his friends Christopher and Grenville Smyth, Edward John Stevenson and John Birkbeck. They were guided by big Ulrich Lauener and three other Bernese guides. Less than one week later, on 7 August, a party of six gentlemen attacked Mont Blanc from Courmayeur, along with porters who halted, as planned, at the Col du Géant, where the Englishmen roped up and continued their climb across the glacier in deep snow. There were no guides. Hudson was accompanied by his friends from Monte Rosa (the Smyth brothers and Stevenson), plus E.S. Kennedy and Charles Ainslie. They spent a very rough night in the Smyths' tent at the Gros Rognon (3,541 metres) near the Col du Midi. In the morning, shrouded in thick, shifting mist, the party advanced behind Kennedy armed with a compass (a technique unknown to guides) and a rather poor map that J.D. Forbes had given them. Nearly forty years later, in 1894, an ageing Kennedy recalled, in a letter to Coolidge, the windy conditions:

> After leaving our sleeping quarters near the Rognon, I was the leading man, the distinction having been conferred upon me for the simple reason that I was the possessor of the map that had been roughly sketched by Professor Forbes. We reached the ice shelf whence we would look down upon the Grands Mulets and the Plateau of glaciers between us and the Dôme du Goûter. Thence Hudson was leader. We had no guide with us but were all roped. A heavy storm was upon us, so loud was the roar of the wind that even with mouth close to the ear of the next man, no word could be heard. Hudson with his customary determination forced his way ahead, while *nous*

autres, we five, allowed the rope to pass through our hands. He was soon out of sight and at the end of his tether, he then unroped and went a short distance further. Upon his return he reported that during a brief lifting of the mist, he had looked down the opposite side of the ridge of Mont Blanc du Tacul, and come to the conclusion that the passage ahead between the two peaks of the Mont Maudit was practicable.

The curtains of freezing mist and fine snow, however, prompted a retreat to the Col du Géant and Courmayeur, where they altered their plan. They would attack from the other slope, via the Col de la Seigne, Contamines and Saint-Gervais.

At 9 a.m. on 15 August everyone at the Hôtel du Mont-Joly in Saint Gervais was at the balcony waving colourful handkerchiefs to see off the party which headed up toward two wretched, roofless stone huts built by chamois hunters at the foot of the Aiguille du Goûter, at a spot called Tête Rousse (3,160 metres). This high plateau had a natural spring and faced the setting sun. The six Englishmen and three chamois hunters (Cuidet, Mollard and Hoste) set out at 4 a.m. and reached the Dôme du Goûter (4,304 metres), a semi-plateau of snow beneath the slopes of the Arête des Bosses, without Mollard, who had returned to Saint-Gervais. The party descended the short, mild slope leading to the Grand Plateau, where the two other hunters left the party of gentlemen after pointing out the usual route up Mont Blanc, between two crevasses.

Their kindness was unnecessary – that route up Mont Blanc was obvious to the gentlemen climbers who, not wanting to waste time and energy in the wind whipping across the Arête des Bosses (a then unknown route), resolutely headed toward the foot of the Mur de la Côte. Albert Smith's show in London had presented this

Crossing the Crevasse du Dôme, by T.D.H. Browne.

feature as a nearly perpendicular wall of ice with a staggering effect upon travellers, a place where any false step would be fatal. The five men studied the slope, hands clutching their weapons. They were well armed, according to their own account. 'Ainslie and Kennedy carried ash poles with steel spikes, which they brought from England; Grenville and Christopher Smyth and Hudson carried haches [*sic*], which are ashen poles from four to five feet in length with iron heads about ten inches long and sharpened exactly like a small pick-axe.' On 14 August 1855, Hudson, Kennedy, Christopher and Grenville, and Ainslie finally arrived at the summit of Mont Blanc. It was 12.35 p.m.

Two of the climbers rowed a boat that bore the motto *Labor ipse voluptas.* 'Effort itself is a pleasure.' That was Hudson's reply to people who asked him if the view from the summit was worth the effort.

Four years later, on 29 July 1859, the Arête des Bosses gave Hudson pleasure step by step. After a night spent in the hut at the Grands Mulets, his party was climbing the ridge he had glimpsed in March 1853. There were four guides, including Melchior Anderegg, and three travellers, who made their way up this ridge of 'bumps' (*bosses*) with no difficulty, enjoying the scenic stroll. Today it is a highway to the summit, the most heavily travelled arête in the chain. Just two years later, the entire Goûter ridge – along the Aiguille, Dôme and Bosses – would be climbed by a party with some of the most famous names of that period: Leslie Stephen, F.F. Tuckett, Melchior Anderegg, Peter Perren, and Johann-Josef Bennen. It was 18 July 1861.

It was common in the nineteenth century to quote famous authors and maxims, as typified by Hudson's choice of title for his account: *Where There's a Will, There's a Way*. As to the text itself, it was simultaneously account, manifesto and brief essay. Hudson addressed all those who dreamed of adventure in the Alps without

*Crossing the glacier
beneath the Grand Mulets,
The Route from Chamonix
to Mont Blanc, print by
Gabriel Loppé, 1855.*

having to pay a guide. The cost was extravagant, and all the more exorbitant in that some guides halted even before the summit was reached. In 1855 the Compagnie des Guides expelled five guides who were struck with panic – or laziness – on the Grand Plateau. The five fellows not only refused to lead but, worse, to follow the party in their charge.

Climbing mountains without guides created a double fracture – in the monopoly of the Compagnie des Guides and in the prestige of guides themselves. Mountaineering was henceforth split into two schools, those who climbed with guides, and those who climbed without them. At the close of the golden age, usually dated 1870, Reverend A.G. Girdlestone, a member of the Alpine club, recounted all his independent climbs – over seventy in total – in *The High Alps without Guides.* Meanwhile, Eugène Rambert's *Les Alpes Suisses,* published in 1864, presented mountaineering without guides as a great game. Rambert recommended this game to readers, but only after a mandatory period of initiation, and always with a companion of one's choosing. He wrote that, 'The tourist will find for himself passages already found by others, he will have the pleasure of making if not original discoveries at least discoveries for himself; in any event, he will have to find his way, and if by chance he manages to open a completely new route, if he stands on truly virgin soil, it will be an additional pleasure, another laurel, a crowning glory.' Rambert felt that the game lost half its appeal when conducted by a guide. It was sometimes said of top-notch mountaineers such as Charles Hudson, 'He's as good as a guide.' The best independent climbers nevertheless acknowledged the superiority of those guides who were hardened by chamois hunting and seasoned by life in the mountains and the regular habit of climbing. A well-known independent climber admitted more than once to Coolidge, who always climbed with a guide, that amateur climbers

THE

HIGH ALPS WITHOUT GUIDES:

BEING

A NARRATIVE OF ADVENTURES IN SWITZERLAND,

TOGETHER WITH CHAPTERS ON THE PRACTICABILITY OF SUCH MODE
OF MOUNTAINEERING, AND SUGGESTIONS FOR ITS ACCOMPLISHMENT.

BY

REV. A. G. GIRDLESTONE, M.A.
LATE DEMY IN NATURAL SCIENCE OF MAGDALEN COLLEGE, OXFORD.

'Qui œtabit optimos cursus contingere autem
Multa tulit fecitque.' HORACE.

WITH A FRONTISPIECE AND TWO MAPS.

LONDON:
LONGMANS, GREEN, AND CO.
1870.

The adventures of an early guideless climber, A.G. Girdlestone.

suffered above all from two weaknesses:

1. The tendency to allow alertness to drop once the major difficulties are behind them.

2: The huge amount of energy required by an amateur to carry his own knapsack, even when divested of everything inessential – whereas guides are accustomed from childhood to carrying heavy loads on their backs.

Life in the mountains in the nineteenth century, when children were charged with hauling and other laborious tasks, was the best training for a profession that involved traipsing up and down, hoisting oneself up, climbing and gritting one's teeth with a load on one's back – for hour after hour. According to Leslie Stephen, it was their hardy childhood in the fresh, high-altitude air that explained the superiority and flair of guides, which he admiringly witnessed more than once in the Bernese Oberland, his own favourite playground. Stephen was led – well led – by the best guides, including the gigantic *capitaine* Lauener and Melchior Anderegg (the guide on Mont Blanc's Arête des Bosses, who shortly afterward, axe in hand, scaled the icy Brenva Spur on the Italian side of the same summit).

Coolidge, who retired to Grindelwald in 1900, watched a lad grow up over several consecutive winters, keeping behind his father in the snow of a steep, 600-metre slope up to the family's pasture chalet. It was one effort among others in a life of slopes near and far. The task of the day was often dictated by the colour of the sky. One learned to keep an eye on the skies, to interpret the movement of clouds, to sense the threat in any change in appearance of a local barometer-peak such as the Wetterhorn. At this particular game, big Ulrich Lauener was unbeatable.

According to Stephen, 'every mountaineer has certain acquired instincts, which are invaluable, and only to be gained by experience. To a man who has been a chamois hunter from his youth, and lived

A hardy childhood in the high-altitude air . . . explained the flair of guides.

on the mountains from his birth, the snows and rocks and clouds speak by signs which we are unable to read.'[3] Someone trained in this school is rarely caught out, argued Stephen. 'A guide's judgment as to the state of the snow and the danger of avalanches is generally infallible. Again, although even a guide very often pronounces a place impracticable, which has subsequently been ascended, he can almost always pick out at a glance the most practicable line of assault.' All commentators agreed that even the best guides were unable to read a map, much less use a compass as amateur travellers did. What guides possessed, however, was a memory of places and a kind of instinct developed by experience. When descending from a climb, all shapes and angles of view of the slope become reversed, yet even in the darkness a guide could distinguish between the three gullies ahead and could choose the right one, to Stephen's great surprise. A good sense of direction thus entailed an ability to follow a route in the opposite direction and in different light. A mountainside, like a face, changes greatly in appearance according to the height and intensity of the sun. Stephen again: 'Another faculty, often very useful, acquired by experience, is the power of retracing without a moment's hesitation a path once taken. It is frequently very puzzling for an amateur to recognise the wilderness of rocks he has passed in the morning, when approaching them at night from the opposite side. A guide can almost always find it, as if he was tracking by a bloodhound's sense of smell.'

Men are not born guides, but being born and living in the mountains, walking on rocks or snow as soon as one learns to put one front in front of the other, acquiring a personal hoard of impressions and feelings at an age when one retains everything, gives a guide that sense of mountaineering which can be learned nowhere other than the mountains. Being born in Chamonix or Grindelwald

3. Leslie Stephen, *The Playground of Europe* (1st edn, London: Longmans, Green & Co., 1871).

On the chaotic glaciers of Mont Blanc, by Edmund Thomas Coleman.

The Aiguille Verte, the Dru and the Glacier des Bois by moonlight, by Jean-Antoine Linck.

was, and still is, an advantage on condition that one has a taste for the mountains, as well as the 'will' so vaunted since Victorian times.

Where there's a will, there's a man.

Reverend Charles Hudson, appointed vicar of Skillington, Lincolnshire, in 1860, married in 1861, the year his friend John Birkbeck took a spectacular fall at the Col de Miage, sliding 400 metres. After honeymooning in Zermatt in 1862, Hudson did not return to the Alps until 1865. His reputation as an excellent mountaineer did not fade during those years of absence; and even had it waned slightly, his ascent of the Aiguille Verte on 5 July 1865, the second just after Whymper's first ascent, would have fully re-established it. Stephen declared that Hudson was the most enterprising mountaineer he had ever met.

Hudson climbed Mont Blanc a third time, on 7 July 1865, with T.S. Kennedy (not to be confused with E.S. Kennedy, Hudson's partner in 1855, and the second president of the Alpine Club), his friend McCormick, and D.R. Hadow (who would make the fatal slip that killed Hudson on the Matterhorn). The guides were Michel Croz and Peter Perren. They left Pierre Pointue (2,038 metres) at 1 a.m., and reached the summit at 8.50 a.m., a few minutes behind a party who had left from the Grands Mulets. The nineteen-year-old Hadow was practically a beginner (having previously attained just one summit, Mont Buet, 3,096 metres), but never asked for a rest or complained about the pace of a rapid ascent of a whopping 2,800 metres in altitude. On the way back down, however, Peter Perren had to belay him here and there, as the weary Hadow began to falter.

The seeds of the Matterhorn tragedy were sown on Mont Blanc: Hadow had done so well.

Hudson's third ascent of Mont Blanc would be his last.

CHAPTER VIII

THE ALPINE CLUB

Peter Perrn of course
(see 'The Club Room of Zermatt' 1864)

Do not know ↓   A. W. Moore ↓   Rev. H. B. George ↓   Russell Stephenson ↓

F. Morshead ↑   Melchior Anderegg ↑   Reginald Macdonald ↑   Christian Almer (I think, but am not sure) ↑

The Alpine Club defended the principle of a sport — of climbing simply for the sake of climbing. The point of an ascent was the ascent itself, not some scientific advance.

The antics of a small band of men who are simply trying hard
to see how near they can come to breaking their necks.

W.A.B. Coolidge

SWITZERLAND MIGHT HAVE FOUNDED EUROPE'S FIRST ALPINE CLUB as early as 1840. Under the impetus of topographers and naturalists, the planting of flags on summits evolved into a movement of enthusiasts. Swiss historian Charles Gos was a valuable disciple of Coolidge. Thanks to his research, we know that in 1840 a Swiss newspaper suggested that explorers of glaciers and virgin peaks unite forces: 'Why not create a federal association for mountain exploration?'

The same idea germinated – and ripened – among the Englishmen of the golden age. A letter from William Mathews (1828–1901) addressed to Reverend F.J.A. Hort, dated 1 February 1857, proposed the establishment of a club for fans of Alpine expeditions. The twenty-nine-year-old Mathews, from Worcester, was a recent convert, his first major summit having been Mont Vélan in 1854. Two years later, he reached the highest peak of Monte Rosa, first conquered in 1855. In 1863 the Swiss would declare that peak, Dufourspitze (4,638 metres), the highest point in Switzerland.

Guillaume-Henri Dufour (1787–1875) was a Swiss general in the engineering corps. He had studied at the prestigious École

William Mathews.

George Spencer Mathews.

Polytechnique in France and had headed all of Switzerland's topographic missions. He devoted twenty years of labour, from 1845 to 1865, to compiling a complete, twelve-map topographic atlas of Switzerland, called the Dufour Map. It was a priceless tool for the men known as 'Alpine climbers'.

Mathews had two younger brothers, Charles Edward Mathews (1834–1905) and George Spencer Mathews (1836–1904). They shared William's enthusiasm for the challenge and vagaries of Alpine travel. We will come across George again on the Brenva Spur of Mont Blanc in 1865.

It was with his brother Charles that William climbed the Combin de Corbassière in Valais in 1856, with a guide recommended by the head guide at Chamonix, Auguste Balmat. That guide was none other than Auguste Simond, famously reputed to be able to lift a man at arm's length.

Mathews praised Simond's zeal, energy and courage in an account that ended in an appeal to minds fatigued by the bustle of industrial society. 'To those who feel wearied – as who does not at times – with the ceaseless mill-work of England in the nineteenth century, there is no medicine so soothing both to mind and body as Alpine travel, affording as it does interesting observation and healthy enjoyment for the present, and pleasant memories for the time to come.'

A new society had emerged between 1800 and 1850, one full of factories, machines and noise, none of which had yet reached the Alps. An Alpine excursion was not just an adventure for body and mind, it was an antidote to another activism of which the English, those pioneers of the industrial revolution, were the first victims, in a way. A trip to the Alps was relaxing for people worn out, aggravated or depressed by this new civilisation. 'Spleen', in the sense of severe boredom or depression in an era of machines, was born on this island of factories and merchants. This notion of spleen, once it crossed the English Channel, settled in the wretched outskirts of Paris and populated the poems of Baudelaire. It became the disease of the age and the curse of large industrial cities.

The Flowers of Evil was first published in 1857. The poet and dandy Charles Baudelaire (1821–1867) was a contemporary of those English gentlemen. 'Fabulous voyagers!' exclaimed Baudelaire in a poem titled *Le Voyage.* The true travellers in that poem left simply for the sake of leaving. Founded shortly afterward, the Alpine Club defended the principle of a sport – of climbing simply for the sake of climbing. The point of an ascent was the ascent itself, not some scientific advance in knowledge of rocks or glaciers. Mountaineering for mountaineering's sake, Alpine travel for Alpine travel's sake – and for the sake of all the sweat, surprises and dangers overcome during that Alpine voyage.

On 3 August 1857, William Mathews ran into E.S. Kennedy in the Hasli valley. Kennedy had been Charles Hudson's friend and companion in the subsequently famous ascent of Mont Blanc without guides. Mathews immediately hit it off with Kennedy, whom he hadn't previously met. The friendship was consolidated by a joint ascent – the first English ascent – of the Finsteraarhorn and by their shared interest in establishing a club for keen Alpine travellers.

The two men met again on 6 November 1857 in Birmingham, England, where they dined at Mathews' home and organised the first meeting of the Alpine Club on 22 December 1857. This first meeting was swiftly followed by the club's first dinner, in February 1858, thanks to Kennedy's energetic correspondence with all the future founding members.

Edward Shirley Kennedy (1817–1898) was unrelated to another member of the Alpine Club, Thomas Stuart Kennedy (1841–1894), with whom he is often confused. E.S. Kennedy had notably inherited a substantial fortune.

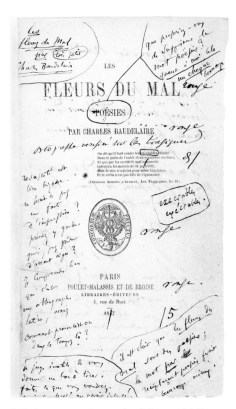

'Fabulous voyagers!' wrote Baudelaire in 1857.

'Many English take delight in exerting ... themselves.'

One of the Alpine Club's first goals was to centralise information, providing members with details on the feasibility – or not – of a given excursion to Alpine peaks, because purely verbal accounts of the early ascents had led to great confusion. For instance, the Englishmen had gone to the Finsteraarhorn in 1857 with the enthusiasm of making an absolute first climb of that peak. Once on the spot, they were disappointed to be told by Oberland guide Johann Jaun that theirs would be the fifth ascent, he himself having scaled it twice.

At first the Alpine Club met only for the occasional dinner. Kennedy was elected vice president during the founding dinner at which Thomas Woodbine Hinchliff (1825–1882), author of an Alpine account,[4] was named secretary. One month later John Ball accepted the presidency of a club that still had just thirty-four founding members. By 1859 the club already had acquired a certain prestige due to its originality and the quality of its members, and it elected the great glaciologist J.D. Forbes as its first honorary member. At that time, the Alpine Club numbered 124 members. In 1893, the way the club worked was explained by Claude Wilson in *Mountaineering,* one of the earliest climbing manuals. By then it had already become the English club most well known on the European continent – in France some philosophers considered it to be the club the most typical of English character, as Hippolyte Taine wrote in 1872: 'For persons of a particular temperament, difficulty, trouble and danger are incentives. Many English take delight in exerting, hardening or forcing themselves to surmount obstacles; the Alpine Club and other associations are proof of this.'[5] The headquarters of the Alpine Club with its rich library of books, maps and documents on all mountains of the world, were located

4. T.W. Hinchliff, *Summer Months Among the Alps* (London: Longmans & Roberts, 1857).
5. Hippolyte Taine, *Notes on England,* trans. W.F. Rae (London: Strachan & Co., 1872).

near Trafalgar Square in London. The club met six times a year and hosted two dinners, one public, the other private. A candidate for admission had to be sponsored by a member who knew him personally. A 'climbing qualification', or list of ascents, was required. This requirement of skill and experience is what made the Alpine Club a very closed, elitist group, unlike the mountaineering clubs founded a few years later on the continent, where payment of dues was all that was required for membership.

In 1871, the Alpine Club had 298 members; there were 361 in 1875, and 444 in 1881. And on the eve of the First World War, in January 1913, the club numbered 730 members. It would be a mistake to take these figures as evidence of the popularity and scope of the mountaineering movement: the Austrian and German alpine clubs boasted 100,000 members, the Swiss alpine club numbered 13,000, the Italian club had 7,500 members and the French club 6,500. One would be equally mistaken to think that all members of these clubs were mountaineers. Count Russell ridiculed that mass of mountaineers who claimed the same status won by members of the Alpine Club with such difficulty. Russell, so sensitive to quality and to solitude on the summit, so allergic to 'populocracy', claimed that only one club member out of ten, among that mass of tourists with hobnailed boots spouting stories at the tables of inns, was a mountaineer worthy of the name.

In the spring of 1859, with the Alpine Club's purpose of informing and documenting in mind, John Ball put together and published accounts of ascents made by various members of the club. The volume was titled *Peaks, Passes and Glaciers.* In 1862, the Austrians, who had preceded the English in exploring the Alps by several decades, founded their own alpine club (Österreichischer Alpenverein). The Swiss finally founded the Schweizer Alpen Club in April 1863, the club they could have established over twenty

Louis Robach and Count Henry Russell in the Pyrenees.

Edited by John Ball in 1859.

127

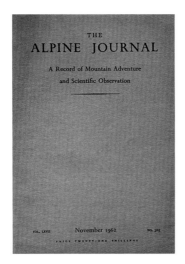

The first issued was published in 1863.

Quintino Sella, by Domenico Morelli.

years earlier. In Italy, Quintino Sella, a wealthy industrialist and an eminent politician from Piedmont, founded the Club Alpino Italiano in October 1863 with his friend, the engineer Felice Giordano. Sella had vowed to do so on 12 August of that same year when he reached the summit of Monte Viso in the company of three 'worthy men' (*valentuomini*).

Alpine excursions had indeed become a new, sociable pastime in Europe for elites who read Saussure, ranging from London to Turin and from Turin to Vienna. In just a few years those same elites would be reading Tyndall and Whymper. More than anyone, Whymper conveyed the impression of a new movement in Europe. The history of mountaineering, which is also the history of a sensibility, includes qualitative leaps forward. The Matterhorn brought one period to a close in a tragic, blinding leap.

The first issue of the *Alpine Journal,* edited by the Alpine Club's third president, H.B. George (1838–1810), was published in March 1863. This quarterly magazine of accounts and scholarly studies was the first periodical solely devoted to the mountains.

The journal served as a model for the later *Annuaire* published by the Club Alpin Français (founded 1874), combining articles of alpine science (glaciology, geology, botany, toponomy, history, etc.) with accounts of climbs. An account of a climb is an apparently easy genre, like travel writing, but soon sinks to commonplaces and clichés if the author lacks talent. The great master of mountaineering writing in France during the early days was Irish by his father and French by his mother: Henry, Count Russell-Killough (1834–1909). The count had a comfortable income and became a passionate explorer of the Pyrenees as well as a founding member of the Club Alpin Français. He launched the club's series of *Annuaires* with a masterful article on the adventurous conditions in which he explored the Pyrenees around 1860 in the company of his friend Charles Packe (1826–1896), a Scottish lawyer, naturalist and member of the Alpine Club. Packe was very keen on the Pyrenees, exploring them with the same unmitigated love as the count. He vaunted the colours of the skies, rocks and light of the Pyrenees to the Alpine Club by publishing the first guide on the chain in 1862: *A Guide to the Pyrenees, Especially Intended for the Use of Mountaineers.*

Packe, Russell, an English photographer named Farnham Maxwell Lyte and French pastor Émilien Frossard (a naturalist who also did drawings in an Romantic-metaphysical style), founded the Société Ramond at an inn in Gavarnie in 1864, which makes it the oldest French mountaineering club. In 1896, in memoirs written after Packe's death, Russell stated that mountaineering had not been a question of 'convulsive gymnastics' for Packe, but rather a kind of religion or cult. Russell had a way with words, and noted that back in 1860 'the Pyrenees were as unexplored as the Mountains of the Moon' (he was alluding to the Rwenzori Mountains, a mysterious chain in the heart of the lakes region of Africa, a largely unknown continent in 1860).

Mountaineering is a product of the exploration of mountains, an offshoot of the great campaign of exploration and conquest carried out by Europe in the nineteenth century. That campaign covered the entire planet. The first mountaineers walked into the unknown realm of summits, peaks and glaciers. They rightly considered themselves to be twin brothers of the great explorers, as well as fans of a new game. E.S. Kennedy described his thoughts on making the first ascent to the summit of Monte Disgrazia in August 1862.

> The view is sublime, and I enjoy it. The top is an object in every way worthy of attainment, and as an heirloom to posterity I would transmit it. The memorial

Charles Packe.

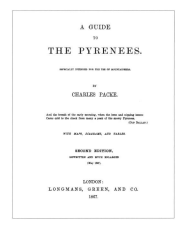

Packe's guide to the Pyrenees.

to succeeding generations raises a feeling gratifying to the pride of man, and I am a partaker in it. The crust of bread recruits exhausted strength, and I devour it; the wine is nectar itself, and I relish it; the pipe is universal, but I nauseate it. The scientific observation is of the utmost importance, and with most unfeigned satisfaction do I behold others trying to keep their hands warm why they are conducting it. But, to my mind, each and every one of the sources of gratification sink into insignificance when compared with the exhilarating consciousness of difficulty overcome, and of success attained by perseverance.

The Club Alpin Français was only founded in 1874. In the case of France, unlike Switzerland and Austria, the late date reflects the real and almost total absence of the French in the field of exploration, with the sole exception of the 1859 ascent of the Grand Combin (4,314 metres) by geologist Charles Sainte-Claire Deville.

In July 1863 John Ball published the first volume of his *Alpine Guide,* being a compilation of descriptions of routes in the western Alps. A second volume, on the central Alps, appeared in 1864, while the third and final volume, on the eastern Alps, was published in 1868. Just as no English tourist ventured into Switzerland without John Murray's *Handbook for Travellers in Switzerland and the Alps of Savoy and Piedmont* (first edition, 1838), after Ball published his guides no English traveller with mountaineering ambitions left without consulting those remarkable volumes, which were similar in principle to Murray's guide but far more specialised.

A guidebook by German physician and geologist Johann Gottfried Ebel (1764–1830) predated Murray's guide, for it was published at the end of the eighteenth century. This already hefty

The Club Alpin Français was founded in 1874.

guide, in German (*Anleitung, auf die nützlichste und genussvollste Art in der Schweitz zu reisen*) even offered a remedy for vertigo. 'Before venturing a difficult step, fill your eyes with the sight of precipices until the impression that they make upon your imagination fades, and you can look at them coolly.'

Murray's guide served as a model for guidebooks in French (Joanne) and German (Baedeker). Ball's volumes meanwhile became the model for mountaineering guidebooks whose role is often crucial in the choice of route. His rather impersonal books do not give a sense of Ball's own voice, however. For that we must turn to the accounts Ball published in *Peaks, Passes and Glaciers*.

There were two series of *Peaks, Passes and Glaciers*. The first, edited by Ball in 1859, was immediately translated into French as *Grimpeurs des Alpes* ('Alpine Climbers'). E.S. Kennedy, the second president of the Alpine Club, edited the second series in 1862 — one of its two volumes included an article by Packe on the Pyrenees. The first series had also included an ascent of Etna. Despite its name, the Alpine Club sought to climb all the mountains of the world with its characteristic curiosity and enjoyment of the game. Universal curiosity went hand in hand with imperial dreams, as indicated in a humorous tone by J.F. Hardy at the start of his description of the ascent of Etna in Sicily, in the footsteps of Saussure. '[T]he Alpine Club, while it derives its name from one familiar group of mountains, is thoroughly Catholic in its principles, and already sees visions of a banner with a strange device floating on the summit of Popocatepetl and of Dharwalagiri, and is hoping by the influence of its enlightened members to drive out the last remnants of the worship of the Mighty Mumbo Jumbo from the Mountains of the Moon.'

Members of the Alpine Club generally enjoyed the liberty afforded by a certain affluence. (Whymper, the plebeian artisan engraver,

John Ball.

Alfred Wills, well equipped, in 1870.

Lucy Walker, the first woman on the Matterhorn, pictured in 1864.

was an exception.) In 1863, the 288 members of the Alpine Club included fifty-seven barristers, thirty-three solicitors, thirty-four clergymen, nineteen major landowners, and fifteen professors. Alfred Wills was a judge later elevated to the peerage – Lord Wills – at a time when the inflation of such honours was being brought under control. A.W. Moore was a senior civil servant with the India Office and a statesman. Francis Walker was an affluent merchant from Liverpool. E.S. Kennedy, the mainstay of the club in its early years, was a man of independent means. Charles Hudson, the Smyth brothers, H.B. George, J. Elliott and J.F. Hardy were all clergymen. T.S. Kennedy was an industrialist and man of means who inherited a fortune. F.F. Tuckett was in the leather trade in Bristol. Leslie Stephen was not only a professor of literature but an eminent literary critic. John Tyndall, the physicist and glaciologist, was one of the best-known scientists of his day, a thinker deeply involved in the debate between science and religion, between reason and faith.

The Alpine Club was a male club, and would remain so even after a few women began playing the gentlemen's game. Lucy Walker (1836–1916), daughter of Francis Walker and sister of Horace Walker (who accompanied Whymper and Moore on the Barre des Écrins), soon showed her mettle during the family's trips to the Alps. After observing Lucy, her father included her on his excursions. In 1864, Francis Walker had the honour of making the first ascent, with guides Jakob and Melchior Anderegg, of the Balmhorn (3,698 metres), a summit in the Bernese Alps. On 22 July 1871, Lucy, a regular member of the Walkers' summer excursions, became the first woman to reach the summit of the legendary Matterhorn. Her father was also present, and was proud of his daughter as well as himself (then aged sixty-five). The guides on this nineteenth ascent of the Matterhorn included Melchior

Anderegg and Peter Perren. But one or two exceptions didn't change the mentality of the day. A men's club must remain a men's club. The first woman was not admitted to the Alpine Club until 1974, over a century after the climbs made by Lucy Walker and fellow mountaineers Meta Brevoort (Coolidge's aunt) and Isabella Straton.

The Alpine Club acquired an immense reputation in very little time. It reflected the influence of a multitude of ascents in the Alps, but also the influence of a country, a culture, an elite. The Alpine Club was a gathering place not only for the mountaineering elite, it was part of the elite which built the Victorian empire, an empire on land and sea, a planet-wide empire of a scope and power unprecedented in history.

Swiss guide Peter Perren showed consideration for his English travellers on the summit of Lyskamm (19 August 1861), by silencing his men when they sang a German anthem. Instead, the fourteen mountaineers sang *God Save the Queen,* the anthem of a nation soon at the peak of its domination.

The summit of the Lyskamm.

CHAPTER IX

JOHN BALL
AND JOHN RUSKIN

John Ruskin's drawing of the Aiguille de Blaitière, one of the needles in the Mont Blanc range above Chamonix.

What sort of human, pre-eminently human,
feeling it is that loves a stone for a stone's sake,
and a cloud for a cloud's? A monkey loves a monkey
for a monkey's sake, and a nut for the kernel's,
but not a stone for a stone's. I took stones for bread …

John Ruskin

As an active politician (having served as a liberal member of parliament for eighteen years), a botanist, a voyager and an author of travel guides, John Ball was highly representative of the figures who founded and ran the Alpine Club. His election as first president of the club in 1858 was no coincidence. For over a decade Ball had been criss-crossing, exploring, and analysing the Alps he loved, both glacial and rocky, as he collected plants and negotiated passes and valleys, forging new passages. A Catholic Irishman like Count Henry Russell, Ball was born in Dublin. After studying classics at Cambridge he served as under-secretary of state for the colonies in 1855, but gave up politics following an election defeat in Ireland in 1858.

He was an early pioneer of the Alps, a lone, umbrella-toting explorer and naturalist. Ball found his umbrella to be highly useful protection not only against the rain but also against the heat of the sun on snow. The Schwarztor (3,374 metres), that 'black gate' between Switzerland and Italy, was a glacier pass above Zermatt between Roccia Nera (4,075 metres) and Pollux (4,091 metres).

John Ball, an early pioneer.

No one in living memory had crossed this pass from the Zermatt side. Ball did so on 18 August 1845, christening it. According to locals, the pass had formerly been used by the inhabitants of Gressoney on pilgrimage to Sion ('the Jerusalem of Valais'), and descended into the Italian valley of Gressoney without serious difficulty. But the Zermatt slope, full of crevasses and seracs, appeared to hold some surprises. Ball always had his opera glasses by his side. He scanned the rugged terrain of the glacier, confirming the need for caution. He realised that he had 'to secure a companion in the undertaking. It is an indefensible piece of rashness to travel alone in the upper region of the glaciers; no amount of skill and experience can avert the almost certain consequences of the yielding of the snow that covers over a concealed crevasse.'

J.B. Brantschen, Ball's steady guide in previous weeks, refused point blank to accompany him on such terrain. Ball reluctantly hired a certain Mathias, a taciturn fellow without initiative, who simply carried gear and was alarmingly awkward in his gait. When two crevasse systems intersected, the two men firmly roped themselves together. Ball walked in front, Mathias behind. In an initial incident, Ball suddenly dropped, sinking up to his shoulders. Mathias paled and begged to turn back. Ball reassured him by repeating that there was nothing to fear with the sturdy rope around their waists. Mathias carried all the provisions, including a small keg of wine, an apparatus for boiling water and three slats of iron designed to fit into two solid alpenstocks, thereby converting them into a temporary ladder or bridge. Indeed, Ball conscientiously informed readers of his personal list of equipment for high-altitude climbs:

> Foremost, I place a knitted woollen waistcoat with sleeves, such as the country people wear in many parts of France; it is invaluable when a night has to be passed in cold or damp quarters after a hard day's walk. A few very

small tin canisters are the best means of carrying a slight provision of tea, chocolate, and raisins. A one-volume Shakspeare [*sic*] is a safe resource for a wet day. I plead guilty to one or two other luxuries, including slippers to rest the feet after long walking. To my knapsack is strapped a stout piece of rope about thirty feet long, with a Scotch plaid and umbrella; the last, though often scoffed at, is an article that hot sunshine, even more than rain, has taught me to appreciate. A couple of thermometers, a pocket klinometer, and a Kater's compass with prismatic eye-piece, may be carried in suitable pockets, along with a note-book and a sketch-book, having a fold for writing-paper, &c.; a good opera-glass, which I find more readily available than a telescope; strong knife, measuring tape, a veil, and spectacles, leather cup, spare cord, and matches. A flask with strong cold tea, to be diluted with water or snow, a tin box for plants, a geological hammer, of a form available for occasional use as an ice axe, with a strap to keep all tight, and prevent anything from swinging loosely in awkward places, complete the accoutrement.

In short, the adventurer's gear of 1845 is not all that outmoded, apart from the woollen waistcoat, veil (against snow blindness) and a few small items (leather cup, matches, etc.), which would not be replaced until after 1945 – that is to say, a full century after Ball's Schwarztor escapade. This list of basic implements responds to specific needs and has not varied, even if industrial advances have modified the materials of which they are made. It is hard to do without a good pair of slippers or light sandals if one wishes to rest one's feet after six or seven hours of hiking over snow and rocks.

Scenes of a mountain excursion, 1845.

Similarly, although countless so-called waterproof jackets have been devised, an umbrella remains an item of great service in the mountains under a steady rain and occasionally under a blazing sun. 'Give me a parasol and I'll go to the top of Mont Blanc,' swore one of the first Chamoniards to attack the 'great molehill' with a conquering stride. In addition to the parasol our good guide took a flask of scent, as he sweltered in the heat and reflected sunlight on the Grand Plateau beneath the summit.

In August 1857, when preparing for the Schreckhorn and an expedition on the glaciers, Eustache Anderson recalled how right that guide was to speak of a parasol in one hand and perfume bottle in the other. The Englishman, protected by a wide-brimmed hat, dreaded the heat of the sun more than the cold of nights. An umbrella can serve not only as parasol but also as convenient protection against the rain either while walking or while pausing for refreshment. It is a portable, travelling roof. Properly opened and properly wielded, an umbrella is as efficient a tool in 2014 as it was in the 1860s, when Parisian ladies would never be without one, any more than shepherds in the Valais.

A wide-brimmed, grey felt hat – and a veil of green or black gauze for the face when necessary – would not necessarily suffice to protect against the reflections of sunlight on snow. In 1856, guide Johann Josef Bennen suffered from serious inflammation of both eyes after an expedition on a glacier. He almost went blind. Two years later, John Tyndall hired Bennen to climb the Finsteraarhorn (4,274 metres) and noted that his guide took extraordinary measures to protect himself from the sun's rays. More than one account describes troubles at the end of a climb due to painful eyes, whether red, blurry and ailing, or even the early stages of ophthalmia or snow blindness (Hirst, Tyndall's companion on Mont Blanc in 1857). These travellers from northern Europe

A portrait by J.E. Millais of John Ruskin, the great artist, inspired thinker and Alpine traveller.

Mont Buet, up which Joseph-Marie Couttet led John Ruskin.

often had pale eyes and were particularly sensitive to solar reflections on the high snows.

John Ruskin (1819–1900), crossing the Mer de Glace in 1844, carefully protected his artist's eyes and his English skin with a large straw hat that he pulled around his ears, plus a veil of two layers of green gauze fastened under his waistcoat, and a pair of huge, dark blue glasses of double thickness. A handkerchief wound round the hat and knotted under his chin completed his outfit. Ruskin noted in his diary that he took delight in being thus accoutred, which was 'enough to frighten anything in the world but Alpine sheep – whom nothing frightens.'

Ruskin – that writer of lyrical if somewhat muddled prose, that artist and art critic, that inspired thinker, that sublime reactionary, that Alpine traveller, that Chamoniard at heart – refused to join a game whose pleasures he had sampled in 1844 on the Mer de Glace and elsewhere in the Mont Blanc chain. In July of that year he climbed Mont Buet with Joseph-Marie Couttet, the 'Captain of Mont Blanc', who taught Ruskin how to use an alpenstock. But Ruskin went no further. He was the contemplative type, all mind and eye. Basically an artist, he was thrilled by the views and he adored the mountains, which he not only drew but was one of the first to photograph, in 1849. Ruskin gazed upon the finest peaks of the Alps the way Romantic poets gazed at cathedrals. In 1856, Ruskin devoted long passages in volume four of *Modern Painters* to this splendour, in a section titled 'Of Mountain Beauty'.

Those stately passages have become famous. '[The mountains] seem to have been built for the human race, as at once their schools and cathedrals; full of treasures of illuminated manuscript for the scholar, kindly in simple lessons to the worker, quiet in pale cloisters for the thinker, glorious in holiness for the worshipper.' Members of the Alpine Club read and reread those pages with the enthusiasm of people recognising their own impressions and sense of overwhelming passion. But Ruskin the writer had his weaknesses: wordiness, disorder, bombast.

The young Whymper stumbled over Ruskin's description of the Matterhorn. Too much jumble, claimed Whymper. Ruskin was not a man of talent, but a genius and a visionary. His diatribe against mountaineering was a diatribe of genius against talent. In the Alpine Club's accounts of exploits Ruskin detected the spirit of a hopelessly secular game, ultimately as common as all displays of sport.

In a preface to *Sesame and Lilies* written after the Matterhorn disaster, Ruskin railed against the vanity and loudness of the members of the Alpine Club, whose acrobatics and unseemly antics shocked him: 'For indeed all true lovers of natural beauty hold it in reverence so deep that they would as soon think of climbing the pillars of the choir of Beauvais for a gymnastic exercise, as of making a playground of Alpine snow.' Invited to dine at the Alpine Club in December 1868, Ruskin was made a member the following year on the basis of his essay 'Of Mountain Beauty'. That book, in Ruskin's curious lyrical-analytical style, remained bedside reading for everyone who loved travelling in the Alps.

The first requirement of any true voyager is curiosity. The second is good humour. One has to smile and joke at every surprise, even unpleasant ones.

In September 1852, after a very hot summer when elections had kept him in Ireland, Ball crossed the Strahlegg pass, at the same time sampling, along with his sugared water, the stinginess of the shrewd folks of Grindelwald: 'Grindelwald afforded me an amusing illustration of the extortionate habits of Swiss innkeepers. On paying my bill the next morning, I found a charge of half a franc for *eau sucrée*. On asking for explanation, I found that after

Ruskin wrote 'of mountain beauty'.

Ruskin's drawing of the needles above Chamonix.
L–R: the Aiguille de l'M, the Grands Charmoz,
the Grepon and the Aiguille de Blaitière.

breakfast I had put a lump of sugar, which I do not use at that meal, into a glass of water; and it was coolly maintained that as the water was not part of the breakfast, I should pay extra for the sugar so consumed.'

In 1854 Ball was the first British traveller to reach the summit of the Grossglockner. In the Bernese Alps in 1857, he attained the southern, or lowest, of the three peaks of Trugberg (3,880 metres), near the Jungfrau, all on his own.

Welcome surprises awaited Ball in the Italian Dolomites. On 19 September 1857 he made the first successful ascent of Monte Pelmo (3,168 metres) in the eastern chain. A chamois fleeing along a ledge had shown him the key passage in the ascent. Nearly a kilometre long, this shelf sometimes narrows to less than one metre wide. It is a very dizzying ledge, and today bears his name – *la cengia di Ball.* Ball was a man of stout heart (by which I mean courage) as well as curiosity, two character traits that go a long way when combined. That day Ball found himself alone, like the chamois on the run. He gathered plants along the way, material souvenirs of that unforgettable ledge.

In the Dolomites once again in 1860, Ball made the first ascent of Punta di Rocca (3,309 metres, in the Marmolada chain) via the glaciers on the north slope. He was accompanied by John Birkbeck, a friend from the Alpine Club. Their guide was Victor Tairraz from Chamonix, enthusiastically brought to the attention of the English by Charles Hudson, and described as a clever Savoyard by Forbes. Tairraz was not only intrepid but learned to speak English. (Marmolada itself – specifically Punta di Penia, at 3,342 metres – fell on 28 September 1864 to the careful assault of Austrian mountaineer Paul Grohmann, a great explorer of the Dolomites who was among the founders of the Osterreichischer Alpenverein, or Austrian Alpine Club, in November 1862).

Paul Grohman founded the Austrian club.

In 1865 Ball climbed Cima Tosa (3,173 metres) – a cairn-building first ascent of this highest peak in the Brenta chain of the Dolomites.

Ball was also drawn to passes, since going from one valley to another was a good way to satisfy his botanical curiosity and expand his herbarium. In 1863 he crossed thirty-two different passes (in forty-eight trips) in major Alpine chains, and 100 passes in secondary chains. The forty-five year-old Ball hardly took things easy – all those passes in a single year represented months of walking during a full season in the mountains.

This Irishman trod so many passes himself, compiling descriptions as soon as he returned to England and later writing guides, that he knew the Alps better than anyone else in the world during that golden age of adventure.

JOHANN JOSEF BENNEN

First Attempts on the Matterhorn

The motto of Valais guide Johann Josef Bennen: 'It has to work!'

E *S MUSS GEHEN.* **It *has* to work.**

That was the motto of Johann Josef Bennen, from Lax in Valais, who was John Tyndall's guide on the Finsteraarhorn (4,272 metres) and the Weisshorn (4,505 metres), and on two attempts on the Matterhorn (1860 and 1862) when the party stood a real chance of success. Bennen also guided Francis Fox Tuckett on the first ascents of the Aletschhorn (4,195 metres) and the Arête des Bosses on Mont Blanc (with Leslie Stephen in 1861), but died young in 1864. Three of those good travellers from England — Tyndall, Tuckett and Hawkins — saw that a memorial stone was erected in his memory at the cemetery in Ernen, near Lax, in the Conches valley.

At the bottom of the stone was a reference to the Book of Job, the relevant passage being chapter 16, verse 22: 'When a few years are come, then I shall go the way whence I shall not return.'

A fine epitaph for a guide.

The poorly maintained stone was restored in 1902, not by John Tyndall as the new inscription suggests, but by his widow, Tyndall having died in 1893 in extraordinary circumstances, accidently

The avalanche spared four men.

poisoned by his wife. The new inscription gave the dates, place of death and profession of one of the most appealing protagonists of the golden age of mountaineering. Bennen, a *Bergführer* (mountain guide), had died one winter day while doing his job.

> *Bergführer Johann Josef Bennen, aus Lax, Geboren 11. November 1819, Verrunglückt 28. Februar 1864*
> *Am Haut de Cry*
> *Errichtet von John Tyndall, F. Vaughan Hawkins und F.F. Tuckett.*
> *Erneuert von John Tyndall, 1902.*

Verrunglückt: 'Died accidentally.' It was on the slopes of Haut de Cry, a summit above Sion in Valais. The chapter on chamois hunters already described the huge wind slab that buried Bennen's party, and the guide's last words as the snow beneath his feet began to move: 'We are all lost!'

Although the avalanche spared four men, Bennen and Louis Boissonet died beneath the snow. The forty-four-year-old Bennen, a bachelor, was due to be married that summer with a woman from his native Valais. He was thirty-eight when first hired by Tyndall, a bachelor of the same age. The physicist was immediately struck by the guide's demeanour and manners. Tyndall described him as 'the strongest limb and stoutest heart of my acquaintance in the Alps'. On 2 August 1858, Bennen was working at the Hotel Jungfrau, near Lake Märjelen. The Aletsch glacier is close by this now-tiny lake. The hotel owner spoke often of Bennen as a man of courage and devotion who would risk his own life to save that of his client. He was forthright, confident, with a glint of good humour in his eye. And he had uncommon strength, which he knew how to manage, thanks to his work as a carpenter. As Hawkins pointed out: 'Carpentering, by the way – not fine turning and planing, but rough out-of-doors work, like Bennen's – must be no bad practice to keep hand and eye in training during the dead season.'

That very night Tyndall and Bennen slept in a cave a three-hour hike up the glacier from Lake Märjelen. The cave was furnished with straw and a fireplace. The porters had headed back, leaving them some pinewood. Bennen claimed that he didn't snore. But he did. Tyndall barely slept that night. Bennen arose at 1.30 a.m. to stir the fire and heat the coffee. They set off at 3 a.m., Bennen with a knapsack of provisions and Tyndall with a knapsack of equipment (telescope, thermometers, water-boiling material).

In the autumn season Bennen tended to chase chamois rather than skirts, but he liked a good story. Once, when they were having difficulty on the steep, rugged Finsteraarhorn, Bennen turned to Tyndall and said, 'Now I'm like the Tyrolean of the tale'. And he recounted the following story: An honest Tyrolean found himself constantly struggling between his love of God and his penchant for women. He confessed as much to his pastor one day. The clergyman said:

'My son, loving women and going to heaven – it just won't work.'

The Tyrolean immediately retorted, 'But Reverend, it *has* to work!'

Bennen concluded:

'*Und so sag ich jetzt!*' (And that's what I say now!)

With those words, Bennen made a great effort and found a way around the difficulty. Tyndall never forgot the story of the Tyrolean and Bennen's motto – It *has* to work! – which was generally ascribed to all the Germanic guides of the golden age, from the most to the less resolute, like Jakob Anderegg.

Es muss gehen. It *has* to work.

John Tyndall.

The Matterhorn, from a photograph by the Bisson brothers.

Tyndall, who studied at the University of Marburg, understood German very well and enjoyed the accents and intonations of his guides, whom he blithely quoted in German in his descriptive accounts.

Beneath the summit of the Finsteraarhorn, prior to attacking the final rocky passage, a thirsty Bennen finished the bottle of tea that Tyndall held out to him. The physicist wanted to begin making his observations, but Bennen dissuaded him.

'Let's get to the summit, *Herr*!'

After heading up a final ridge, he cried:

'*Die höchste Spitze!* (The highest peak!)'

In August 1860, the pair decided to attack the legendary Matterhorn. The weather had not been good. For weeks a southern wind had brought clouds and rain. The local papers read by Hawkins complained of *der ewige Südwind,* 'the eternal southwind.' This fifth attempt on the Matterhorn would be Bennen's first. The guide was keen to climb a peak whose reputation for invincibility had practically paralysed the people of Zermatt. No attempt from the Zermatt side had been mentioned, while the people of Breuil in Valtournenche on the other slope had already made three assaults. The previous summer, 1859, Hawkins and Bennen had reconnoitred the Matterhorn from various angles, making a complete tour of the mountain armed with telescopes. Bennen was confident that the mountain could be scaled, and made a date for the following year.

Due to the weather once again, they had to wait until 20 August 1860 before attacking the Matterhorn via the Lion ridge on the Italian side. At Breuil they had recruited Jean-Jacques Carrel, the best mountaineer in Valtournenche. Carrel was a good-humoured, shaggy chamois hunter, whose relatively advanced age (nearly fifty years old) surprised Hawkins. It was Carrel who had had the bold idea of making the first assault on the Matterhorn in 1857 with his thirty-year-old nephew, Jean-Antoine Carrel (known as 'the Bersagliere' subsequent to his career in the Piedmontese army, later to conquer the Matterhorn just after Whymper), and a young seminarian named Amé Gorret (1836–1907). The three men from Valtournenche thus were the first to reach the peak known as the Tête du Lion (3,723 metres).

In October 1865, Abbé Amé Gorret described that first attempt on the Matterhorn in a local paper. The winds had been changing in Valtournenche, and the idea of climbing the Matterhorn was in the air. Along with an engineer, Felice Giordano, Gorret was one of the masterminds of the Italian camp. His account is enlightening. He was a local lad, having been a shepherd in the high chalets of Cheneil before entering the seminary. 'A taste for excursions and ascents is quite recent where I live; although surrounded by magnificent mountains we ignored them, and only chamois hunters were familiar with the passes. We viewed tourists who passed through with wonder.'

What an admission of how isolated these valleys were, how paradoxical was the clash of sensibilities and viewpoints. The shaggy natives of Valtournenche marvelled at the tourists. Gorret continued: 'The Matterhorn – that proud, handsome mountain we could see every day – would bring up visitors short, struck with admiration. We were not struck by the Matterhorn. It was so little known that I recall being told on several occasions that what we call the Col du Lion, between the Tête du Lion and the pyramid of the Matterhorn, was the Col d'Hérens, beyond which lay Hérens, and other things of that sort.'

The idea sprang from the attitude of the ever-increasing number of tourists in Valtournenche. 'During the summer of 1875,' wrote Gorret, 'when tourists, especially English, were travelling across

Jean-Antoine Carrel, known as 'the Bersagliere'.

Abbé Amé Gorret.

Jean-Antoine Carrel (seated) with a guide.

Valtournenche in much greater numbers than before, someone talked about an ascent of the Matterhorn. At the time I was on holiday from the seminary, and the idea of an ascent, which made everyone smile wryly, so mad did it seem, this idea of an ascent appealed to me, as well as to Jean-Antoine and Jean-Jacques Carrel.'

A conspiratorial secrecy surrounded that first skirmish with the rocks of the Matterhorn, as Gorret recounts. 'Without daring to announce the goal of our excursion, one day we left the chalet of Avouil with a small axe to cut steps in the ice, a piece of black bread in our pockets, and some brandy.'

After 1857, all eyes remained fixed on the Matterhorn. Abbé Gorret, with his seminarian's sense of distance, later referred to 'Matterhornmania.' Like many clergymen in Val d'Aosta, he was an enthusiastic mountaineer, and became a historian of mountaineering.

In 1858, during a second attempt, Jean-Jacques and Jean-Antoine Carrel made it somewhat higher than the previous year, reaching the Grande Tour at roughly 3,800 metres.

Jean-Jacques made a very good impression on the Englishmen in 1860, following their first moment of surprise at his tousled, colourful, aged appearance. The Bennen-Carrel offensive might well have threatened the summit that year if the two men had spoken the same language. Carrel spoke only the Valdotain dialect and could understand only Italian. Bennen could speak and understand only Swiss German. The two men had to communicate via gestures. On that day, 20 August 1860, Carrel walked behind the party as soon as they reached the first snowfields, and was of almost no use to Bennen. At 5 a.m., a very careful Bennen began advancing along a very narrow ridge of snow, hard as rock. A few moments later, the four men methodically roped up. On studying the Matterhorn the previous day and noting the fresh white snow, Bennen made himself understood by all, in words and gestures. Snow on the rocks was the worst situation, the thing he feared most. Now amidst these rocks that occasionally gleamed with ice and stalactites, Bennen turned and gave a long speech – here Hawkins was reminded of Thucydides' generals – on the need to use extreme care when placing their feet on the rocks, and urged them to pay constant attention: '*Wohl immer achtung!*'

Beneath a rock step even steeper than the chimney of black ice up which he had just been hoisted, Hawkins refused to go on. Leaning against a slab alongside Carrel, who smoked a pipe, Hawkins watched his friends continue to climb, and saw a rock as large as a human body come tumbling down. It crashed in a nearby couloir of snow. Although he could climb like a cat, Bennen advanced very slowly, and stopped climbing shortly afterward, around 3,960 metres high. It was noon. Time to turn back.

Highly impressed with Bennen's confidence and conduct of the operations, Hawkins began his account of the ascent with praise for Bennen and other Oberland guides. Hawkins did not hide his preferences, and dealt the guides from Chamonix a severe blow:

> John [*sic*] Joseph Bennen, of Laax [*sic*], in the Upper Rhine Valley, is a man so remarkable that I cannot resist the desire (especially as he cannot read English) to say a few words about his character. Born within the limits of the German tongue, and living amidst the mountains and glaciers of the Oberland, he belongs by race and character to a class of men of whom the Laueners, Melchior Anderegg, Bortis, Christian Almer, Peter Bohren, are also examples – a type of mountain race, having many of the simple heroic qualities which we associate, whether justly or unjustly, with Teutonic blood, and essentially different from – to my mind, infinitely superior to – the French-speaking, versatile, wily Chamouniard. The

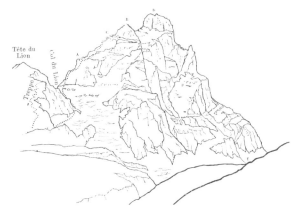

The Matterhorn seen from Breuil.

'After 1857, all eyes remained fixed on the Matterhorn.' José Mingre, oil on wood (first half of the twentieth century).

names I have mentioned are all those of first-rate men; but Bennen, as (I believe) he surpasses all the rest in the qualities which fit a man for a leader in hazardous expeditions, combining boldness and prudence with an ease and power peculiar to himself, so he has a faculty of conceiving and planning his achievements, a way of concentrating his mind upon an idea, and working out his idea with clearness and decision, which I never observed in any man of the kind, and which makes him, in his way, a sort of Garibaldi. Tyndall, on the day of our expedition, said to him, '*Sie sind der Garibaldi der Führer, Bennen*' ('You are the Garibaldi of guides Bennen!'); to which he answered in his simple way, '*Nicht wahr?*' ('Am I not?'), an amusing touch of simple vanity, a dash of pardonable bounce, being one of his not least amiable characteristics.

Ruskin claimed that men of the Alpine valleys suffered from a kind of 'mountain gloom', which he ascribed to the local atmosphere. Bennen, a devout Christian, displayed neither religious gloom nor mountain gloom, nor the somewhat haggard visage of men obsessed with chamois hunting, his favourite pastime. Both Hawkins and Tyndall considered Bennen 'a perfect nature's gentleman'. His cool-headedness and control in difficult circumstances dispelled any idea of fall or misfortune due to a false move or error in judgment.

Hawkins concluded with a platitude, but one that turned out to be premonitory: nothing could bring Bennen to grief – except an avalanche.

CONQUERING
THE WEISSHORN

The Weisshorn: a long, high-altitude route along ridges culminating in a pyramidal island in the skies over Valais.

O N 19 August 1861, one year nearly to the day after its attack on the crags of the Matterhorn, the Bennen–Tyndall team brilliantly shattered a zone of ignorance by conquering the Weisshorn, 4,506 metres high. The high-altitude route along ridges culminated in a pyramidal island in the skies over Valais.

It was a three-man party: Tyndall and two guides – Bennen, and Ulrich Wenger from Grindelwald.

The Matterhorn is a twisting, four-ridged pyramid with marked breaks. These abrupt edges give it a somewhat strange shape, as though worked by the chisel of some Romantic artist. The Matterhorn is the perfect summit for anyone with a Romantic bent, but a rickety pyramid for anyone who likes straight lines. On arriving in Zermatt in 1844, Ruskin initially turned up his nose at the sight of 'this strange Matterhorn'. Later, however, in *The Stones of Venice,* he elevated it to the rank of 'the most noble cliff of Europe'. As early as 1849 Ruskin made the first daguerreotypes[6] of the Matterhorn. 'The first sun-portrait ever taken of the Matterhorn

6. An early form of photography, invented in 1839.

John Ruskin.

(and as far as I know of any Swiss mountain whatever) was taken by me in the year 1849.'

The Weisshorn, in comparison, was more classic in shape. It formed a three-sided pyramid whose ridges conveyed a thrust of great scope and regularity. According to Tyndall, it made 'a deeper impression of majesty and might than the Matterhorn itself'. For a man who failed twice on the Matterhorn but conquered the Weisshorn, the conclusion seemed obvious: 'The Weisshorn [is] perhaps the most splendid object in the Alps.'

The Weisshorn's stature thus made it a feared adversary. In July 1857, unfamiliar with the seracs on the glacier du Géant and as helpless as his guide (a young porter clearly terrified by the seracs), Tyndall urged himself onward with the thought 'that what man has done, man may do' – a good motto for bucking up courage and confidence during tricky passages. Reversing that motto, however, conveys the difficulty faced by a party during the golden age of mountaineering on the steep ridges of the totally virgin summits of the Weisshorn and Matterhorn. The known and the unknown are totally different in nature, which gives full reign to 'fanciful' imagination. It is certainly incautious, and probably mad, to go there where no one has ever preceded you. What man has never done, no man may ever do. And it might even be foolish – perhaps what man has never done is not, in the end, worth doing.

That is why the first mountaineers encountered a wall of disbelief and incomprehension in remote Alpine villages. The summits were not worth the trouble – much less the life – of any man with common sense.

Even mountaineers of today sometimes have a moment's hesitation as they stuff their backpacks: what's the point? Suddenly the game seems a little pointless – it loses the meaning it once had, upon awakening one sunny morning or in the first flush of summer.

So the perplexity of the peasants of 1850 can be imagined. Among that high-altitude population, only a handful of men – a few shaggy chamois hunters or an occasional clergyman (young ones like Amé Gorret or older ones like Johann Imseng) – indulged in the recreation of travellers who arrived from the cities equipped with thermometers and telescopes. But little by little, in villages where wealth was measured in cows, people began to realise three things: The game could be a source of income; it could bring honour to the region; it could even bring fame.

That was the drift of a conversation between Tyndall and his guide Bennen at the foot of the Italian side of the Matterhorn on that day in August 1861. Bennen, having descended after an afternoon of lone reconnoitring above the high pastures of Breuil, stated that any attempt would be futile. A route nevertheless appeared to lead to the large shoulder of the Matterhorn (4,241 metres, later named Tyndall Peak), already approached by the party in 1860 and considered a subsidiary summit.

'We can, at all events, reach the lower of the two summits,' commented Tyndall.

'Even that is difficult,' replied Bennen, 'but when you have reached it, what then? The peak has neither name nor fame.'

Even Bennen – the Garibaldi of guides – did not think it worth the energy and physical danger to reach a subsidiary peak, even if it was on the Matterhorn. In contrast, the Weisshorn – 'White Horn' – was not a peak lacking name and fame. It was a giant of Valais, a summit with the same fame as the peaks of Jungfrau and Finsteraarhorn, its neighbours across the Rhone. The failures of several parties on the Weisshorn, including the great team of Melchior Anderegg and Leslie Stephen, made it clear that the mountain would not give up easily even when approached by a party of experienced mountaineers.

The Weisshorn, by Edward Theodore Compton.

John Tyndall, 1857.

Melchior Anderegg.

Melchior Anderegg (1828–1914) from Meiringen was one of the great guides of the golden age. His calmness and caution were proverbial, summed up by an anecdote and a motto the reverse of *Es muss gehen* ('It *has* to work'). On reaching the summit of the Dent d'Hérens, Anderegg appeared to contemplate the rocks of the Matterhorn.

'*Es geht?*' (Might it work?), asked his companions.

'*Ja, es geht, aber ich gehe nicht.*' (Yes, it'll work, but I won't.)

Many accidents in the mountains are caused by vanity and the inability to reply as Anderegg did. His cousin, Jakob Anderegg, was also a great guide but steel-willed, a tenacious believer in *Es muss gehen* who constantly ploughed ahead.

On 15 August 1861 – the day of the Assumption of the Virgin – Tyndall drank his milk on the summit of the Sparrhorn (3,021 metres), an easy-to-reach scenic viewpoint above Belalp on the right bank of the Rhone. Bennen, who had already been retained along with Ulrich Wenger from Grindelwald, was preparing the attack in the village of Randa, beneath the cliffs that hid the top of the Weisshorn being admired at that very moment by Tyndall on his high-altitude stroll. On 18 August, the party set out from Randa at about 1 p.m. Tyndall had been unwell in the hotel the previous night and lagged behind his guides, suffering from intense thirst despite the shade of the pines on the lower slopes. Tyndall liked milk. On reaching the chalet on the high pastures of Schallenberg after two hours of hiking, the shepherd brought Tyndall a pail of fresh milk. 'The effect of the milk was astonishing,' wrote Tyndall. 'It seemed to lubricate every atom of my body, and to exhilarate with its fragrance my brain.' He was ready to follow Bennen anywhere.

Wenger, meanwhile, was felicitously described by Tyndall as 'a man rich in small expedients' – including the ability to grill cheese over a fire. Once the party reached its bivouac on a ledge overlooking a natural amphitheatre, Wenger took out a large piece of cheese and held it over the fire of pine. As the cheese softened and melted, he scraped it off with his knife.

Having dined, Tyndall placed his knapsack beneath his head and stretched out between two pairs of rugs that he had had sewn together to form two sacks. However, awakened too early by the cold and the moonlight, the three men had to wait over an hour for dawn before they could set off.

The ascent began at 3.30 a.m. and took ten hours during a hot, sunny, cloudless and windless day posing no threat of storm. A couloir of snow and rocky rubble, which had appeared terribly steep to Bennen by telescope the day before, led to the rocks of the east ridge. This long ridge, occasionally dotted with cornices of snow, was interrupted and masked by pinnacles known as gen-darmes. Bennen gripped a spike of rock with his two carpenter's hands. The real rock climbing had begun. As Tyndall recalled: 'For both mind and body the discipline was grand. There is scarcely a position possible to a human being which, at one time or another during the day, I was not forced to assume. The fingers, wrist, and forearm were my main reliance, and as a mechanical instrument the human hand appeared to me this day to be a miracle of con-structive art.'

Ascending the ridge sometimes on the left, sometimes on the right, and sometimes on its razor edge, the men experienced an illusion: the summit at the top of the ridge always appeared to remain the same distance away. Nothing can seem longer than a mountain ridge that constantly forces you to one side or the other of its lip. There was not a breath of wind; the air shimmered in the torrid heat. The men paused, and prematurely opened a bottle of champagne. Dribbling a few drops on snow gave them a sorbet

'My dear sir, the summit is still far off!'

The Weisshorn seen from the Furgg glacier above Zermatt, by Edward Theodore Compton.

to suck. Bennen declined the champagne – he wanted to keep his eyes sharp. Tyndall turned to him:

'You have now good hopes?'

'I do not allow myself to entertain the idea of failure,' he replied.

But Bennen was exhausting himself by cutting step after step in the ice on the slopes when the gendarmes had to be flanked. They paused on a ledge. Bennen leaned wearily on his axe.

'*Leiber Herr, die Spitze is noch sehr weit oben.*' (My dear sir, the summit is still far off.) That was the decisive moment: to go on, or to turn back. While debating, Bennen ate a morsel of bread and drank a gulp of champagne. Ten seconds later, he was reassured.

'*Herr! wir müssen ihn haben.*' (Sir, we must make it.)

Both guides now assured Tyndall that the silvery pyramid standing against the blue sky, the pyramid that seemed so close, was indeed the summit and not yet another subsidiary peak masking the real one. They reached it at 1.30 p.m. Bennen raised his arms and gave a wild, Valaisian cheer, hoarsened by thirst and ten hours of climbing. Wenger gave the shriller yell of his native Oberland. After this outburst of victory, Bennen regretted that he had no suitable flag to deploy, to convince all the quibblers in Randa and Zermatt. Tyndall and Wenger suggested that he use the handle of his ice axe as a flagstaff. The red pocket handkerchief he tied to the top could still be seen the next day from the Riffelberg Hotel, to Bennen's enormous satisfaction.

THE RACE TO THE MATTERHORN

John Tyndall and Edward Whymper

A drawing by John Ruskin, startled at seeing what he called 'this strange Matterhorn'.

After his victory over the Weisshorn, Tyndall's hopes soared. *Es muss gehen.* There was no time to lose. Given the hot summer, the rocks on the southern slope of the Matterhorn should be in excellent condition. Bennen was sent to Breuil to reconnoitre, notably seeking a spot to bivouac halfway up the mountain.

On the evening of 23 August he came striding back down to the high pastures of Breuil, where Tyndall awaited him. His report was negative – very negative – and delivered in a solemn tone that Tyndall found unusual from the lips of his cherished guide.

'Herr,' he said at length, in a tone of unusual emphasis, 'I have examined the mountain carefully, and find it more difficult and dangerous than I had imagined. There is no place upon it where we could well pass the night. We might do so on yonder col upon the snow, but there we should be almost frozen to death, and totally unfit for the work of the next day. On the rocks there is no ledge or cranny which could give us proper harbourage; and

The 'dash and intensity' of the twenty-year-old Edward Whymper.

starting from Breuil it is certainly impossible to reach the summit in a single day.'

Bennen was dead set against any attempt. Tyndall hadn't expected this disappointment, and was almost irritated with Bennen, whose pride seemed satisfied with the axe he had firmly planted on the summit of the Weisshorn. They decided to return to the Matterhorn the following year. Tyndall spent the nine months of his academic year in London preparing for the assault, ordering a special rope from the best ropemaker in the capital, as well a collapsible ladder, long iron nails and a hammer.

This attempt, Bennen's second, was done in a palpable atmosphere of a race for the summit, following ten other assaults by serious competitors since his first foray of 1860. Edward Whymper had notably entered the ring. The twenty-year-old Whymper brought the dash and intensity of his youth, that impatience to reach a goal which lent an air of forced march to some of his ascents. Whymper was an intense 'wanter', to use the term (*vouleur*) employed by Jules Vallès in his 1886 novel, *L'Insurgé* (The Rebel). Mountaineering isn't war, but grappling with those high walls called for the energy and fury of war or insurrection. At twenty, Whymper was two decades younger than Bennen and Tyndall, both of them war-hardened but already of another generation over the venerable age of forty.

Whymper on the Matterhorn was like the young Napoleon Bonaparte on campaign in Italy, imparting energy and speed to the whole movement. Whymper was the legendary angry young man who upset the applecart. Mountain conquest accelerated with the arrival of this totally unexpected outsider, still unknown in 1860 to the tiny group of gentlemen who met in London to discuss their summers in the Alps.

Of Dutch stock, Whymper's modest family numbered eleven children – nine boys and two girls. Edward was the second child. Having left school at fourteen, he worked hard as an apprentice draughtsman and engraver in his father's workshop. From fifteen to nineteen he kept a diary. The teenager's main ambition was to become the best engraver in London, 'and with God's help, not only to draw well, but [to] draw better and better and, if possible, *better than all!*'

In passing, it is worth noting the harshness of winters in the mid nineteenth century. On 15 January 1855, according to Whymper's diary, the Thames was so frozen at Richmond, to the west of London, that thousands of people flooded on to it to skate and stroll. One of the direct consequences of these cold winters was the size and beauty of glaciers in the Alps and their polar impact on the landscape, which should never be forgotten when reading accounts of the golden age of mountaineering. The first sight of the Alps with its glaciers dazzled Whymper as it had so many others.

A London publisher, William Longman, noticed young Whymper's drawings and commissioned him to do a series in the Alps for a large illustrated book. Longman was particularly interested in the Dauphiné chain, an Alpine region little known to the English. The remote peak region was where Napoleon, that ogre so detested if admired by the English, had made his hundred-day comeback in 1815.

Whymper thus left for the Alps in the summer of 1860. He was a focused hiker with a singularly lively step. People noticed him. His normal pace, which he maintained well beyond the age of forty, was a fast eight kilometres per hour. In the Alps he walked, drew and kept a journal. He was amazed that people had written so much about a common sugar loaf: 'Saw of course the Matterhorn repeatedly; what precious stuff Ruskin has written about this, as well as about many other things. When one has a fair view of the

The Écrins seen from the Col du Galibier, by Whymper.

An excerpt from Whymper's list of exploits.

Two mountaineers and their tent at the Col du Lion.

mountain as I had, it may be compared to a sugar loaf set up on a table; the sugar loaf should have its head knocked on one side. Grand it is, but beautiful I think it is not.'

When Whymper returned to the Alps in late August of 1861, his ambition no longer focused on engraving. The Matterhorn, that huge loaf of sugar, had been the focus of his attention ever since he learned that the Tyndall–Bennen team had made it to the top of the Weisshorn. The young man had lost that race. But he could still beat them to the Matterhorn, and he was unaware of their pessimistic reconnoitring mission of 23 August. So Whymper bivouacked on the Col du Lion (3,580 metres) in a very bad Galton tent with a Bernese guide who was dreadfully shaken by a terrible explosion high on the mountain around midnight.

'My god, we are lost!' exclaimed the guide.

The Matterhorn roared with a distant, but dreadful, crash in the silence of the night. Small fragments of rock whistled as they flew near the tent. The demoralised guide was unable to go back to sleep, punctuating the remainder of the night with moans of '*Schrecklich!*' (Terrible!). The next day, advancing up the Lion ridge, they reached an obstacle called the Chimney (3,885 metres), some ten metres of vertical rock. Whymper managed to climb it, but his guide refused to follow. Whymper called him a 'coward', and the guide responded in terms that Whymper decided not to record for posterity, any more than he recorded the name or place of origin of his guide. Recovering his calm, Whymper climbed back down the Chimney with the help of his guide.

After 1861, the race to reach the top of the Matterhorn took on an almost official character in the countries involved. Canon Georges Carrel of Aosta (uncle of Jean-Jacques Carrel) wrote to Francis Fox Tuckett (1834–1913) at the Alpine Club to ask whether a reward might offered for the first successful ascent of the

Matterhorn, as Saussure had done in his day for Mont Blanc. But Tuckett replied that he 'did not think it right to tempt poor men with promises of money to risk their lives on an expedition which was without any scientific aim.'

In July 1862, as Tyndall was stoking up his energy on a few summits in the Bernese Alps, Whymper made five attempts on the Matterhorn in that month alone. All were made from the Italian side. On one trip, with no one from either Breuil or Zermatt being either able or willing to accompany him, he risked a solo climb on the Lion ridge, getting as far as the spot called the Cravate (4,084 metres), higher than Bennen–Tyndall or any other previous team.

On the way back down Whymper fell while rounding a corner of rock, groping across a sheet of ice into which he had not be able to cut steps. His feet probably slipped out beneath him, but as he later wrote, 'I cannot tell how it happened.' He had left his axe – not a Bennen-style ice axe but an old navy boarding axe – in the tent on the Col du Lion fifty metres above. As he tumbled he lost his alpenstock. He tried to grasp the rocks as he bounced six or seven times in a fall that finally ended some seventy metres lower, just at the edge of a precipice. Whymper described this fall in his *Scrambles Amongst the Alps.* A footnote he added proves more interesting than the tale, for he offers surprising revelations about his state of awareness and insensitivity during the fall:

> As it seldom happens that one survives such a fall, it may be interesting to record what my sensations were during its occurrence. I was perfectly conscious of what was happening, and felt each blow; but, like a patient under chloroform, experienced no pain. Each blow was, naturally, more severe than that which preceded it, and I distinctly remember thinking 'Well, if the next is

Whymper's fall.

Whymper claimed that a fall in the mountains was not to be feared.

harder still, that will be the end!' Like persons who have been rescued from drowning, I remember that the recollection of a multitude of things rushed through my head, many of them trivialities or absurdities, which had been forgotten long before; and, more remarkable, this bounding through space did not feel disagreeable. But I think that in no very great distance more, consciousness as well as sensation would have been lost, and upon that I base my belief, improbable as it seems, that death by a fall from a great height is as painless an end as can be experienced.

In short, Whymper claimed that a fall in the mountains was not to be feared on the condition of remaining in this strange state of anaesthesia. The last blow will make you lose consciousness. Or else, like Whymper, you will come back to life in pain and blood.

The battering was very rough, yet no bones were broken. The most severe cuts were one of four inches long on the top of the head, and another of three inches on the right temple; this latter bled frightfully. There was a formidable-looking cut, of about the same size as the last, on the palm of the left hand, and every limb was grazed, or cut, more or less seriously.

Whymper applied a block of snow to his temple, slowing the flow of blood. A few minutes later, he fainted on a ledge. That he was then able to descend 1,700 metres after reviving, in the sunset and then at night, says a great deal about the man's capacities. Back in Breuil his wounds were washed with hot wine mixed with salt despite his protest. Contrary to Whymper's assertion, it is not all that rare to survive such a fall; what *is* rare is returning to battle after such a whipping. Yet after a week's rest, head bandaged, Whymper returned to attack the same rocks twice. The local Breuil remedies worked. His wounds, treated with salted wine, healed. Making a concession to prudence, however, Whymper no longer went alone. He charged Jean-Antoine Carrel with hiring a cousin, César Carrel, and a porter named Luc Meynet. Meynet, a short, deformed peasant called 'the hunchback', had crooked legs but the agility of a monkey, and he remained remarkably good humoured and humble beneath his load. The party nevertheless turned back at the spot called the Crête du Coq (4,032 metres).

For Whymper's next attempt the Carrels were off hunting marmots (highly popular in the nineteenth century) so he climbed with little Luc, clearly his favourite person in Breuil due to the man's lively manner and selflessness. Whymper's memoirs painted a sentimental, Dickens-like portrait of Meynet. The cautious Whymper nevertheless decided to halt at the level of the Cravate, a long streak of snow (or rubble, depending on the season) at roughly 4,100 metres. On their way back down, during the difficult passages, Meynet kept repeating merrily, 'We can only die once.'

Whymper promised to return with a ladder.

Whymper, Tyndall, Bennen and all serious contenders for the inaccessible summit felt that the Matterhorn's weak point was the Lion ridge on the Italian side, where the thrust of the pyramid looked broken and fractured. From the Zermatt side, three attempts had been made on the Hörnli ridge – by Alfred, Charles, and Sandbach Parker in July 1860 and July, and T.S. Kennedy with guides Peter Perren and Peter Taugwalder the elder in January 1862 (midwinter!). They seemed to confirm the general feeling that this route was impossible, the highest point reached by the Parker brothers having been 3,700 metres.

Luc Meynet, 'the hunchback'.

The Parker brothers, members of the Alpine Club, were talented mountaineers who climbed without guides. Strangely, when he met the Parkers, Whymper did not follow up on their comments, which were not all that discouraging: 'In neither case did we go as high as we could. At the point where we turned we saw our way for a few hundred feet further; but, beyond that, the difficulties seemed to increase.' Had the Parkers' statement aroused his curiosity, Whymper might have made it to the top of the Matterhorn in July 1862. At the end of that month of July Tyndall hired not only his loyal Bennen and one of Bennen's best friends, the fine guide Anton Walters, but also the two bold lads from Breuil, Jean-Antoine Carrel and his inseparable cousin, César.

Whymper, still present in Breuil, suppressed his vexation and made his tent on the Col du Lion available to the party. The game is up, he thought, seeing the size of the army and its equipment (rope, grappling hooks, ladder).

The Carrels performed their duties as porters and supported the efforts of the two Germanic guides – but without excessive zeal. Yet Jean-Antoine could have laid claim to a leading role. Once again communication had to be carried out in sign language, during an ascent interrupted by a bivouac on two ledges far above the Col du Lion at roughly 3,800 metres. Two tents were erected. They set off again at 4 a.m. Walters and Bennen, alternately in the lead, pushed and pulled one another along. As described by Tyndall, 'Walters, holding on to the narrow ledges above, scraped his iron-shod boots against the cliff, thus lifting himself in part by friction. Bennen was close behind, aiding him with an arm, a knee, or a shoulder. Once upon a ledge, he was able to give Bennen a hand.'

On the first peak, later named Tyndall Peak (4,241 metres), the party planted a flag in a first flush of elation – the final summit seemed within reach. 'In an hour,' said Bennen, 'the people at

Zermatt shall see our flag planted yonder.' These hopes were soon dashed by a precipitous gap in the ridge. Everyone pronounced the giddy passage impossible – except Bennen, who never uttered the word impossible. But rather than attempting it, he pointed out another possible route to Tyndall. It was up to Tyndall to decide whether they push on or head back. In moments of doubt or hesitation Bennen preferred that the responsibility for retreat and failure fall upon his cherished client. Tyndall coolly pushed the ball back into Bennen's court with modesty as courteous as it was shrewd:

'Where you go I will follow, be it up or down.'

It took Bennen half an hour to make up his mind. After dithering, he finally gave up and renounced the attempt to cross the cleft (now known as the Enjambée). None of these men, whether from Valais or Valtournenche, were familiar with the roping-down technique now known as 'abseiling'. So beneath the broad horizontal ledge on the Italian side, dubbed the 'Cravate', the party affixed the long thirty-metre rope made by the best ropemaker in London, and slid down a wall that would have been impossible to descend without a rope.

Canon Carrel, uncle of Jean-Jacques Carrel (the shaggy chamois hunter from Breuil), concluded his brief account of the attempt with the following words. 'After five and a half hours of climbing from the tent, Mr Tyndall and his companions sat on the ridge that now bears his name. There they erected two pyramids of stones, and attached two large batons with little flags. They held a consultation, eyes mournful, heads down – time was racing by, they had to head back down to the hotel.' Getting as far as Tyndall Peak was nevertheless a victory, which Canon Carrel recognised as such. 'Mr Tyndall's ascent was a first, if not total, victory. The rope he affixed to the hardest passage greatly assisted the ascents

Walters and Bennen on the cliff.

After 1861, the race to the top of Matterhorn became official.

made in the years 1865, 1866 and 1867. It should nevertheless be mentioned that the lower end of the rope had been somewhat displaced by the wind and has been replaced by a cable by Commander F. Giordano, engineer.'

The 'Grande Corde' (or 'Corde Tyndall') is still up there, so to speak, although replaced by cables several times since the memorable assault made by the 'Garibaldi of guides' almost succeeded.

Bennen and Tyndall saw each other for the last time on 22 July 1863 when crossing the Oberaarjoch (3,212 metres) in the Bernese Alps. It was a glacier route, and when they were caught in a thick fog Tyndall was amazed at his guide's sense of direction. As Bennen said, '*Herr, ich bin hier zu Hause; der Vieschergletscher is meine Heimat.*' (Sir, I'm in my own house. The Viesch glacier is my home.)

In March 1864, Tyndall opened *The Times* and read that a Swiss guide had died in an avalanche. He only discovered the man's name the next day. Bennen was the first of the great guides of the golden age to die, the first black flag to flutter until the disaster on the Matterhorn. But Bennen was known only in a few valleys, and to a few travellers. His death went unremarked in European cities.

Snow hounded the men of the Matterhorn party. On 30 July 1864 it was Tyndall's turn. During his descent of the Morteratsch (3,754 metres) in Engadin, he and his four companions were swept over a bergschrund and several crevasses, carried along for some 300 metres with surreal slowness by a huge, heavy snowslide. As he bumped up and down in the avalanche, Tyndall thought of Bennen.

'It is now my turn.'

A slight ease in the steepness of the slope saved the party from a final precipice. Tyndall had lost his watch, a fine chronometer. Sixteen days later, a search at the foot of the avalanche recovered it. Tyndall inserted the key and wound it. The watch started immediately.

JOHN TYNDALL

(1820–1893)

John Tyndall, by Florence E. Haig. This intellectual discovered his hands — their anatomy and how they worked — when climbing the Weisshorn.

THE MORE ONE SPECIALISES IN A GIVEN FIELD, the further one gets from the broader view and actions that characterised the humanism of certain nineteenth-century individuals. Accounts of excursions written by the likes of Tyndall and Hawkins are remarkable for their qualities of observation and analysis, of literary reflection and lofty distance. Super-specialisation had been one of the drawbacks, among others, of twentieth-century society.

John Tyndall was simultaneously a first-rate thinker and a top-notch mountaineer in the decade from 1858 (the Finsteraarhorn, Monte Rosa twice) to 1868 (the first complete traverse of the Matterhorn). He had no particular training for the latter, but benefited from a cool head and youthful attitude. The intellectual Tyndall discovered his hands – their anatomy, how they worked – when climbing the Weisshorn in August 1861. He was one of the first mountaineers to delight in climbing, an athletic exercise still unknown to his compatriots. The starchy stiffness of the British was mocked at inns throughout Europe as soon as those gentlemen's backs were turned. A broom handle was said to be more flexible than an English tourist, that taciturn character who seemed to personify the haughtiness of his island and empire. Humorists like Töpffer mocked the English as 'No-No' tourists, those stilted, monosyllabic visitors of panoramic viewpoints. There was, however, one class of tourist said to be even more rigid than an Englishman – namely, an Englishwoman.

Tyndall was not just a glaciologist but a highly influential intellectual in England who promoted the sciences. He invented, among other things, a sterilisation method that was of great service to milk drinkers like himself, Tyndallisation being a process similar to pasteurisation.

Tyndall felt that reason and science should take precedence over faith. The world order was a rational order. Everything could – or would – be explained through natural phenomena, with no recourse to miracles or the glories of providence.

In the mountains, Tyndall was a physicist who studied ice, in the footsteps of Saussure as well as his fellow Briton, James D. Forbes. For Tyndall, mountaineering adventure meant scientific observation. It was not a game. When members of the Alpine Club made fun of the overly scientific articles he published in the *Alpine Journal,* he resigned from the club, never to return.

As a scientist, he was a figure of particular significance in the birth of mountaineering. His writings shed great light on the golden age and the race for the Matterhorn. Thanks to Bennen, the lion-hearted guide from Valais, Tyndall might have pipped Whymper, that hungry young man, at the post.

The first complete traverse of the ridges of the Matterhorn – ascent via the Lion ridge, descent by the Hörnli ridge, on 26 and 27 July 1868, with two guides from Valtournenche, Jean-Joseph and Pierre Maquignaz – revealed to Tyndall the vestiges of his

Guide Jean-Joseph Maquignaz from Valtournenche.

own great attempt of 1862: ends of rope, shards of fabric, metal bars and even the upright of a ladder planted in a snowfield like some flag pole. He also noted the ropes and cables placed in difficult spots by the Valtournenche guides – the steep wall had lost some of its wild grandeur, so striking in 1860 during Tyndall's first attempt with his beloved Bennen, who liked to say '*Wohl immer achtung!*' (Pay constant attention!) It was a moment of inattention that would later – much later – kill Tyndall himself.

The beauty of the mountains filled Tyndall with a feeling of admiration and adoration of Nature's works. On reaching the Weisshorn after a ten-hour climb, silence and meditation had seemed the only appropriate response: 'I opened my notebook to make a few observations, but soon relinquished the attempt. There was something incongruous, if not profane, in allowing the scientific faculty to interfere where silent worship seemed the "reasonable service".' (An allusion to Paul's Epistle to the Romans.)

The risks of mountaineering, which Tyndall practised as an amateur but with great talent, struck him as minimal provided one remained cautious, dexterous, and attentive. It was a lapse in attention that led to beginners' mistakes.

As Tyndall put it:

> In fact, the dangers of the Alps can be almost reduced to the levels of the dangers of the street by the exercise of skill and caution. For rashness, ignorance, or carelessness the mountains leave no margin; and to rashness, ignorance, or carelessness three-fourths of the catastrophes which shock us are to be traced. Even those whose faculties are ever awake in danger are sometimes caught napping when danger seems remote; they receive accordingly the punishment of a tyro for a tyro's neglect.

John Tyndall, scientist and glaciologist.

Overleaf:
The Mont Blanc massif mapped out by Anthony Adams-Reilly during the course of his ascents alongside Whymper in 1864.

189

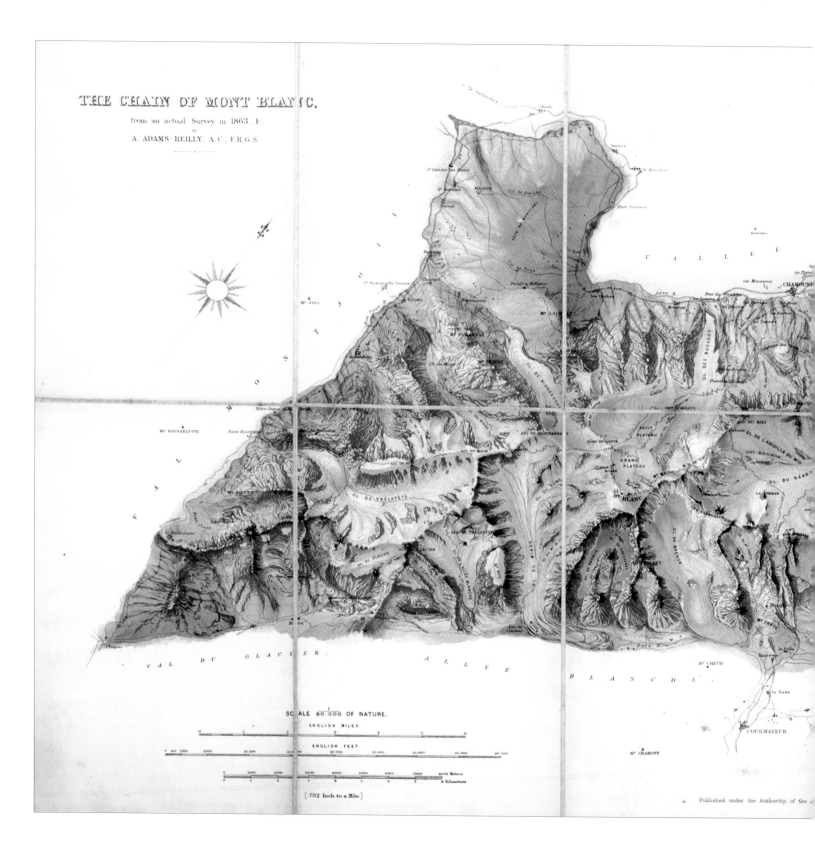

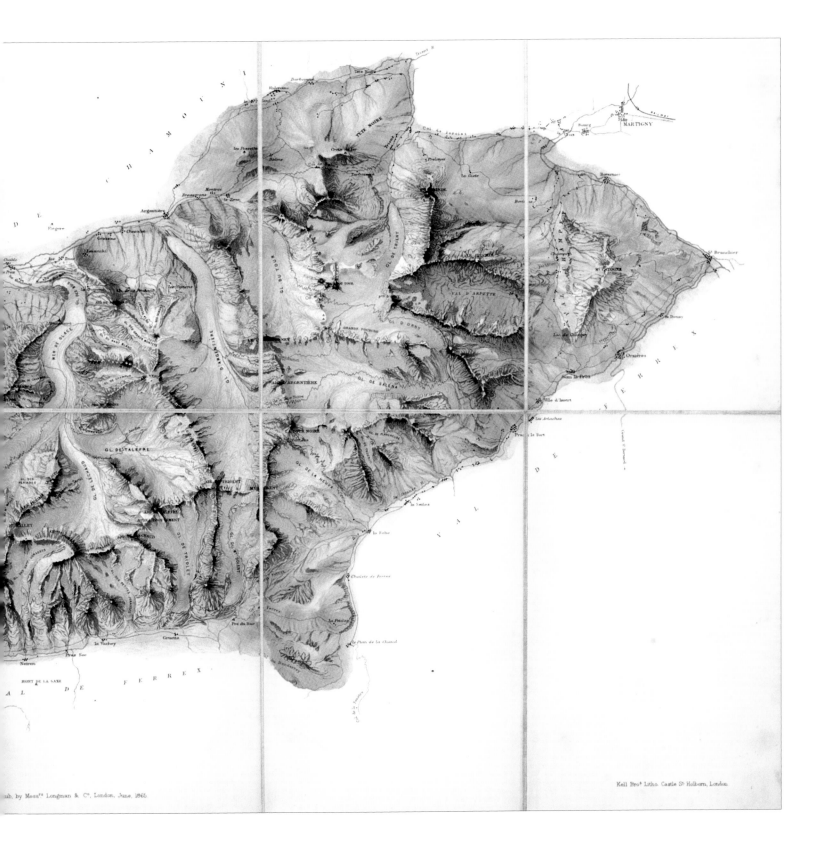

Pub. by Mess.rs Longman & Co. London, June, 1865.

Anthony Adams-Reilly, cartographer and friend of Whymper.

Tyndall's accounts of mountaineering, published in three books including the scientific milestone of *The Glaciers of the Alps*, are among the finest of the golden age. He was good at recounting, explaining and generalising, jumping from Bennen's confident step on to a razor-ridge of snow to the physics of the cosmos. He was a scientist and scholar in the best sense of the term, not one of those ridiculously specialised researchers of the twentieth century. He was a thinker who pre-dated scientific jargon – a clear, understandable thinker, just as his Enlightenment mentors had been.

Tyndall was Irish. That was one of the ways he resembled John Ball, the first president of the Alpine Club. But Tyndall was an Irish Protestant – another indication of the ecumenical nature of the mountains. Mountaineering was not a Protestant invention, much less an invention of Londoners, as pointed out in a recent book by Frank Nugent on Irish mountaineers of the golden age, *In Search of Peaks, Passes and Glaciers: Irish Alpine Pioneers*. Nugent discusses Ball, Tyndall and the cartographer Anthony Adams-Reilly. He might also have mentioned Count Russell, of Irish blood through his father and, like Ball, a Catholic, and of a Romantic sensibility like all his peers at the Alpine Club, nurtured as they were on the poetry of Byron, Shelley and Wordsworth.

'To me, high mountains are a feeling,' wrote Byron somewhere or other.

The high mountains were a feeling widely shared in the nineteenth century. From 1854 onward, the stimulus of the race to the great virgin summits extended it even further. This feeling for the high mountains was, more broadly, a feeling for nature.

Tyndall was born on 2 August 1820 in Leighlinbridge, County Carlow, south of Dublin and to the west of the Wicklow Mountains. Large swathes of heathland provided a perfect playground for fox. Tyndall's father, a Protestant Orangeman, worked for the

Royal Irish Constabulary and sent the lad to the village school, where he studied little more than English grammar until the headmaster noticed his intelligence one day and encouraged his efforts at self-education.

In 1839, Tyndall, by then a young geometer, was hired by the Ordnance Survey. There he studied to become an engineer during his missions and late into the night, enabling him to spend seven years working on the railways then sprouting all over Britain. The money that he put aside every week paid for his education in physics at the University of Marburg in Germany, where he matriculated at age twenty-eight. While a student there, Tyndall made his first trip to Alps, by coach and on foot, into the heart of Switzerland, from Basel to Zurich, Zug, Arth, the summit of Mount Rigi (a popular viewpoint), the Furka and Grimsel passes, the Grosse and Kleine Scheidegg, and the Wengernalp. Tyndall courageously stayed in modest inns, where all the beds were infested with fleas – notoriously dubbed 'kangaroos' by Genevan wit Töpffer. In 1842 a tourist waiting for a steamer on Lake Geneva had vented his spleen to Töpffer in the following terms: 'What a foul country! Full of fleas, and not a decent cigar to be found!'

Walking stick in hand, without a guide, eschewing wine and cigars, Tyndall gorged himself on milk and bread and put up with the 'kangaroos', passing himself for a Swiss on promenade. He spent little and returned happy from a land where so many glaciers and pretty girls could be viewed for no money. 'Trusting to my legs and mountain stick,' he wrote, 'repudiating guides, eating bread and drinking milk, and sleeping when possible in the country villages where nobody could detect my accent, I got through amazingly cheap.'

Completing his education with a doctorate in physics, Tyndall was noticed and praised by leading colleagues right from his first

John Tyndall (bottom, centre), member of the Royal Institution.

Tyndall taught at the Royal Institution from 1853 onward.

lectures in London. He began teaching at the Royal Institution in 1853. In 1856 he made a second trip to Switzerland with a leading scientist of the day, T.H. Huxley. The two men stayed at the Jungfrau hotel in the Wengern Alp near Berne. Tyndall wanted to study 'the veined structure of ice'. The next day, on 10 August 1856, he headed up the Guggi glacier on his own, for the first time treading the substance that so sparked his physicist's curiosity.

In the summer of 1857 he camped at Montenvers, above Chamonix, for six weeks, studying the Mer de Glace and its tributary glaciers. Tyndall was as bold as he was curious. That very first season he climbed to the summit of Mont Blanc via the Corridor and the Mur de la Côte with his friend Thomas Hirst and guide Édouard Simond, who not only needed encouraging but also help in cutting steps on the Mur de la Côte. The following year, Christian Lauener guided Tyndall across the Strahlegg pass (3,351 metres) in the Oberland and up Monte Rosa in Valais. One week after that ascent Tyndall went back to the summit on his own, in a burst of enthusiasm and vitality upon waking up in his hotel and seeing the peaks from his window: 'As I looked from my window the unspeakable beauty of the morning filled me with a longing to see the world from the top of Monte Rosa.'

On 13 September Tyndall repeated his ascent of Mont Blanc via the Corridor and Mur de la Côte, his party being guided this time by a man from Chamonix we know well, Auguste Balmat, whose hands were seriously frostbitten.

Tyndall made his third and last ascent of Mont Blanc on 21 August 1859, when he camped for twenty hours a few metres beneath the summit with the same Balmat. In the morning he carried out a series of sometimes droll experiments, notably on the propagation of sound. As he described it:

The Glacier des Bois and the Aiguilles du Charmoz depicted from Le Chapeau, by Jean-Antoine Linck.

Tyndall slowed down after Bennen's death.

The explosion of a pistol was sensibly weaker at the top than at a low level. The *shortness* of the sound was remarkable; but it bore no resemblance to the sound of a cracker, to which in acoustic treatises it is usually compared. It resembled more the sound produced by the expulsion of a cork from a champagne-bottle, but it was much louder.

That same year, in late December, he explored the glacier in winter by spending three days in the hut at Montenvers: 'The glacier excited the admiration of us all: not as in summer, shrunk and sullied like a spent reptile, steaming under the influence of the sun, its frozen muscles were compact; strength and beauty were associated in its aspect.' Shortly afterward, Tyndall finished his book on glaciers, which he published in 1860.

Having slowed down after the death of Bennen, Tyndall joined the club of celebrants and contemplatives, and had a chalet built for himself at Lusgen Alp near the Belalp Hotel in upper Valais. It was on a promontory of pastureland that looked north to the Aletsch glacier, the largest in the Swiss Alps, and south toward the Valais peaks of Dom de Mischabel (4,545 metres), the Matterhorn and the immaculate crown of the Weisshorn. The majesty, power and glory of the Alps fortified the silence surrounding chalet and scientist as he strolled along, meditating on the high pasture.

Tyndall married the year he built the chalet, and spent every summer at Lusgen Alp with his wife. On reaching seventy, chronic, cruel insomnia and abdominal pains brought him low. He died of an overdose of chloral erroneously administered by his wife, Louisa, who mistook one drug for another. The daughter of a lord, she had been thirty-one the day she married Tyndall, then fifty-six. A memorial stone to Tyndall was erected in Belalp, at a spot where he liked to halt. The slab was 4.75 metres high, with his name etched on one side and two inscriptions on the other. One was in English: 'Raised to her all-beloved by Louisa his wife, to mark a place of memories.' The other was in German, which Tyndall spoke fluently: 'The community of Naters dedicates this spot that he so loved to its honorary citizen, the noble English naturalist.'

Louisa Tyndall lived for another forty-seven years after the death of her husband, dying in 1940 aged ninety-five. For forty-seven years she postponed publication of the book she wished to write about her husband. Several biographers offered their services. She refused to give them her deceased husband's correspondence and papers. On Louisa's death it was discovered that she had amended her own diary and eliminated everything concerning her relationship with her husband. *Honni soit qui mal y pense.* Posterity will quibble endlessly on the secrets of the Tyndall couple, and on an overdose of chloral administered to an aging scientist by his pretty wife during a moment of inattention.

Wohl immer achtung! as Bennen used to say: pay constant attention. One day it was a sheet of ice; another day, a minor slip – one drug instead of the other from the fair hands of a woman above suspicion.

'Louisa, you've killed me!' Tyndall allegedly had the strength to whisper.

Louisa Tyndall.

CHAPTER XIV

SHAGGY NATIVES, GENTLEMEN TRAVELLERS

Nutrition and Health

What fuel did travellers and guides of the golden age rely on?

Wine so bitter …
it would curl your hair.

Joris-Karl Huysmans, *The Vatard Sisters*

W HAT FUEL DID TRAVELLERS OF THE GOLDEN AGE rely on, what was their indispensible stimulant? Tea, of course. Yet tea was not enough. Nor was black coffee, also often mentioned.

And what remedies were employed by shaggy chamois hunters, mountain-mad clergymen, and eccentric English gentlemen to ward off sudden fatigue, altitude sickness, dizziness, flu, tummy troubles, sunburn, frostbite, blisters, cramps, thirst or hunger? What drugs did they use? How did a super-athlete nourish and cure himself if he came from Chamonix? Or if he came from London?

In 1842 John Ruskin's guide – Joseph-Marie Couttet, a fifty-six-year-old veteran of Napoleon's army and former 'captain' of Chamonix guides – told Ruskin, as they were sharing a good jug of wine, that in Chamonix people drank absinthe as a cure. If someone came down with a fever, he was taken up to Montenvers or La Flégère and made to drink absinthe until dead drunk, following which he was put to bed to sleep off the drink and vanquish the fever through rest. According Ruskin, Couttet claimed that this remedy never failed. Meanwhile, the cultivated, affluent gentleman

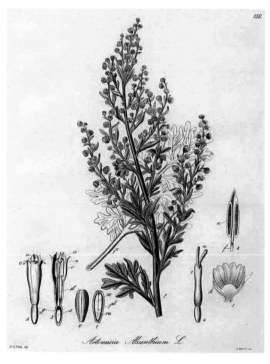

Artemisia absinthium – *absinthe. Eighteenth-century plate.*

from England, who read the reports in the Alpine Club, relied on calomel (mercuryl chloride) as a purgative and a few drops of laudanum (a tincture of opium) for insomnia and headaches.

Absinthe, it might be recalled, was a powerful alcohol distilled from a type of wormwood (*Artemisia absinthium*). Although considered 'green magic' by poets, its manufacture and consumption were outlawed in 1915. A French mountaineering handbook published in 1904 (*Manuel d'Alpinisme*) devoted a chapter to 'Drink' in which it took issue with poets and fans of aperitifs (absinthe was also drunk as an aperitif), boldly declaring that 'absinthe kills'. A few lines later, in capital letters, it added: 'DEATH TO ABSINTHE'.

French historian Hippolyte Taine asserted that William Pitt the Younger (1759–1806), who masterminded all the coalitions against France and Napoleon, drank at least two bottles of port at dinner. Two bottles of port!

Journalist Albert Smith apparently consulted Pitt's shades before climbing Mont Blanc in 1851 with three companions and more bottles than guides (of whom there were sixteen):

    60 bottles of Vin Ordinaire
    6 bottles of Bordeaux
    10 bottles of St George [Burgundy]
    15 bottles of St Jean
    3 bottles of Cognac
    1 bottle of syrup of raspberries
    6 bottles of lemonade
    2 bottles of champagne.

The rest of Smith's list tells us something about their anxieties. These brave gentleman were apparently concerned by problems of constipation rather than an excess of meat and wine.

20 loaves
10 small cheeses
6 packets of chocolate
6 packets of sugar
4 packets of prunes
4 packets of raisins
2 packets of salt
4 wax candles
6 lemons
4 legs of mutton
4 shoulders of mutton
6 pieces of veal
1 piece of beef
11 large fowls
35 small fowls.

Those packets of prunes are revealing, and their usefulness was confirmed by Viollet-le-Duc. Held to be the leading cause of illness by nineteenth-century doctors, constipation was a common phobia of climbing parties during the golden age of mountaineering. Which may seem surprising: what were they worried about, given that digestion is accelerated by legwork? The steepness of Mont Blanc's slopes ensured the intestinal transit of all those fowls.

The people who came after Smith displayed a certain prudence in what they ate and drank. When Tyndall, that lone glacier explorer, climbed Monte Rosa (4,634 metres) in 1858, he did so soberly – not a drop of alcohol, just a ham sandwich. Tyndall, like Whymper and a few others, was an early voice against having one for the road: 'I had neither brandy nor wine, but I knew the immense amount of mechanical force represented by four ounces of bread and ham, and I therefore feared no failure from lack of nutriment. Indeed, I am inclined to think that both guides and travellers often impair their vigour and render themselves cowardly and apathetic by the incessant "refreshing" which they deem it necessary to indulge in on such occasions.'

Pedestrianism

Like many of his compatriots, Tyndall was a great walker in the plains and countryside. A penchant for competitive walking, called 'pedestrianism', became a national rage. Highly popular in Britain in the late eighteenth and nineteenth centuries, pedestrianism probably contributed to the attacking strength of members of the Alpine Club. Captain Robert Barclay Allardice became known as 'The Celebrated Pedestrian' for a money-earning stunt that could be summed up in three figures: he said he would walk 1,000 miles in 1,000 hours — one mile each and every hour — for a prize of 1,000 guineas. Captain Barclay, as he was known, walked from 1 June to 12 July 1809 to claim his reward. This challenge is much easier, I think, than walking 100 miles in less than twenty-four hours, as was regularly done in pedestrianism circles in the nineteenth century.

Walking was these gentlemen's first — and last — form of training. Some of them, like Whymper, walked so quickly that they did not have time to eat. Throughout his life a man like Whymper was a champion walker in terms of speed and distance. His diary, partly published in Francis Smythe's biography of Whymper, is full of specific references to distances he managed to cover at a very young age, by day and by night, in every kind of weather (including torrential rain), without complaining and without affectation. Aged seventeen, Whymper recorded his longest distance in a day's walk in the Sussex countryside — thirty-five miles — and the longest distance without a halt — twenty-seven miles. On the evening of 7 November 1857, he happily noted a speed record all the more gratifying in that the roads were bad and he was wearing new shoes: twenty-five miles in seven hours. During the first hour he managed to cover nearly six miles.

Walking was common exercise among all classes throughout Britain. Stendhal claims that a young English woman walked further in one week than a young Roman woman in a year, a comment repeated and confirmed by Taine in 1872 in his *Notes on England*.

Whymper's pace: 5½ miles per hour

In 1879 Whymper was still attentive to his pace on England's paths and had two assistants check his speed – down to the second – prior to leaving to explore the volcanoes of Ecuador. He covered seven miles in seventy-seven minutes and twenty-five seconds, or an average of almost nine kilometres (5½ miles) per hour. That is a lively, bracing pace, as swift as can be, but hard to maintain over long distances day after day, given fatigue and wear on the feet.

Today's walkers are happy when they cover six kilometres (3¾ miles) per hour, carrying a light backpack on a perfectly flat road. Hitting seven kilometres per hour requires lengthening the stride and focusing on keeping up the rhythm. A full day at that pace – say, forty-two kilometres in seven hours – is a sign of outstanding shape for an ordinary walker, since speed generally drops after midday.

Whymper walked a mile – 1.6 kilometres – in eleven minutes. That was his usual pace, he told his assistants, as a forty-year-old man in everyday clothing. Over eight kilometres (five miles) per hour! His pace as a young man in the Alps must have been stunning. During his first trip to the Alps, he made faster progress from Bourg-d'Oisans to Grenoble than the stagecoach, which dawdled and often halted. Whymper preferred to advance at his

Whymper walked a mile in eleven minutes.

The Col du Lautaret.

own impatient pace on the high road of Lautaret. As Rimbaud put it in *A Season in Hell* in 1873, it was 'the open road in all weather, supernaturally sober'. The open road, whatever the weather – that was Whymper at twenty.

Below is a passage from Whymper's diary, quoted by Smythe in his biography of the mountaineer. The fragment is highly enlightening on Whymper's character, swift pace and travel conditions in the Alps in 1860, the age of stagecoaches. On 30 August of that year Whymper, who had been patrolling the Alps since 27 July, relaxed in the village of Courmayeur after a sixty-five-kilometre hike from Bionaz in Val d'Aosta, representing sixty-five kilometres of steadily climbing path. On 14 September, in Briançon, all the seats in the stagecoach for Grenoble being taken, Whymper made a snap decision:

> As there remained nothing for me but to walk to Grenoble [112 kilometres away], I set about it at once. I started at a quarter to two. Got to Le Monestier easily in 2¼ hours; fed and went on to the Col de Lauteret, passing several rather wretched villages on the way; did it in 2¼ hours (rather fast), the last half-hour in nasty rain. There appeared to be some very good views at the top but the rain and darkness prevented my seeing anything. Went into a wretched stone cabin at the top which was crowded with workmen (more than 30 men in a little vaulted room of the dirtiest description). They, however, gave me a very civil reception and I had wine and got hot water for tea for sixpence.

Whymper was nothing if not impatient:

> Started against [the workmen's] remonstrances for La Grave at eight. It was pitch dark, and to render the

road more difficult to keep, it came on after a while raining very heavily. I got very wet, of course, before I got to La Grave at ten minutes to ten. Found a fair inn, but when the diligence passed there was still no place, so I had the choice either to stay there or else march on. Now it is probably easy to continue walking through rain when one is once wet; but it requires very considerable pluck to start at nearly midnight, when it is raining in torrents, on a 50-mile walk on a road you do not know. So I was over-persuaded and went to bed. The man, of course, did not wake me and indeed I had hard work to wake *him;* therefore I did not start till a quarter to six; disgusted with him I punished myself by having no breakfast till I got to Le Dauphin at twenty-five minutes to eight. Let no one stop at Le Dauphin, the incivility of the people combined with the bad fare was an almost unique specimen to me. There are some remarkably fine mountain views both between La Grave and Le Dauphin and Le Dauphin to Bourg and the whole country has the appearance of being very well worth exploring. Started from Le Dauphin at twenty minutes past eight and got to Bourg-d'Oisans at 20 minutes to 11; had some wine; found the diligence from there was so slow as to be useless and walked on. This path downwards was very dismal, rain came on and when I got to Uriage I was out and out drenched. Fed and started at five minutes to four and went plodding on with the chance of more rain. The attractions of a diligence which was going more than six miles an hour proved too much for me and a little outside Vizille I got up and rode the rest of the way to Grenoble.

The village of Bourg-d'Oisans.

Infantryman and grenadier of the 3rd regiment of the Imperial Guard.

In those final lines, Vizille and Uriage should probably be reversed, otherwise his itinerary is incomprehensible. Nevertheless, nourished only on a poor breakfast at Le Dauphin and a glass of wine at Bourg-d'Oisans, the young man covered the entire distance from La Grave to Vizille on foot – seventy-five kilometres. The day before, muddy and drenched by icy rain on the Lautaret pass (2,057 metres), Whymper walked from Briançon to La Grave – thirty-eight kilometres. And the day before that, having left from Mont-Dauphin for Vallouise (1,200 metres), Whymper had descended late in the afternoon to sleep in Briançon – fifty-six kilometres.

A trooper's pace

At twenty, Whymper marched like a trooper. With a little effort, he would have matched the exploit of the grenadiers of Napoleon's Imperial Guard, those veterans of the forced march of Napoleon's return from Elba. It might be recalled that the grenadiers carried weapons (rifle and bayonet) and military kit that averaged twenty kilos in weight. One thousand soldiers marched with Napoleon from Golfe-Juan to Grenoble – 320 kilometres – in six days, from 2 to 7 March 1815. During the last leg, from Corps to Grenoble, the guard paraded before taking up its quarters in Grenoble itself. Napoleon dined and slept on Rue Montorge, a stone's throw from the public square where his enemies would have willingly erected a gallows to hang the Corsican 'ogre'. But his faithful grenadiers had covered sixty-nine kilometres in a day. Whymper's pace almost matched the Imperial Guard on campaign. So, as a general rule, never underestimate men of the past.

The young Englishman was willing to make whatever harsh, prolonged effort was required on the monotonous incline of a corridor of snow or slope of scree. After all, what's a moraine in the cirque de Bonnepierre or any other of the heaps of scree so decried in the Oisans to anyone who can swallow and digest 170 kilometres on the open road in only three days?

Like Whymper, the Pyrenean pioneer Count Russell trained by walking long distances on the open road. 'To get myself in shape in 1858, I went on foot from Bagnères-de-Bigorre to Luchon (70 kilometres) in one day, in torrid heat.' The next day, Russell made the entire ascent, from Luchon, of the Pico de Aneto (3,404 metres).

Certain guides from Chamonix and elsewhere were not to be outdone. The nineteenth century brought to a close millennia of travel on foot and by beast. Before the arrival of trains – the first mechanical form of transport – the sound of a motor was never heard in the countryside. All peasant farmers were footsloggers and haymowers. They worked hard in summer, from sunrise to sunset, from father to son. Sometimes a family produced a prodigy of strength or endurance whom a magazine might feature as a curiosity in its pages, with no commercial intent, slotted between the monstrance of Belem or a chart of the historic and religious traditions of ancient Mexico. In 1868, for instance, the *Magasin Pittoresque* featured Édouard Balmat. That encyclopaedic publication was a hodge-podge of erudition which, that same year, included a description of the town of Sion; its lists of walks are as extraordinary as they are instructive, given that they concern Chamonix guides whom Whymper probably encountered here or there.

Édouard Balmat, having left Paris to join his regiment in Genoa, reached Chamonix on the evening of his fifth day. Distance covered: 564 kilometres. That's 110 kilometres per day. A few years later, the same Balmat left Bains de Loèche (today Leukerbad) at 2 a.m. and arrived at Chamonix at 9 p.m. the same day – roughly

The Ascent of Mont Peter Botte on Mauritius, engraving published in Le Magasin Pittoresque, 1833.

120 kilometres in nineteen hours. Those 120 kilometres included a descent from Loèche to the Rhone Valley at Susten (shortly after Sierre on the road to Brig), a stretch along the Rhone Valley via Sion as far as Martigny, the crossing of two passes (Col de La Forclaz, 1,526 metres, and Col de Balme, 2,204 metres), and then the descent to Chamonix.

The waters of Loèche are rich in sulphate and have been used for baths, showers, and drinking since the early Middle Ages to cure rheumatism and skin diseases. In those days, people taking the cure would paddle in the waters of the resort's pools for three to six hours a day. Balmat, after that kind of preparation, was ready to pull out all the stops on his return voyage. His average pace was more than six kilometres an hour even though his route included the slopes of two passes, Forclaz and Balme, representing 2,000 metres of verticality after having covered 66 kilometres since setting out from Loèche. What persistence! One wonders what he had to do the next day — make hay, perhaps? Those Savoyard peasants were real muzhiks, tougher than the muzhiks from the Russian steppes. They were incredibly hardened to suffering and effort. Napoleon won his battles and built his empire on the legs and backs of such peasants.

They would have brushed aside with a shrug of the shoulders all those issues of health and nutrition that would soon be surfacing in Alpine reviews.

Bathing for the skin, absinthe for fevers, nothing else.

The pedantic notion of 'health and nutrition' was an invention of bourgeois travellers, who were more fragile than might appear at first sight when one sees the knapsacks worn by the Smith party.

Nervous tension and fatigue weigh on the stomach. The effect of a slice of dried sausage that is too fatty, or a sip of coffee that is too strong, can be surprising. Weight on one's back is only one

Eugène Viollet-le-Duc, a founder member of the Club Alpin Français, mapped the Mont Blanc chain.

Viollet-le-Duc, an 'old mountain rambler'.

aspect of the question. There is also the weight on one's stomach. In general, the less one eats in the thick of the action, the better one walks – digestion, after all, is hard work.

The recommendations of an old rambler: Viollet-le-Duc

Four years after the Club Alpin Français was founded in France (1874), Eugène Viollet-le-Duc (1814–1879), a self-described 'old mountain rambler', published his observations in the club's *Annuaire* under a typically nineteenth-century title: 'Hygiene for Travellers in Alpine Lands'. Viollet-le-Duc was not only the architect who supervised famous restorations (including the medieval city of Carcassonne, the cathedral of Notre-Dame in Paris, the chateau of Pierrefonds, and the cathedral of Amiens), a friend of Prosper Mérimée and a professor of art and aesthetics, but he was also one of the founding members of the Club Alpin Français. In the France of 1878 no one was more familiar with the geometry and aesthetics of Mont Blanc than Viollet-le-Duc. He drew up a map of the chain over a seven-year period, 1868–75, season after season, from passes, panoramic peaks and glaciers. This map, his finest claim to fame in the golden age of mountaineering, required 200 days of hikes and observations in the field.

The recommendations of this old-timer remain valid today: get an early start after a light breakfast of black coffee and a chunk of bread (to avoid a heavy stomach). According to Viollet-le-Duc, 'The cold morning air is singularly conducive to walking, if the stomach is not overly heavy.'

Maintain a steady pace when walking uphill – accelerate only on the flat, should one wish to gain time.

Avoid intense effort – skirt obstacles. Don't insist if overcome by faintness or sickness; instead, return to the attack several days later, after steadily hardening oneself on other walks. Viollet-le-Duc:

'I have seen people struggle to reach 3,000 metres, then two weeks later surpass that altitude with no difficulty if, in the meantime, they have gradually accustomed themselves to ascents.'

At the end of his essay, Viollet-le-Duc returned to this idea of thresholds, of reaching higher altitudes in stages, without doing violence to one's nature or temperament. If one wishes to walk in the mountains free from risk, free to observe, admire and benefit from the effort, storing up good memories that encourage a return, then it is important not to push oneself too far.

He used a more general term when discussing acute mountain sickness, namely, 'cerebral phenomena that occur during higher ascents'. These could be avoided if one gradually habituated oneself to ascents by remaining at an altitude of at least 1,000 metres between ascents. 'Whereas,' warned Viollet-le-Duc, 'leaving Le Havre to arrive at Chamonix thirty hours later and the next day attempt an ascent of Mont Blanc is, one can be sure, an imprudence at the very least.' Thus although the verb 'to acclimatise' does not figure in Viollet-le-Duc's article, he clearly expressed the idea and repeatedly practised it in his years of walking in the mountains. He was also familiar with the research of Dr Paul Jourdanet.[7]

Viollet stressed regular training: every day, climb higher at a steady pace, sticking to a rhythm that suits one's own lungs and above all prevents stopping and starting.

Eat little but often, especially when walking at high altitude.

Drink little but often. If possible, drink something hot to quench the thirst – tea with a little cognac, weak coffee, hot wine.

Never drink milk on the way up – it weighs on the stomach.

The first-aid pouch should contain: a bottle of tincture of arnica (for bruises); a flask of laudanum (a tincture of opium widely used

Altitude sickness: early observation of symptoms, 1875.

7. Paul Jourdanet, *Influences de la pression de l'air sur la vie de l'homme* (Paris: G. Masson, 1875).

'Viollet-le-Duc fretted over a traveller's stools ...'

as a remedy for all sorts of ailments in the nineteenth century, and very effective for headaches, according to Thomas De Quincey[8]); a phial of ether; a phial of alcohol, a phial of spirit of ether, despite its volatility, for nausea (according to Viollet-le-Duc); a few tablets of diascordium (for diarrhoea); some virgin wax; rosin; and gum diachylon (for fractures).

Viollet-le-Duc applied rosin to his feet before an ascent, to protect against cold and frostbite. He mixed the rosin with wax and olive oil, making a pomade that he smeared on his feet. The first concern of all hikers is the state of their feet and maintenance of their shoes. As he wrote: 'The excursionist must take great care of his feet, since the least graze can bring him to a halt for days on end. The nails must not be too long nor too short, and they must be cut straight, taking care to round the corners with a file.'

Once the excursion was over and shoes removed, it was suggested that the shoes be stuffed with hay or dry grass if they had become damp. Above all readers were advised not dry them by the fire, but in the open air so that the leather would retain its softness and avoid cracking, which might irritate the feet.

Viollet-le-Duc fretted over a traveller's stools – it was an important subject that he discussed, for that matter, before getting to feet and shoes: 'There is an essential matter that I feel I must bring to the attention of mountaineers. The modest amount of nutriment that one generally takes when making sustained ascents, the quality of that nutriment, and the rapid evaporation to which the body provokes, among some travellers, persistent constipation – which must be remedied at all costs.'

Indeed, according to Viollet-le-Duc several days of constipation could trigger serious ailments in the traveller, as he witnessed

---

8. Thomas De Quincy, 'Confessions of an English Opium-Eater', *London Magazine* (September/October 1821).

himself on more than one occasion: headaches, congestion, vomiting, and physical and mental prostration. Therefore it was important to take along a light, handy syringe which he felt was less dangerous than the laxative pills used by English travellers.

Finally: alcohol. English accounts of the golden age of mountaineering often place it front and centre, whether hot wine first thing in the morning, a little drink for the road during halts, a sip at the bivouac or a toast at the summit.

Viollet-le-Duc founded a different school. He was probably the first mountaineer in France to explicitly discourage the use of alcohol in the mountains, including white wine and champagne. All alcohol was discouraged, except red wine with a meal. 'Brandy and rum should be avoided. Kirsch is the least pernicious, but it is better to abstain altogether, during an ascent, from any alcoholic liquor that weakens the legs and provokes drowsiness and dizziness even at small doses. One day, at an altitude of 3,800 metres, I came across a traveller who, having drunk the equivalent of one glass of pure brandy, found it impossible to place one foot in front of the other. White wines, especially the kind of Champagne wine supplied to travellers in the Alps, are veritably crippling. The same is true of gassy lemonades, which should be avoided, especially since the more one drinks the thirstier one gets.'

Only red wine was tolerated, basically in the hut, with a lunch that included eggs and roast meat or ham. Guides from Chamonix were wary of white wines – most particularly, it would seem, of white wines from Valais.

'One for the road' on the steps of an inn.

Only red wine should be drunk at a meal, claimed Viollet-le-Duc.

The Grand Combin: wine, snow, and sugar

As soon as the two Mathews brothers arrived in Châbles in Valais in August 1856, with the summit of the Grand Combin in view,

Enjoying a drink at the summit, celebrating success and the vista with snow-chilled wine, was a tradition among travellers of the golden age.

they ordered provisions for a three-day excursion by five mountaineers (themselves, a guide and a porter from Valais, and a guide from Chamonix). They took six loaves of bread, some cheese, a huge piece of cold chamois meat, chocolate, sugar and – inevitably, although very hard to carry – ten bottles of wine. Which, for that matter, was an absolute minimum: a little over half a litre per day for each member of the party.

Mathews himself acknowledged that he had a hard time passing up on sorbets made of wine, snow and sugar; he found them as invigorating as they were delicious. But Auguste Simond, the guide from Chamonix, was worried – the party was taking white wine, not the red wine he was accustomed to drinking during an ascent. White wine, said Simond, renders you legless. Fortunately, that did not turn out to be case.

The Allalinhorn, 28 August 1856:
All praise to red wine from Valais
Enjoying a drink at the summit, celebrating success and the vista with snow-chilled wine, was a tradition among travellers of the golden age. It was a habit that both travellers and guides were keen to maintain – wine at the summit dispelled any anxieties about the descent. In the midst of an assault on the Allalinhorn on 28 August 1856, on a rocky ridge that plunged directly onto the Allalin glacier, E.L. Ames suddenly felt dizzy to the point of paralysis. He sat down, determined to go no further. His lead guide, Andermatten (who ran the Monte Rosa Hotel in Saas) was far ahead and refused to turn back even though the other guide, Imseng, hastened to convey Ames's desire to him. Things might have turned serious if Ames hadn't recovered his wits, or had taken umbrage at that refusal. Ames clung to the rocks on the narrow ridge, a bottle of wine in one pocket of his shooting jacket, a flask of some

The Finsteraarhorn seen from the lower Grindelwald glacier.

execrable Valais beverage in the other. The passage wasn't difficult, but very dizzying. The bottle of wine swung to the left, above the void, hampering his movements. The party reached the summit an hour and a half later. In the freezing cold, Andermatten uttered jubilant shouts. '*Aach, Der Herr Pfarrer sucht uns gewiss mit dem Spiegel!*' (I'm sure the Reverend is watching us through his telescope!) In fact, a few days earlier Joseph Imseng, the old clergyman from Saas who was himself a high priest of local exploration, had studied the summit with them.

Apprehensive about the descent, Ames shared the wine with his two guides. The wine, the victory and his earlier ascent changed his view of the edge of the ridge. 'One is apt to suppose that what is difficult to ascend must be still more awkward to descend, but it seldom proves so; partly, perhaps, from the difficulties being known, and partly because no doubt can arise as to the necessity for surmounting them. But, on this occasion, I think some virtue must be ascribed to the red Valais wine, which had infused a little extra courage before starting.'

Ames never forgot that 28 August 1856. His account, published in *Peaks, Passes, and Glaciers,* was far from the only one to vaunt the merits of the modest wines of Valais.

The Finsteraarhorn: Libations in the sun

J.F. Hardy reflected on this subject during an ascent of the Finsteraarhorn (4,275 metres). The sun was rising, its morning rays thawing the party. It was time for libations. As Hardy recounted:

> Throwing off the rope, we hastened to fill our cups and horns with some of the Valais wine, and drained off our bumpers of that rather unpalatable and decidedly thin liquid, as though it were the choicest grape of Burgundy.
>
> And truly, though I seem to sneer at it now, it is but

seeming, for I am fully convinced that it is the proper drink for the mountains, and that cold tea or milk on the one hand, and brandy on the other, are equally a snare and a delusion. The former are not sufficiently invigorating, and though brandy should always be carried in case of illness, it should never be administered except as a medicine.

The Schreckhorn (4,078 metres): A pipe at the summit

On the Schreckhorn, Leslie Stephen and his three Oberland guides only unleashed their final assault after having downed a shot of whisky. Once at the top, Stephen sat and filled his pipe. The air was wonderfully calm and the horizon spread out beneath his thoughtful eyes as the smell of tobacco scented the air. Stephen was smoking a 'peace' pipe.

Stephen succinctly described the tacit agreement of these English-Oberlander parties and their shared penchant: 'The guides of Oberland have an occasional weakness, which Englishmen cannot condemn with a very clear conscience, for the consumption of strong drink.'

At the summit, as in the valley, whether for relaxation, pleasure or morale, wine and tobacco were basic substances that no one wanted to give up. Why deprive oneself of a swig of whisky before the moment of truth? As to tobacco, whether pipe or cigarette, no one batted an eyelash at it in the nineteenth century. Drinking wine and smoking a good pipe were signs of a highly personal and private contentment.

Butter for thirst

More or less all gentlemen climbers had their recipe for abating thirst, something that would prevent them from drinking too much or too often. Whereas Viollet-le-Duc advised drinking often,

The Klein and Gross Schreckhorn seen from the Mettenberg.

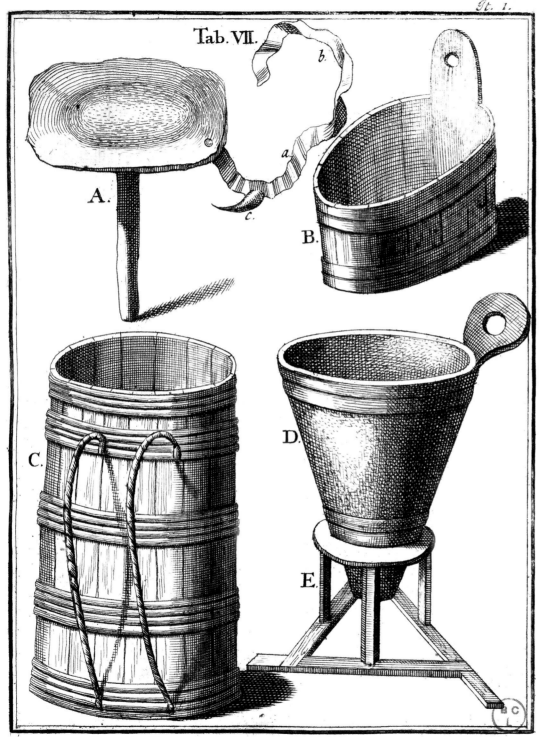

Pl. 1.

A.

B.

C.

D.

E.

a.

b.

c.

Utensils used
for making milk
and cheese.

Ames was wary of water from the glaciers and he espoused a different school. Ames preferred butter. As he wrote:

> The idea had been suggested to me on the Furca, by a waitress of discerning mind and great administrative talent in the commissariat department, on the occasion of a recent ascent of the Galenstock, where it had proved so desirable a condiment that I determined thenceforth always to take a supply with me on similar expeditions. If tightly packed in a glass tumbler, or any other vessel, with a paper cover, it may be carried for hours in a knapsack without melting, or if the surface should be a little affected by the heat, a handful of snow, or cold water (if any is to be had), will soon restore it to its former solidity. As a preventative of thirst, it is invaluable on the upper glaciers and high rocks, where no water can be found; and even where water is abundant its merits will be readily appreciated by any old traveller who knows that drinking frequently during a long ascent is a pernicious habit, more easily denounced than resisted.
>
> I mention this, because butter is rarely thought of as an item in the provision list, and is decidedly preferable in every way to its usual substitute, cheese.

Milk, which Viollet-le-Duc advised against, was Tyndall's favourite drink. Tyndall was a big drinker of milk – the milk of Alpine pastures, a fresh, strong, creamy milk.

During ascents, Oberland guides usually ate something every three hours. Writing of local habits, Tyndall mentioned an Oberland superstition not shared by Bennen. Many guides thought one would sleep forever if one dozed atop one of the tall peaks in their region – a belief probably based on a fear of lightning.

SHAGGY NATIVES, GENTLEMEN TRAVELLERS

Early Equipment and Techniques

Chamois hunter seen here on ice with crampons on his shoes, by Édouard Pingret (nineteenth century).

I N 1861, WHYMPER COOLED HIS HEELS IN THE VILLAGE OF BESSÉE for the arrival of the only baton, or staff, which would enable him to reach the summit of Mont Pelvoux, according to his friend Jean Reynaud, the district surveyor. This baton was famous throughout the area but at that moment was in the possession of the post-master, who was proving hard to find. He was finally located, half drunk, toasting France and its wonderful batons. This particular staff was a branch of young oak about one and a half metres long, gnarled and twisted. Whymper was not sure it would be of any use, but Reynaud convinced him to take it along.

In their attempt on the Matterhorn in 1857, the three men from Valtournenche – Jean-Jacques Carrel, Jean-Antoine Carrel, and Amé Gorret – took a staff of ash without a metal tip but with a curved iron blade at the top, plus a small woodcutter's axe which Jean-Jacques carried between his shirt and jacket, like a miner. The ash baton was not really a mountain staff. The curved metal head was used to hook marmots and draw them from their holes. These details of their tools were mentioned in a letter Gorret wrote to his countryman Guido Rey (1861–1935), a historian and inveterate Matterhorn enthusiast who worshipped 'the great pyramid'.

The alpenstock used in the Oberland.

The British travellers of the golden age swiftly adopted the alpenstock used in the Oberland, which was perfectly suited to the terrain according to Alfred Wills in his account of the ascent of the Wetterhorn. Use of the alpenstock in Switzerland was mentioned as early as the sixteenth century by Josias Simler, a Swiss humanist who wrote *De Alpibus Commentarius.* The Latin name given to the staff was *alpinus baculus.* It was the long baton with an iron tip at one end seen in the hands of the guides who conquered Mont Blanc in 1787 – Balmat's alpenstock was some three metres long, while Saussure used a shorter one measuring two and a half metres. A good alpenstock was supposed to be longer than its user, a length that came in handy when crossing snow bridges: if two guides held each of its two ends steady, it could be used as a handrail. In other cases, it could be placed right on the snow with each end more or less anchored, occasionally twinned with another alpenstock – or extended with iron fittings, as John Ball did – to strengthen the bridge. Everyone would then cross on all fours, one after another, as though on a bridge of crystal. Sometimes they even crawled, making themselves so very, very light. Crossing a snowbridge whose fragility leapt to the eye (and knotted the throat) was almost the first thing mentioned in the first account published in *Peaks, Passes and Glaciers.* As described by Wills during his 1857 expedition on the Glacier du Tour, 'We … crossed many a crevasse over which it was prudent to pass not so much on our hands and knees as crawling *au ventre* [on our bellies], with the alpenstock laid lengthwise in the snow still more to distribute the weight.'

Often, the man walking in front would probe the snow with his baton, which might be used as pole for rescue should the snow collapse. John Ball described such an incident during his excursion on the Schwarztor glacier in 1845: 'At the very first bridge the snow yielded under both my feet, and I fell through as far as the waist, but with the help of the alpenstock, laid flat upon the surface, I had no great difficulty in scrambling back again.' As late as 1885, when use of an ice axe had become common, some old timers in Germanic regions still preferred a long alpenstock when crossing a glacier, according to Emil Zsigmondy.

Ball recommended holding the baton horizontally in both hands when climbing slopes of soft snow. He employed that technique on the Col de Strahlegg in September 1852. 'I took the lead, as I was anxious to test of a mode of mounting steep slopes of soft snow, which I may venture to recommend as advantageous in such cases. You hold the alpenstock horizontally with both hands, the point being turned to the left side, and thrust it forward, with a somewhat oblique movement from right to left, so as to bury it in the snow transversely, at about the height of the chest.'

In 1865, the Englishmen climbing the Brenva spur of Mont Blanc were armed with alpenstocks, yet things would have gone badly without the ice axes of their guides Melchior and Jakob Anderegg. An alpenstock had neither the driving power nor ability to harpoon or anchor hard ice. When descending rocks, however, Austrian mountaineer Emil Zsigmondy made skilful use of an alpenstock's long reach. But he claimed that even three years of mountaineering were insufficient for learning to master this technique:

> During a descent, with one hand you drive the steel tip into the ground a few paces ahead, with the other you grasp some outcrop; in this fashion, you can descend steep slopes where the feet find no hold. In certain specific cases, you can also slide along the length of the alpenstock, gripping it with both hands, and being very careful not to let your weight swing forward, which would make the alpenstock pivot in a semi-circle and fling the traveller into the abyss.

A woodsman's hatchet was sometimes used as an ice axe.

The English tent designed by Galton in light canvas.

The tent was sometimes used as a blanket.

Zsigmondy's friend Purtscheller had often told him of the marvellous skill of hunters from Salzburg and Bavaria who used this technique of sliding down an alpenstock.

An alpenstock, which was generally shortened to about 1.8 metres by 1860, could be used in all kinds of ways. On 29 August 1861, Whymper erected a tent on the Matterhorn's Col du Lion. It was an English tent of light fabric devised by Francis Galton, which opened like a book. One end was closed but the other had flaps. Two alpenstocks served as tent poles, while cords on the lower edges (weighted by stones) and a rope that passed through iron rings on the alpenstocks (then tied to pegs) were designed to secure it. Unfortunately, strong winds obliged Whymper to collapse the tent and use it as a blanket instead. He was disappointed that a tent which appeared so fine in London was so useless in the first mountain gust. The next year Whymper returned to the Col du Lion where he slept under a tent most of whose features he had revised and perfected. This camp on the Col du Lion on the eve of a bold solitary attempt on the Matterhorn has remained famous in mountaineering history ever since Whymper published an illustrated account in his memoirs. Whymper reflected a good deal on the issue of bivouacking in the mountains.[9] Although still young, he already had extensive experience in nights spent outdoors at respectable altitudes (over 3,000 metres), whether under an outcrop of rock or on a bed of quickly gathered pebbles, in the twilight, during an evening storm. In 1861, on Mont Pelvoux, Whymper spent four consecutive nights out of doors.

Charles Hudson and his friends used the alpenstock in a highly original way – as a balance pole on glissades in the snow, braked by the feet rather than the alpenstock itself (as standard, quasi-instinctive technique would have it):

---

9. Edward Whymper, 'Camping Out', *Alpine Journal* (March 1865).

In glissading these and similar slopes, the feet of a skilful slider are placed flat upon the snow, about twelve inches apart, and parallel to each other, while his knees are kept slightly bent, with body and head erect, and the alpenstock carried nearly horizontally in both hands, after the manner in which a balancing pole is poised by a tight-rope dancer. If the slider be able to check his speed, and ultimately to stop his onward motion, by the usual mode of raising his toes and driving his heels into the snow, the steepest descent need not alarm him; for should these expedients prove insufficient, he would rapidly bring his alpenstock into use, and then by thrusting the point into the snow about six inches behind him, somewhat as a kangaroo uses his tail, and by throwing the weight of his body backwards upon the pole, he would be able to arrest his course.

When it comes to ice axes, we know the shape of the original one used in Chamonix. In 1787, some of Saussure's guides on Mont Blanc drew hatchets from their belts when they ran into steep breaks in the ice, into which they cut steps. And in 1888, spurred by the recent centenary of the ascent of Mont Blanc, Joseph Vallot sorted through old tools in a barn belonging to Monsieur Cachat, owner of the Hôtel du Mont Blanc and grandson of Jean-Paul Cachat, nicknamed 'Needle', who had been one of Saussure's guides. It was an inspired idea, for one of the tools found by Vallot was none other than the old guide's axe.

According to Vallot, it represents the oldest known ice axe. From blade to tip, it measured 1.16 metres. The roughly forged axe head was set on a baton thirty-five millimetres in diameter. A large nail twisted around the handle held this crucial feature in place. Like an alpenstock, the ice axe had a steel tip at the other

Saussure crossing a crevasse on his backside.

end. As Vallot noted, what distinguished it from modern ice axes was the direction of the blade, which was angled vertically, like a conventional axe, rather than horizontally.

As early as 1863 the *Alpine Journal* devoted an article of several pages to the best model of ice axe. It was signed by six authorities in the Alpine Club – Kennedy, Grove, Cowell, George, Hall and Nichols – but it was impossible to find any two club members in *full* agreement on this important subject. Everyone defended his own ice axe. The article described at least three distinct models, including one for travellers and another, much heavier one, to do the cutting work expected of guides. It was recommended that the handle be made of ash or walnut. Alpenstocks were also made of ash, other woods such as oak and locust being considered too heavy, not stiff enough or too brittle. The ice axe was designed to cut steps in ice and icy snow, which explains the importance of the pick and the blade (called an adze).

In August 1855, during the first ascent of Mont Blanc without guides, Englishmen had to cut steps in the Mur de la Côte using various tools. As described by Hudson:

> Ainslie and Kennedy carried ash poles with steel spikes, which they brought from England; Grenville, Christopher, Smyth, and Hudson carried *haches,* which are ashen poles from four to five feet in length with iron heads about ten inches long and sharpened exactly like a small pick-axe. The guides who ascend Mont Blanc from Chamonix always carry two or three of these instruments, which need not be heavier than a short staff, and are lighter than the poles usually used.

This bladed 'instrument' of 1.5 to 1.8 metres in length, and lighter than an alpenstock, was nothing other than an ice axe. Whether

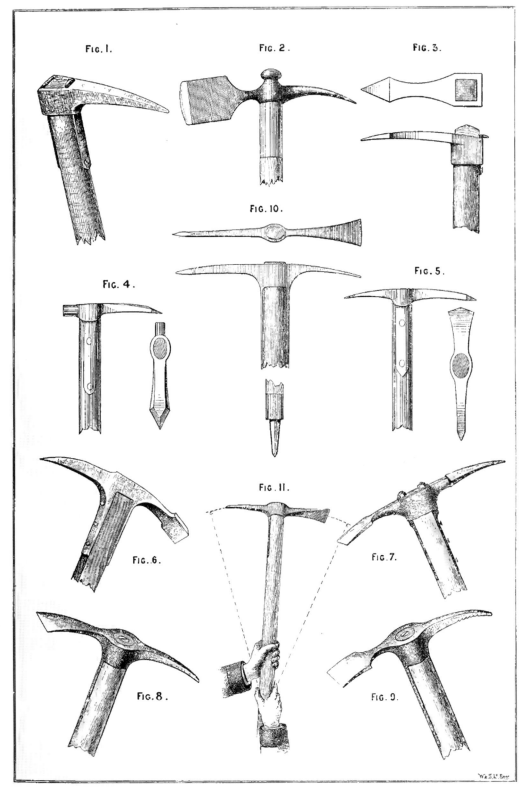

Types of ice axe.

Leslie Stephen with his alpenstock.

wielded in the huge hands of rustic guides or the gentlemanly hands of explorers – or gripped in the tongs of blacksmiths and toolmakers – the shape, materials and uses of the ice axe evolved during the golden age of mountaineering and the following decade. It thus steadily replaced the alpenstock, which was certainly much older than its earliest recorded description.

The ice axe used by Chamonix guide Michel Croz, for example, was closely related to the pick-axe employed by Cachat and exhumed by Vallot – its curved blade was vertical and its very sharp pick was straight. Melchior Anderegg from Brenva, meanwhile, used an ice axe with a triangular, straight pick and an adze that was nearly horizontal. Josef Bennen, the guide on the Weisshorn, used an axe oriented vertically.

In Tyndall's account of the Weisshorn, the protagonists used an ice axe that was the object of a footnote in the French translation of 1876: 'A short-handled mountain pike topped by an axe head and a pick tip, with a soft steel tip at the bottom.'[10] This was a perfect definition because it described the tool without specifying the angle of the axe blade.

Leslie Stephen was one of the first – if not the very first – gentlemen climbers to carefully screw a small pick-axe on the large square head of his alpenstock. E.S. Kennedy is also mentioned among the small group of inventors spurred by the excitement of climbing and the instinctive need for a cutting tool on the ice. A pendant piece was needed for the adze, a head that acted as counterweight, plus a shorter handle to make the tool easier to wield when cutting steps. Apparently the axe used by Mathews was terribly heavy – the weight made it easier to cut steps but wearied the arms. It was important to be able to work with either arm. The most difficult task that befell a guide was to cut steps on the way down an icy slope

10. John Tyndall, *Dans les montagnes,* trans. Louis Lortet (Paris: Hetzel, 1876).

– all positions for cutting downward were particularly tiresome. It was precisely on the descent of the Col du Dolent in 1865 that Whymper recognised and admired the controlled efforts made by his two guides, Michel Croz and Christian Almer.

Tyndall probably employed a Valais-type ice axe – used by his guide Bennen – when he made his solo ascent of Monte Rosa in 1858. The axe played the role of partner in the absence of a rope. Tyndall became painfully aware of this fact at the summit, when an awkward move pitched his axe down the slope:

> Once indeed an accident made me shudder. While taking the cork from a bottle which is deposited on the top, and which contains the names of those who have ascended the mountain, my axe slipped out of my hand, and slid some thirty feet away from me. The thought of losing it made my flesh creep, for without it descent would be utterly impossible. I regained it, and looked upon it with an affection which might be bestowed upon a living thing, for it was literally my staff of life under the circumstances.

Who first came up with the idea of rotating the axe blade and turning it into the adze so typical of an ice axe? As early as 1865 Whymper sketched an ice axe very similar to the standard model. This type of ice axe triumphed in the following decade and was used for the next five or six generations, the main modification being the length of the handle.

Indeed the ice axe became the characteristic tool of the mountaineer, whether guide or amateur, for it could be used in many ways, even on rocks where it could hook on to flakes, around spikes or into cracks and other small holds. Zsigmondy often employed it on granitic rock. 'In the granite mountains … one frequently encounters smooth, steeply sloping rocks crossed here and there

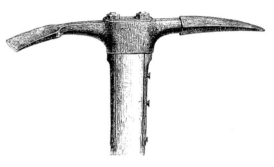

Kennedy's ice axe, drawn by Whymper.

An ice axe designed by Whymper.

233

Émile Javelle.

by cracks into which the pick of the ice axe can be inserted; in this way passages that offer no projecting hold and could not otherwise be climbed, may be crossed. In such circumstances, the longer the ice axe the better.' Zsigmondy's own oak-handled 'Ampezzo'-style axe measured 1.3 metres, which some people found too long – a 'Zermatt' ice axe was 1.2 metres in length.

Among other advantages, Zsigmondy pointed out that an ice axe was easy to haul at the end of a rope during rock climbing passages, unlike an alpenstock.

An ice axe is called *Eispickel* in German, *picozza* in Italian, and *piolet* in French. Where does the French name come from, and how did it become common parlance? Émile Javelle, a Frenchman living in Switzerland (at Vevey, on the shore of Lake Geneva), was still using a hatchet (*hache*) that became a bother while climbing the Matterhorn in 1870. He left it under a rock. That hatchet was indeed a *piolet*. The entry for *piolet* in an authoritative etymological dictionary of the French language (*Dictionnaire Historique de la Langue Française,* edited by Alain Rey, 1992) gives an erroneous description of the implement. The dictionary claims that *piolet,* introduced into the French language as early as 1860 by Littré's dictionary, refers to 'a mountaineer's pole of metal, equipped with a metal tip at one end and at the other a small metal pick [*pioche*].'

It might be recalled that the first entirely metallic ice axe was not forged until a century later, in Scotland, by Hamish MacInnes. The French dictionary's erroneous and incomplete definition overlooks the famed axe head – the future adze so typical of the ice axe – just as it is mistaken about the handle, which was still of wood at that time. As to the term itself, the dictionary locates its origin in the Valdotain dialect, where *piolet* referred to a 'hatchet'.

It might be wiser to look for the word's roots in Romandie, the French-speaking part of Switzerland. Eugène Rambert,

Belaying techniques were still very rudimentary.

Passage d'un Crevasse.

Travelling across crevasses and seracs on the Bossons glacier, by Jean-Philippe Linck.

a mountaineer from Lausanne, used the term *hache à piolet* in his writings, while his fellow Swiss, Morsier, called it a *hache-bêche*.

Meanwhile, Louis Spiro, a clergyman and guide who discussed the topic in an excellent monograph published in 1911, said he was certain that the word came from Gryon or the Ormonts Valley in the canton of Vaud, where *pioleta* referred to a small, handy hatchet used to cut pine branches. By analogy, the term was applied to the implement used by chamois and crystal hunters, which combined hatchet and pick in a single head on a short handle. The final vowel, *a,* was dropped when the word became common in French-speaking lands after 1870.

A guide's role and craft was to cut: to cut steps and thus to pave the way. But in that heroic age it sometimes happened that a guide was not up to the task for one reason or another – fatigue, lack of interest, bad will, etc. An example of this behaviour occurred during an ascent of Mont Blanc in 1857 by Tyndall and Thomas Hirst with guide Édouard Simond. The small party set out from the Grand Mulets and struggled above the Grand Plateau, on the first slope of the Corridor. The crusty snow so irritated the guide that he willingly let Tyndall take over, returning to the lead when crossing a crevasse. Further up, however, breathless on a steep slow of icy snow, Simond let Tyndall take over again. Hirst, much further back, remained motionless, quietly smoking a cigar. Tyndall wrote, 'I hewed sixty steps upon this slope, and each step cost a minute, by Hirst's watch. The Mur de la Côte was still before us, and on this the guide-books informed us two or three hundred steps were sometimes found necessary. If sixty steps cost an hour, what would be the cost of two hundred?'

Cutting steps was hard, exhausting, laborious work, which at least had the advantage of keeping the leader nice and warm. The climbers aligned on the slope behind him waited in more or less

On such a step a mountaineer would place a 'mountain' shoe.

comfortable positions depending on the terrain. Sixty steps – which took an hour in this case – was little more than twenty metres.

All the legendary stoicism of nineteenth-century Englishmen was required to bear this ordeal on steep, north-facing slopes where the cold bit hard. It took just a little breeze – not to mention really foul weather – to chill the almost motionless mountaineers more or less anchored by the tips of their ice axes. Once the fatigue of ascent set in, the man in the lead laboured with less speed and skill. Ten to twenty blows were no longer sufficient to hew a safe step. And the difficulty of the task increased on glassy ice. British climber Clinton Dent, who conquered the Grand Dru in 1878, noted that one day his guide needed over sixty blows to carve a single step in a slope of hard ice. On such a step a mountaineer would place and then very carefully secure a so-called 'mountain' shoe. These shoes were the boots worn by chamois hunters, a well-studied piece of equipment given its crucial role in the mobility and safety of those mountaineering hunters. Tschudi observed that the choice of shoes was of the utmost importance since they provided security in critical positions, and he claimed that good shoes could save a hunter where ordinary shoes might lead to his death. A hunter's mountain boots were made of cow hide, their thick soles set all around the edges with one or two dense rows of nails with pointed heads; sometimes they were also studded in front and under the heel in a horseshoe shape. This arrangement provided the entire foot with a solid and extraordinarily reliable base. During a trip to the Alps in the summer of 1868 the French writer Théophile Gautier lingered in front of the window of a cobbler in Chamonix. He noted the indispensible nailed boots worn by climbing parties. 'They are sturdy shoes of raw leather, with thick soles studded with nails, and aglets for lacing. They are very supple despite their coarse appearance. They are greased with lard, which is similar to polishing them.'

These boots were indispensible, perhaps, but were also awkward and of doubtful use when climbing over smooth or rounded rock, because the nails, instead of biting and gripping, would slide along the rock face, whether of granite, gneiss, schist or limestone – they slipped across all rock. According to Whymper, the guides of the golden age drove too many nails into their leather shoes, from a concern for sturdiness. They thereby diminished the friction effect of the soles, as Whymper told Georges Casella, the last French journalist to see and interview him.

The nails in the shoes of golden-age mountaineers discouraged climbing on rock faces to such an extent that it was not rare for the leader to remove his boots. Removing footwear in order to climb barefoot was a common practice in many Alpine valleys, not merely in the canton of Schwyz where Tschudi noted it in conjunction with the use of resin to make the toes and sole stickier.

That shaggy guide from Valtournenche, Jean-Jacques Carrel, took off his boots during one attempt on the Matterhorn, and tied them to his belt. But one shoe fell while he was climbing, so Carrel was obliged to descend with a piece of rope wound around his foot. Upon reaching the snow of the glacier beneath the Col du Lion, he further padded the rope with a large handkerchief, then slid or limped between the crevasses.

On the Matterhorn, the Carrels – driven by personal pride, bubbling with the patriotism of a finally united and independent Italy, and equipped and encouraged by engineer Felice Giordano – used every means at their disposal to conquer the mountain. In addition to their own physical resources, they called upon iron grapples and hooks and steel pegs, as stressed by Guido Rey in a footnote to his monograph on the Matterhorn (*Il Monte Cervino*).

Giordano also recruited another shaggy local, Jean-Joseph Maquignaz. Although it was Maquignaz's first Alpine campaign, his

Fig. 647.—Mountaineering Outfit.

1, Helmet; 2, gloves; 3, ice-axe; 4, compass in case; 5, rücksack; 6, hat, with goggles; 7, puttees; 8, boots, showing nails in soles; 9, rope.

An Alpine traveller's kit.

*A double-toothed
grappling hook.*

profession as a miner and stonecutter commended him – his skills would come in handy when it came to driving steel pegs into the rock. All means were fair when attacking the inaccessible. Whymper himself used a steel grappling hook, although his main contribution to mountaineering technique was a rudimentary abseiling system for recovering the rope. A rope had already become a climber's best and most loyal friend, according to John Ball – the Irishman was perhaps the first mountain traveller to castigate the carelessness, ignorance or arrogance of parties of guides and excursionists on glaciers who overlooked the security of a properly knotted rope.

Of the seventy-two mountaineering accidents – in the strict sense, excluding heart attacks that felled gatherers of edelweiss and 'fancy' tourists climbing the stairs to some scenic viewpoint – that were recorded in the quarter century from 1856 to 1882, ten were unambiguously attributed to falls into a crevasse, representing roughly one-seventh of the total. For example, on 9 August 1864 a porter named Ambroise plunged into a crevasse just a few steps away from a party of Austrians on Mont Blanc's Grand Plateau. The obvious cause: he wasn't roped up. Either they didn't have a rope, or they didn't rope up in time upon reaching a zone of crevasses and ledges, or they weren't properly tied on.

Zsigmondy provided specific examples of cases where parties were 'insufficiently attached', to use his term. By which he meant that the guide or guides, after having knotted the rope around the client's waist, did not tie themselves to the rope but merely held it in hand, and were obviously caught out by the violent jolt and pull. In July 1856, Édouard de la Grotte dropped into a crevasse on the Findelen glacier near Zermatt in Valais and was killed; his two guides were holding the rope in their hands.

In August 1860 an accident below the Col du Géant (on the Italian side) resulted in four deaths. The party was composed of three

English travellers, roped up, and three guides who were not tied on but held the rope at both ends and in the middle. When one of the Englishmen slipped on a steep slope of soft snow, he knocked over his compatriots and they all carried off the guide in the middle, Frédéric Tairraz. The rope whipped through the hands of the other two guides.

This accident, as stupid as it was bitter, created ructions in the Alpine Club. Tyndall even travelled to the spot to question a guide from Courmayeur in order to get explanations for the disaster and to draw some lessons.

Rescuing a member of the party.

> Consider now the bearing of the mode of attachment above described upon the question of rescue. When the rope is fastened round the guide's waist, both his arms are free, to drive, in case of necessity, his spiked staff into the snow. But in the case before us, one arm of each guide was virtually powerless; on it was thrown the strain of the falling man in advance, by which it was effectually fettered. But this was not all. When the attached arm receives the jerk, the guide instinctively grasps the rope with the other hand; in doing so, he relinquishes his staff, and thus loses the sheet-anchor of salvation. Such was the case with the two guides who escaped on the day now in question. The one lost his baton, the other his axe, and they probably had to make an expert use of their legs to save even themselves from destruction. Tairraz was in the midst of the party. Whether it was in his power to rescue himself or not, whether he was caught in the coil of the rope or laid hold of by one of his companions, we can never know.

That is a very lucid analysis of an accident and the consequences of a given technique. On 29 August 1868, Count Louis de Combacérès

A tricky passage across a snow bridge.

was killed by falling into a hole on the Trient glacier – the party hadn't taken a rope.

An accident at the top of the Corridor in August 1870 was extensively discussed in the *Alpine Journal.* The party included Mr and Mrs Marke, Miss Wilkinson, two guides from Valais and a young porter from Le Trient, Olivier Gay, who had been taken on at the Grands Mulets hut. The ladies tired and decided to halt at the summit of the Corridor (4,350 metres). There, attended by Gay, they waited while the rest of the party completed the ascent. Mrs Marke began shivering with cold just ten minutes after the party had left for the summit. Gay lent her his arm to take a short stroll – and both suddenly disappeared into a crevasse. Miss Wilkinson, the broken end of the rope dangling before her, set up a great cry. The party heard her screams and returned to discover the horror. The loose rope snaked across the snow – it had broken all the more easily on impact since it had been used for years to carry wood up to the Grands Mulets hut. The bodies of the two victims were never found despite the efforts and operations of a rescue party, which worked for six hours at a depth of thirty metres to try to widen a gap. Mrs Marke was the first female fatality on Mont Blanc. The editor of the *Alpine Journal* had harsh words for the poor lad, accusing him of being only too happy to feel a lady's arm upon his own:

> The porter gives one lady his arm, and walks across a snow-field notoriously full of crevasses. The catastrophe which occurred was that which every experienced traveller would have predicted as highly probable. I will not enquire whether, in this case, any blame attaches to the traveller; but it is difficult to imagine that anyone with the slightest pretensions to act as *guide* could have committed the folly to which it was owing that the porter lost his own life and that of his companion.

In his defence, the young man might have argued that the lady had gone pale and seemed on the verge of fainting from cold if he hadn't immediately revived her by taking a short stroll.

In *Peaks, Passes and Glaciers* John Ball memorably referred to the rope as his 'constant friend' when crossing crevasses that otherwise would have frightened him stiff: 'I own that I should have found it nervous work but for the security afforded by that constant friend of the Alpine traveller – the rope.' On 17 August 1858, Tyndall made his second ascent of Monte Rosa with great aplomb – and without a guide or other companion, in a solitude that he happily abandoned during the descent by joining a party. Toward the end of his account Tyndall solemnly warns all those who might think that glaciers are harmless and the dangers of the Alps are pure charlatanism. As he wrote in *Glaciers of the Alps,* 'The dangers of Mont Blanc, Monte Rosa, and other mountains, are real, and if not properly provided against, may be terrible. I have been much accustomed to be alone upon the glaciers, but sometimes, even when a guide was in front of me, I have felt an extreme longing to have a second one behind me.' Tyndall who, along with Whymper and Moore, was one of the most determined gentlemen of the Alpine Club, was no fool regarding his luck during his outbursts of boldness. He deemed a rope – a properly tied rope – with one or two guides to be necessary, and not only on crevassed glaciers.

Some guides, whose skill and conscientiousness were unimpeachable, rejected the practice of mutual roping up in all circumstances. A week before his solo ascent of Monte Rosa in 1858, Tyndall had climbed it with a Swiss guide, Christian Lauener, who only took out his rope during the descent. Tyndall was uncomfortable being belayed by a guide who refused to tie himself on, merely looping the rope around his arm:

A.W. Moore.

This to me was a new mode of attachment. Hitherto my guides in dangerous places had tied the ropes round *their* waists also. Simond had done it on Mont Blanc, and Bennen on the Finsteraarhorn, proving thus their willingness to share my fate whatever that might be. But here Lauener had the power of sending me adrift at any moment, should his own life be imperilled. I told him that his mode of attachment was new to me, but he assured me that it would give him more power in case of accident.

The guide's reply provoked a rush of blood in Tyndall. 'It could neither be called anger nor pride, but a warm flush ran through me as I remarked, that I should take good care not to test his power of holding me.' This technique died out after numerous accidents in which the rope slithered like a trout – along with the tourist – from the hands of one or several guides. There was a pithy exchange on the crowning ridge of the Finsteraarhorn between Chamonix guide Auguste Simond and his client, J.F. Hardy, who wished to be roped up. Simond refused, saying that 'it would be worse than useless here, for that the weight of any unfortunate who slipped would certainly drag the others down'. Somewhat cynical in his naiveté, Simond even added, 'Here, sir, it is everyone for himself.'

Fortunately, added Hardy, Simond did not actually adhere to 'this principle, for he was always ready to give a hand to anyone who wanted it'.

Where, and when, should a rope be pulled out? And when should it be put away? No implement in the mountaineer's arsenal raises so many technical issues (knots, handling, belaying) and questions of conscience. Why rope up if one can't brake a fall? The risks of error in analysing the situation and the possibility of a fall can never be excluded. *Errare humanum est.* Even the

Monte Rosa.

Giving a leg up, a common technique for scaling rock.

best guides make mistakes. Yet a guide is paid – handsomely – to keep the client safe, rather than say, 'here it is every man for himself'.

During the golden age a team of three on a rope was considered ideal. In a letter published in *The Times* in 1882, the president of the Alpine Club, T.G. Bonney, stressed that there should never be more than five, nor fewer than three, people roped together. Three was clearly a good figure for all kinds of terrain: a tourist between two guides or between a guide and a porter. The common technique of giving someone a leg up when climbing a rock wall was much easier if done on the shoulders of two men.

When facing the rock steps on the Italian slope of the Matterhorn, Whymper put the issue succinctly: 'No man could expect to climb [the Matterhorn] by himself. A morsel of rock only seven feet high might at any time defeat him, if it were perpendicular. Such a place might be possible to two, or a bagatelle to three men. It was evident that a party should consist of three men at least.'

Yet too many people roped together meant a loss of cohesion and flexibility in manoeuvres.

One party of six men had no guide to lead the foray, but was sufficiently experienced to act prudently and cohesively. On 7 August 1855 those six Englishmen – Hudson, Kennedy, Stevenson, Ainslie and the two Smyth brothers – found themselves on the Col du Géant after deciding to climb to the summit of Mont Blanc without the cost or nuisance of a guide from Chamonix. The party rested at the col, where its porters – seven hunters from Courmayeur carrying tent and provisions – turned back. The Géant glacier glinted in the sun before the Englishmen. It was 12.30 p.m. Hudson described their preparations:

> On leaving the Col, the rope which we used on all occasions of difficulty was attached to belts fastened round our

waists, and we advanced single file. Nor was this precaution unnecessary, for following the directions which the chasseurs had given us before their departure from the Col, we endeavoured to skirt the northern angle of the peak of red granite called from its shape La Tour Ronde, when C. Smyth, who was at that moment in the van, slipped up to his middle through a treacherous coating of drifted snow by which a deep crevasse running transversely to our line of march was concealed. Stevenson, who was the second in the line, by planting his alpenstock firmly in the snow, was able to keep the rope perfectly tight whilst the leader was extricating himself from his perilous position.

Techniques for advancing and belaying were thus steadily developed depending on the type of climbing terrain (rocks, snow, etc.) and the number of people on the rope. In his account of an attempt on the Matterhorn from the Italian side with his guide Josef Bennen in 1861, Tyndall provided a good explanation of how two mountaineers advance in alternation on difficult terrain, mutually belaying one another with the rope, in turn:

> Our mode of motion in such circumstances was this: Bennen advanced while I held on to a rock, prepared for the jerk if he should slip. When he had secured himself, he called out, '*Ich bin fest, kommen Sie*'. [I'm fast, you come on.] I then worked forward, sometimes halting where he had halted, sometimes passing him until a firm anchorage was gained, when it again became his turn to advance. Thus each of us waited until the other could seize upon something capable of bearing the shock of a sudden descent. At some places Bennen deemed a little extra assurance necessary; and here he emphasised his statement

On the usefulness of a rope in the mountains.

247

that he was *'fest'* by a suitable hyperbole. *'Ich bin fest wie ein Mauer'* [I'm as solid as wall] — *fest wie ein Berg, ich halte Sie gewiss* [I'm as solid as mountain, I can certainly hold you], or some such expression.

Returning to glaciers, we have an example of good judgement, but judgement acquired only after an error and recognition of that error. On 18 August 1856, Auguste Simond (the Chamonix guide who had climbed the Wetterhorn), Benjamin Felley (a well-known hunter from Val de Bagnes) and their two clients, the brothers William and Charles Edward Mathews, were descending the Petit Combin by its southern slope, cheerfully making their way, one after another, in the soft snow of a snowfield. The only measure of caution apparently necessary on this last strip of glacier was to remain in single file.

William Mathews turned on hearing a strange sound. He saw the waving arms of his brother, who had sunk up to his neck in snow. A snow bridge had collapsed under the weight of the third man after William and Felley had already crossed it. William grabbed one of his brother's hands and yanked him from the abyss. 'He had a most providential escape,' wrote William, 'and described the sensation of his legs dangling in the cleft as something the reverse of agreeable.' William came to the logical conclusion: 'If we had been tied together, such an accident would not have been attended with the smallest danger; and we were very imprudent in crossing the *névé* [snowfield] without using the rope.'

In 1856, for that matter, the shaggy guides of the upper valleys hardly bothered to carry a rope, which was used only to accompany the occasional Englishmen. The scraps of rope that they pulled out to lead reluctant goats or drag the corpse of a chamois hardly inspired confidence among the foreign gentlemen. That is why the latter equipped themselves at a good ropemaker in London before setting out for the Alps. As John Ball recounted in his 1852 crossing of the Strahlegg, 'We had a stout rope, which I generally carry with me strapped to my knapsack, in preference to relying upon the worn-out articles that are sometimes provided.' Similarly, William Mathews noted that his party had ample rope in 1856 because they had brought 100 feet from England.

Those ropes were made of Manila hemp, which was sturdier, more supple and easier to handle than ordinary Piedmont hemp from Italy. It was made from a plant related to the banana family, *Musa textilis,* which originally grew in the Philippines – hence its name. The sailors in the British navy used ropes of Manila hemp. The first rope to be formally recommended by the Alpine Club to its honourable members was thirteen millimetres (half inch) in diameter and thirty metres (100 feet) long.

Crampons are rarely mentioned in early accounts. That is a curious detail in the technical history of mountaineering. British mountaineers of the golden age – the likes of Ball, Stephen, Tyndall and company – advanced over ice and snow without using crampons, even though crampons had long existed. Chamois hunters commonly used them on glaciers in the eighteenth century. Saussure, the famous Saussure, not only tried them but found them so useful he sought to improve them. They became his standard equipment. Whymper was one of the few Englishmen of the golden age to have tried crampons. But crampons, considered too rudimentary and too fragile, were not used by the great guides of the Western Alps, regardless of their valley of origin. Michel Croz from Savoy, like the Germanic guide Jakob Anderegg, preferred to rely on the axe. His technique was described by Whymper on the Col du Moming in 1854: 'One, two, three went his axe, and then he stepped on to the spot where he had been cutting.'

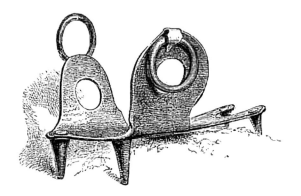

Four-point crampon, drawing by Whymper.

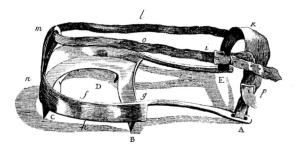

Saussure's crampon.

It was the Austro-Germans, and the Tyroleans in particular, who slowly reintroduced crampons, first in Switzerland. The Tyroleans had never totally abandoned these implements, mentioned in chronicles as early as the sixteenth century and sometimes called by the evocative name of *graffe*. There were iron *graffes* for the feet. These four-clawed *graffes* were probably like the ones used by chamois hunters, as Saussure described in his *Voyages*. During an ascent of Mont Rochemelon in 1588, the lord of Villamont had iron *graffes* on hands and feet in order to climb straight uphill on the snowy slope. Why would people scorn a device of obvious appeal, commonplace among chamois hunters of the eighteenth century? Or why did they not at least seek to perfect it, as Saussure did in his day?

Here we must turn to Emil Zsigmondy, the young author of a key guide to the dangers of a pastime that eventually cost him his own life:

> Tittle-tattle would suggest that Swiss guides' dislike of crampons can be explained by the fact that they could no longer brag about the enormous number of steps they cut, and that their high wages would subsequently be reduced.
>
> I think the primary reason that the Swiss do not use crampons is simply that they do not know them. When they saw some during our stay at Zermatt, this instrument pleased them a good deal, and François Burgener asked Professor Schulz to procure some for him. A few men nevertheless use them in winter for the hunt. M.F. Lochmatter, the innkeeper at Macugnaga, showed me his cross-shaped crampons of roughly worked iron; they were not hinged, and were attached by a single strap. He told us that he feared our crampons were too weak

for him and would break under his weight, he would have to have stronger ones made. Crampons like the ones used by Lochmatter are not to be recommended; first of all, they have only four teeth, which is totally insufficient, and then they do not attach firmly, so that they compromise sureness of step rather than increasing it.

By 1880 the young Zsigmondy was using Kaprun crampons, with six points and hempen straps, which were fairly reliable assuming that a few precautions were taken. The so-called 'Allgäu' crampons, widely used in the Tyrol, had ten points and two hinges. According to Zsigmondy, 'The English naturally share the opinion of their Swiss guides when it comes to crampons, and Whymper's comments are still considered authoritative. He received a pair from Mr Kennedy and included a drawing of them in his book. This is what he said about them: "They are the best variety I have seen of the species, but I only feel comfortable with them on my feet in places where they are not of the slightest use, that is in situations where there is no possibility of slipping, and would not wear them upon an ice-slope for any consideration whatever. All such adventitious aids are useless if you have not a good step in the ice to stand upon, and if you have got that, nothing more is wanted except a few nails in the boots."'

With the arrival of the Belle Époque, opponents of crampons were still numerous in the British and French mountaineering worlds, prior to the adoption of Eckenstein crampons. During that period of rivalry between the major Western nations and the growing power of the German Empire, the acceptance or rejection of many techniques was based on purely chauvinistic considerations.

In contrast, the ice axe was adopted by all. Every mountaineer came to use one, starting with guides, followed by tourists.

An advert featuring nailed mountain boots for women.

LESLIE STEPHEN

The Schreckhorn

Leslie Stephen admired guides and enjoyed contradictions: 'I utterly repudiate the doctrine that Alpine travellers are or ought to be the heroes of Alpine adventures.'

I was at the centre of a paradise of snow!
My enthusiasm bordered on madness.

Henry, Count Russell

L
ESLIE STEPHEN PREFERRED THE OBERLAND to all other chains of the Western Alps, just as he preferred Grindelwald to Chamonix and Zermatt. His was an aesthete's preference for the originality and majesty of the geological architecture beheld by walkers in the valleys of Lauterbrunnen, Grindelwald and Hasli. Stephen even preferred the names of Oberland peaks, such as Mönch (Monk), Jungfrau (Maiden), Schreckhorn (Terror Peak), Wetterhorn (Weather Peak) and Eiger (Ogre).

The Schreckhorn was one of Stephen's finest conquests, not forgetting the Bietschhorn (1859), Eigerjoch (1859), Rimpfischhorn (1859), Oberaarhorn (1860), Blümlisalphorn (1860), Lyskamm (1861), Mont Blanc's Arête des Bosses via the Aiguille du Goûter (1861), Jungfraujoch (1862), Monte Disgrazia (1862), Zinalrothorn (1864), and finally two superb ascents in the Mont Blanc chain, Mont Mallet (1871) and the Col des Hirondelles (1873).

The Schreckhorn is a sharp peak entrenched behind glaciers of the same name. Having been converted to mountaineering in 1857 when he crossed the Col du Géant in the valley of Chamonix in 1857, Stephen had already acquired a certain skill when he

Christian Almer.

attacked the Schreckhorn. *Le capitaine* Lauener having demurred – *that* Lauener! – Stephen was obliged to hire a number of guides, to his annoyance. There were three: Peter Michel, Christian Michel and Christian Kaufmann.

At 4 a.m. on 14 August 1861 Stephen found himself under a rock, by the light of a candle, waiting while the eldest of his guides, Peter Michel, sitting opposite, placidly munched bread, cheese, meat and butter with his poor teeth. Stephen had no appetite at that hour. But the meal took half an hour!

Back in 1842, the party of Édouard Desor (the disciple of Agassiz, both men having scientifically investigated the Aar glacier) had given up at the sight of a crescent-shaped ridge of sharp rocks some 300 metres long, separating the southern summit from the highest, northern, one. In August 1857 it was fresh snow that finally got the better of the two best guides in Grindelwald, Christian Almer and Peter Bohren, and their client Eustace Anderson. Anderson began his account in *Peaks, Passes and Glaciers* with a quotation from Byron: 'This most steep fantastic peak.'

The north summit of the Schreckhorn is 'big above and little below', as 'Captain' Lauener liked to trumpet. Stephen's three guides seriously annoyed him by repeatedly drawing out their little flask of brandy and a hunk of bread during the first two or three hours, until 7 a.m. when the real work began. Finally, at 11 a.m., the party shared a little brandy to lend them the courage to crawl along the final stretch of rocks. They were only able to stand again when two steps away from the platform crowning the Schreckhorn. After they issued their shouts of victory, Stephen smoked his pipe beneath the large black flag they had hoisted on the summit – the party had no intention of dealing with sceptics or hairsplitters on its return. Stephen mused. A man on a summit is a man at the centre. The tall peaks of the Oberland – Finsteraarhorn, Jungfrau,

Mönch, Eiger, Wetterhorn – formed a vast ring of ancient snows and rock walls around the man dreamily smoking his pipe. As Stephen put it:

> You are in the centre of a whole district of desolation, suggesting a landscape from Greenland, or an imaginary picture of England in the glacial epoch, with shores yet unvisited by the irrepressible Gulf Stream. The charm of such views – little as they are generally appreciated by professed admirers of the picturesque – is to my taste unique, though not easily explained to unbelievers. They have a certain soothing influence like slow and stately music, or one of the strange opium dreams described by De Quincy.

There is a god of mountaineers. That god awaits them at the summit when they forget their watches, forget the passing time (their ultimate master). In 1864 Melchior Anderegg and his cousin, Jakob Anderegg, guided Stephen and his friend F.C. Grove on the Zinalrothorn. In the final rocky passage, the four men stretched like elastic bands on miniscule holds. There was no slow and stately music on the summit. Wearied by the mountain's difficult rocks, Stephen showed little concern in the landscape but great concern for the descent during his twenty minutes at the top of Zinalrothorn. During an earlier ascent – the Eigerjoch in 1859 – Stephen had admitted, 'Bodily fatigue and appreciation of natural scenery are simply incompatible'. Thus the first pipe of the day at Zinalrothorn was enjoyed not on the summit but back at the foot of the mountain, in the sunshine, as Melchior pointed out eleven different routes – eleven possibilities – for scaling the Grand Cornier, a still-virgin peak (which Whymper would vanquish in 1865).

Stephen was a perspicacious traveller who admired his guides, to whom he paid tribute in his account of the ascent of the

Melchior Anderegg and Leslie Stephen.

The great novelist Virginia Woolf was Leslie Stephen's daughter.

Schreckhorn. He did not consider tourists like himself to be heroes. 'I utterly repudiate the doctrine that Alpine travellers are or ought to be the heroes of Alpine adventures. The true way at least to describe all my Alpine ascents is that Michel or Anderegg or Lauener succeeded in performing a feat requiring skill, strength, and courage, the difficulty of which was much increased by the burden of taking with him his knapsack and his employer.' This was an admirable spirit of gratitude toward the guides who were sometimes described as more boring than a rainy day.

Leslie Stephen (1832–1904) was as tall and lanky as he was modest. In his long face one immediately seeks resemblance with his daughter, Virginia Woolf, the famous writer who terminated her intimist novels with her own suicide. For Woolf, the excursion ended at the lighthouse. Or at Montenvers, we might say.

Stephen wrote one of the first personalised books to come out of the Alpine Club, with a fine engraving by Whymper on the frontispiece. It shows the party of climbers on the Rothorn – as described by Stephen to Whymper – performing acrobatics on the final stretch of rocks. The title of Stephen's book was well chosen: *The Playground of Europe.* It cocked a snook at Ruskin, whose genius was not necessarily acknowledged by Stephen. Ruskin had spouted too much foolishness for Stephen's taste when the two men met. In a letter of 1876 to Gabriel Loppé – artist and mountaineer – Stephen wrote, 'Ruskin is sometimes incredibly stupid, but he is also droll, and when I see you I will recount some of his absurdities.' Ruskin felt that the Alps represented altars and cathedrals. But for the younger Europeans, they constituted a playground.

Whymper's book, meanwhile, bore a clearer, if more banal, title: *Scrambles Amongst the Alps in the Years 1860–69.* Published in London by Murray in 1870, the first edition of *Scrambles* sold out in a matter of days. Illustrated with five maps and ninety-two engravings, it was a huge hit. Adolphe Joanne, a future founder of the Club Alpin Français who spoke English and who authored travel guides similar to the Murray guides, translated Whymper's book into French, publishing a few excerpts, accompanied by a brief introduction, in a travel magazine, *Le Tour du Monde,* in 1872. *Scrambles* is an extremely lively and vivid book. Its narrative is not interrupted by the author's reflections as often as Stephen's accounts were. Both books imparted a new thrust to the mountaineering movement, according to Coolidge, who was a good judge in the matter. Alpine literature, which Coolidge pored over with his aunt, Miss Brevoort, was a major influence on his first steps and youthful enthusiasm.

Stephen found it easy to express ideas. He was a literary critic, a contributor to national papers and a historian of literature and philosophy who authored a dozen books, such as *History of English Thought in the Eighteenth Century,* which, unlike *The Playground,* have never been translated into French. Stephen was also a major contributor to the colossal *Dictionary of National Biography.* He was an intellectual with a keen intelligence but without Ruskin's inspiration, and he had a melancholy streak inherited by his daughter. The heron-like Stephen, born under the sign of Saturn, left the Anglican Church at age thirty. He married twice, his first wife dying after seven years of marriage; he had four children by his second wife, who died in 1895.

His daughter Virginia, born in 1882, committed suicide in Sussex on 28 March 1941. Her drowning had nothing to do with the war, which in fact came as a healthy jolt to her, a diversion from her chronic depression of previous years. But melancholy got the better of her as spring approached, and drove her into a river in the English countryside. Her father had died of illness long before, on 22 February 1904, at the age of seventy-two, an age that Virginia herself did not have the strength to attain.

W.A.B. Coolidge.

The heron-like Leslie Stephen, born under the sign of Saturn.

Walking can be a lifesaver for melancholy types. The simplest remedies are often the best. The lanky-legged Stephen was a great walker, but perhaps didn't sufficiently demonstrate the benefits of walking to his daughter. When in the Alps, Stephen disdained, out of principle, mules and carriages and above all 'that lowest depth to which human beings can sink, and for which the English language happily affords no name, a *chaise à porteurs* [sedan chair].' Feeble snobs, fancy tourists, and telescope-wielding 'cockneys' all got on Stephen's nerves like a screechy violin. What were those fools doing in the Alps, that sublime theatre of his mania?

The Alps were not cathedrals for Stephen, who was only too happy to give his book a secular title and do away with Ruskin's grandiloquence and ceremony. Yet the term 'playground' – which still reflects the current state of the Alps and today's mountaineers – may be misleading. The Alps meant much more to Stephen, they were an 'elixir of life, a revelation, a religion', stated one obituary upon his death. He had been a member of the Alpine Club since 1858, and served as its vice-president and president as well as editor-in-chief of the *Alpine Journal*. A regular attender of club meetings, he would come from far away – on foot. Stephen also came up with a law that swiftly became as popular as the title of his book. Whereas entropy – the steady decline of energy – is a law of physics, Stephen's dictum was a psychological one confirmed by experience and general consensus: any difficult mountain will inevitably 'pass through the successive stages denoted by the terms "inaccessible", "the most difficult point in the Alps", "a good hard climb, but nothing out of the way", "a perfectly straightforward bit of work"; and, finally, "an easy day for a lady."'[11]

11. Translator's note: This passage appeared in the first edition of Stephen's *Playground of Europe* (1871), but not in subsequent editions. Stephen's law was later popularised through A.F. Mummery's pithier version in *My Climbs in the Alps* (1895): 'All mountains appear doomed to pass through three stages: an inaccessible peak, the most difficult ascent in the Alps, an easy day for a lady.'

Those lines were written after the Matterhorn had been slain, and a series of increasingly easy ascents were made from both sides, Swiss and Italian. The nineteenth ascent of the Matterhorn nevertheless raised eyebrows in mountaineering cycles. Miss Lucy Walker, the thirty-six-year-old sister of Horace Walker, dragged her skirts to the summit, becoming the first woman to ascend the Matterhorn on 21–22 July 1871. That haughtiest peak in the Alps thus dropped through every grade of difficulty in just six years. It might be noted that the climbing party included no husband (Lucy Walker was unmarried) but rather a father, Francis Walker, of the venerable age of sixty-five. The ascent was a double exploit by a woman and a man old enough to be a grandfather; Francis, for that matter, had already climbed the Brenva spur on Mont Blanc at the age of fifty-nine, also worthy of the record books.

In July 1865, those two first ascents – the Brenva spur and the Matterhorn – brought the golden age to an end even as they shed light, in contradictory ways, on Stephen's dictum. The dangers and difficulties of an unknown mountain are largely illusory. But not entirely – appearances on Brenva were a reality, and even now in 2014 the spur remains a difficult, feared ascent involving high-altitude commitment and seracs that any guide will charge a good deal to lead you through. The Matterhorn, in contrast, has become a family excursion, assuming that the weather is favourable and the rocks are dry on the Hörnli ridge.

In that same summer of 1871, a second skirt swept the summit of the Matterhorn, guided by Christian Almer and his son Ulrich. Miss Meta Brevoort accompanied her nephew, Coolidge, on the party that climbed the mountain on 4–5 September 1871. Shortly after this ascent, Lord Wentworth had his two guides from Valtournenche arrange a bivouac among the rocks of the summit, the better to contemplate the setting and rising of the sun. Wentworth

Meta Brevoort, Coolidge's aunt, was the second woman on top of the Matterhorn.

How can the true difficulty of a mountain be assessed when
so much depends upon the imagination? The Matterhorn,
by Albert Bierstadt.

was Lord Byron's grandson: 'High mountains are a feeling.' Englishmen of the golden age were even more Romantic in spirit than Germans. What more was needed for the summit of the Matterhorn to figure in Murray's travel guide under recommended outings?

Stephen's quip was a witty expression of one universal truth: the unknown frightens and magnifies all difficulties, whether viewed from near or afar, with the naked eye, John Ball's opera glasses, or the 'fancy' tourist's spyglass. The unknown and its effect on the human imagination aggrandises the epic. As Stephen put it, 'I have almost been induced to believe at times that there is no real difference between mountains, except that which results from our imaginations, the new mountain being always more imposing than that with which we have become familiar.' Stephen himself would never scale the Matterhorn – the Zermatt guides he approached were too nervous after the disaster of 1865. Peter Perren – who guided the Walker family to the summit alongside Melchior and Jakob Anderegg – was the first Zermatt guide to venture on to the slopes after that fatal day.

How can the true difficulty of a mountain be assessed when so much depends upon the imagination? In 1874, Georges Devin, a member of the Club Alpin Français founded that very year, published an account of his ascent of the Matterhorn in the club's *Annuaire.* His blasé tone may have startled some of his fellow members. The ascent of the Matterhorn was so well known – and, ultimately, so easy – according to this Parisian, that it was hardly worth recounting. 'The steepest inclines never give the impression of a drop from a fourth-floor balcony, and apart from the difference in height, which is only a question of imagination, it is easier to worm one's way up an upright rock than it is to walk along a balance beam in a gymnasium.' Easier, perhaps, but more dangerous:

in the event of a fall, the difference between a rock cliff and a gymnasium floor will soon be noticed.

On 25 July 1868, one of the most active members of the Alpine Club, Reverend J.M. Elliot, made the first repeat climb of the Matterhorn from the Zermatt side. Although it was the tenth ascent, it was the first to exorcise the curse of the Hörnli ridge. One year later, on 27 July 1869, Elliot slipped on the icy ridge of the Schreckhorn – without a rope. The bold, twenty-seven-year-old reverend had refused to rope up with his guide, Franz Biener. He tumbled down the steep snowy slope to his death.

So Stephen's quip is also just that – a quip. A previous ascent, indeed countless previous ascents, will never reduce the danger of one false step.

FRANCIS FOX TUCKETT

At the Height of the Golden Age

The high mountains, where climbers became schooled in snow …

T HE SHAGGY GUIDES OF THE GOLDEN AGE are our brethren. Even shaggy chamois hunters liked a fire and some hot water at a bivouac. Where required, porters carried wood aloft for a fire before the morning's attack. When it came to bivouacs, one of Leslie Stephen's great friends, Francis Fox Tuckett (1834–1913), elected to the Alpine Club in the spring of 1859, was one of the club's most organised members. Tuckett's 'boiling apparatus', made to his specifications by a Mr Stevenson of Edinburgh, burned 'spirits of wine' (alcohol) and was endowed with a thermometer making it possible to calculate altitude (based on the actual boiling temperature) as well as preparing food. He never headed into the mountains without his apparatus, described in a note at the conclusion of his account of his ascent of the Aletschhorn (18 June 1859) where his party set up a comfortable bivouac on the approach glacier. Tuckett's three guides were our friend Johann Josef Bennen, Peter Bohren from Grindelwald (who, as usual, lustily sang Oberland songs at the campsite) and Victor Tairraz from Chamonix. On the way back down, Tairraz led the way on a forty-degree slope of deep, crusted snow. On hearing

Francis Fox Tuckett.

him give a cry, his companions hastily drove their alpenstocks deep into the snow, anchoring the staggering Tairraz as the top layer of snow swept beneath his feet. 'We came close to great misfortune,' commented Tairraz once the party had safely moved off the slope – the avalanche had swept over a precipice of seracs and would have spelled the end of one of the finest climbing parties of the golden age. The great Bennen would have died in 1859 of the snow he so feared, a feeling all members of the Alpine Club would soon share.

The high mountains were where climbers became schooled in snow, that endlessly changing substance – like a turbulent sky – which in an instant could alter the luck and effort required by an ascent. What would it have taken for the entire slope, rather than just the top layer, to have turned into a massive avalanche that killed Tuckett's entire party? A mere extra hour of sunshine?

A few days later, Tuckett's party was camped on a windy ridge of the Grivola (3,969 metres), a virgin mount thrusting up from the Gran Paradiso chain. In addition to Tairraz (Tuckett greatly valued the shrewd Savoyard), he was accompanied by Jean Tairraz (Victor's brother) and two hunters recruited from Valsavarenche, Ambroise Dayné and Chabot. Having run out of alcohol to fuel his apparatus, Tuckett recalled a recent encounter in the hotel beneath the Jungfrau. An ordinarily silent guest at the hotel approached Tuckett one morning asked about the machine. 'The personage in question had amused us for some days by appearing every morning in a mackintosh, his waist encircled by a piece of stout string, and his throat by two, and sometimes three, towels, whilst a conical nightcap of ample proportions completed an *ensemble* that would have done honour to an alchemist.' Tuckett recorded their conversation, in French.

'Monsieur is a man of science?'

'No, sir,' replied Tuckett, 'although it is true that I dabble in meteorology, as an amateur.'

'So you are probably familiar with radiant heat?'

'Most certainly, sir.'

'Well, then, I shall let you in on something that I would not confide to just any old one.'

'I would be most honoured,' replied Tuckett as the highly excited, half-crazy gentleman explained the theory of his invention.

'Heat exists everywhere, radiates everywhere. So here is my idea. By means of a little apparatus of my own invention, I manage to extract all the radiant heat emitted by all bodies, and I use as much as I wish … '

Radiant heat being a property of solid ice, the crank saw no obstacle to the preparation of a steaming-hot meal on every glacier.

'You and your friends, for example, make an excursion high on the Aletsch glacier, and you wish to prepare dinner, or supper, or some light refreshment, anything at all. But what can you do? Nothing but ice all round. No coal, no wood, absolutely nothing to burn. That is the truth, is it not? Well, now, listen to me: if you use my apparatus you will be able to extract the radiant heat from the glacier, and presto! there you will have your chocolate, tea, coffee, eggs, beefsteaks, whatever you wish, instantly. Isn't science wonderful?'

It transpired that a few 'perfections' remained to be made, but the wonderful machine would soon be made available to the Alpine Club. The kindly, polite Tuckett furnished the man with the address of the club's secretary.

The summer of 1859 was a fair one throughout, from the first days of July to the end of September. Tuckett nevertheless came a cropper on the Grivola, successfully climbed a little later (23 August 1859) by his compatriots John Ormsby and Robert Bruce. Three guides participated, including two who had been on the first attempt (Jean Tairraz and Ambroise Dayné), along with Zacharie

A party camps in a tent beneath the rocks.

The Grivola.

Cachat form Chamonix. The rubbly pyramid of Grivola ultimately offered them a superb view of Mont Blanc and the Matterhorn capped by what Ormsby described as a 'a long thin pennon of cloud … like a fleecy flag of defiance.' Enthused by his victory over the Grivola, Ormsby felt that the Matterhorn, that grand old peak of the Valais, was posing itself as a challenge. All round the party there stood virgin mountains, beginning with the Gran Paradiso, that imposing snowy peak, the highest point of the chain of the same name, which Tuckett had noted as a potential target. What a glorious period! To the east and south of the Grivola were the tall summits of the Vanoise and Maurienne chains: Grande Casse (3,852 metres), Mont Pourri (3,779 metres), Dent Parrachée (3,684 metres), Pointe de Charbonnel (3,750 metres) and Albaron (3,638 metres) had never even been the object of campaigns. The maps of the Graian Alps used by the Englishmen were worse than the Dufour maps of the Swiss mountains. Travellers had long been intrigued by Mont Iseran (4,061 metres), a major summit marked on the maps, which in fact turned out to be the eastern peak of Mont Levanna (3,615 metres), to which the altitude of Gran Paradiso had been assigned. William Mathews realised this error when crossing the Col d'Iseran in September 1859 with a guide from Tignes.

'Where is the snowy peak called Mont Iseran?' Mathews asked the guide on reaching the top of the pass.

'There is no peak, Monsieur' came the reply, 'it is just a mule track.'

At that time there was no better way of clearing up such mistakes than by conducting a local investigation. The men of the high pastures, the hunters, the innkeepers and even better, the local clergyman – usually better informed than his parishioners – were all consulted.

Mathews, a founding member of the Alpine Club alongside E.S. Kennedy, shed crucial light on the western Graian Alps the following year by crossing several passes and scaling the Grande Casse (3,852 metres) with guide Michel Croz and a certain Favre on 8 August 1860. Their ascent is now memorialised by Pointe Mathews, one of the peaks on the Grande Casse.

A week later, Frédéric Tairraz died along with three English travellers in the disaster on the Col du Géant — he and the other two guides were not attached to the rope to which the Englishmen were tied, but merely held it in their hands. Jean Tairraz, who ran the Hôtel du Mont Blanc in the town of Aosta, spoke at length of his cousin and the sad consequences of that roping technique to his partners during their attack on the Gran Paradiso on 4 September 1860, namely John J. Cowell, William Dundas, and Chamonix guide Michel Payot. A blizzard drove them from the summit. Tairraz returned a few days later with Cowell — it was fine summit for training for snow and altitude, asserted Cowell on his return, annoyed at not having seen an ibex, that rare animal protected and hunted by the king of Italy.

Tuckett climbed the Gran Paradiso in 1861 with Bennen and Perren before joining his friends Leslie Stephen and Melchior Anderegg for the first complete ascent of the Arête du Goûter up to Mont Blanc (comprising Aiguille, Dôme and Bosses). The English had been seeking this famous alternative route for a decade, in order to escape the demands of the guides from Chamonix. In 1862 Tuckett's explorations moved distinctly southward, to the Alps of the Dauphiné region. His dear compatriot William Mathews had performed a masterstroke by scaling Monte Viso (3,841 metres) on 30 August 1861 with Frederic Jacomb and brothers Michel and Jean-Baptiste Croz. Although Monte Viso is a heap of rubble, unlike the Grivola it rises above the Piedmont and is not diminished

Monte Viso.

*The Chamonix guide
Michel Auguste Croz,
so admired by Whymper.*

by the proximity of other giants. That is why it was one of the first Alpine summits to be clearly distinguished and named, even in antiquity. Further north and west of Monte Viso, the Dauphiné region boasted a summit that was the highest point in France prior its annexation of Savoy (similarly, Lac Paladru was long the largest lake in France). This poorly defined, never-attempted summit was called the Barre des Écrins (4,102 metres). In 1862, Tuckett engaged Perren from Zermatt and Michel Croz from Savoy, whose reputation was beginning to spread following his ascents of the Grande Casse and Monte Viso.

Croz was a man who acted decisively. On 4 October 1961 he had even raced up the bastion of Mont Pourri on his own. Wielding his axe, he was ready for the hand-to-hand combat and gut-spilling tactics of a grenadier of the Garde Impériale, singing:

> *On va leur percer le flanc*
> *Rantanplan, tirelire*
> *On va leur percer le flanc*
> *Rantanplan tirelire lan!*
> (We shall split their sides
> Rat-a-tat-tat, tiddly-o
> We shall split their sides
> Rat-a-tat-tat, tiddly-i!)

It took Croz eight hours from the last high-pasture chalet to the summit and back, in the October light that changed the appearance of everything down to the moraines. 'He is one of the best walkers I have ever seen,' wrote Mathews in Croz's log following their first campaign together in the Graian Alps in 1860.

This was the height of the golden age. Energy was at its peak. The most determined travellers and the best guides – those shaggy mountaineers – came together and spurred one another with a

Francis Fox Tuckett.

shared enthusiasm. Jean-Baptiste Croz climbed the Dent Blanche (4,357 metres), that giant peak in the Valais, with T.S. Kennedy, William Wigram and Johann Kronig on 18 July 1862, just as his brother Michel was completing his campaign in the Dauphiné with Tuckett.

Tuckett's crucial exploration of the Dauphiné lasted ten days, from 7 to 16 July 1862. He would never return to the chain known as the Oisans. That strange fact could be explained by his life and temperament. As a globetrotting conqueror of virgin peaks and passes, Tuckett extended his playground to the entire planet. Obviously, if one's ambition is to see everything in this vast world, returning someplace to do – or redo – something seems like a waste of time. On only one day in 1885, twenty years after that memorable campaign, did Tuckett lay eyes again on the Oisans, that chain of arid slopes, from the window of a train taking the globetrotter through the Alps. It was the Grenoble to Veynes line, affording Tuckett one last glimpse, perhaps beyond Le Trièves, of the southern edge of the Oisans before disappearing into the tunnel at Croix-Haute.

Tuckett and Coolidge saw one another, appreciated one another and wrote to one another. Coolidge referred to the elder Tuckett as his 'Alpine godfather'. In letter to Coolidge dated 1891, Tuckett told him that his own list of carefully recorded and numbered excursions reached the thrilling number of 1,000. A thousand climbs in every country, at every altitude, of every level of difficulty. Tuckett was a typical example of what the mountaineering community of the day called an 'ex-centrist', namely the most mobile and least homebound of mountaineers. A 'centrist' focused on one point in the Alps – Chamonix, Grindelwald, Interlaken, etc. From there, comfortably installed at an inn free of rats and fleas, a centrist ventured out to surrounding summits. An 'ex-centrist', meanwhile, roamed from valley to valley. Once an ascent had been made, whether of pass or summit, the ex-centrist turned his back to the familiar slopes and headed for the joy and surprises of marching ahead into the next valley.

Tuckett ran a leather business in Bristol, which he abandoned for three months of each year. He was a champion of passes. His 1891 list included 289 summits, of which ninety-eight were major peaks, and 687 passes, indicating a preference that he shared with his elder, John Ball, the first president of the Alpine Club. Tuckett's list of passes includes two major cols in the Oisans: the Col des Écrins (3,367 metres) and the Col du Glacier Blanc (3,286 metres). They are the two gateways to the Glacier Blanc (called the Encoula glacier on maps of the day). The Barre des Écrins is cloaked by this magnificent glacier, the finest in the Dauphiné region. On 7 July 1862, even before launching his Écrins campaign from Ville-Vallouise, Tuckett had taken his revenge on the Grivola and pointedly spent a night on the summit of Monte Viso.

On 9 July, Tuckett reached the summit of Mont Pelvoux (3,946 metres) via a wide couloir of snow still known as the Couloir Tuckett. For three hours Tuckett took all kinds of measurements enabling him to verify or correct the documents he had been given in Paris by the War Office. Thanks to influential connections, Tuckett had obtained the map of the Briançon area at a scale of 1:80,000, and a copy of the same map at a scale of 1:40,000. Using a barometer, Tuckett confirmed the assumption that the Barre des Écrins stood higher than the double-headed Pelvoux.

On 12 July, after spending a night in the chalets of Ailefroide, the party climbed the Glacier Blanc to the upper basin. The slope steepened. With snow above his knees, Tuckett recalled the incident on the Aletschhorn and headed toward a marked gap, the Col des Écrins, which he crossed. The descent toward Bonnepierre

Rocks crashing down the Matterhorn.

T.G. Bonney.

*The Königspitze (3,851 metres) was first
ascended by F.F. Tuckett on 3 August 1864.*

was easy thanks to the snow, but much lower down, at a ford in the Bonnepierre mountain stream, the party found itself in a tight spot and wound up drenching themselves.

At the hamlet of La Bérarde, Rodier father and son, good shaggy mountaineers in that corner of the world, offered them beds of fresh hay, free of bugs (a great luxury in the Dauphiné notorious for its 'kangaroo' fleas). The next day, the Lord's Day, was a day of rest – Tuckett was from a Quaker family. On 14 July (not yet proclaimed France's national holiday), the party returned to Ville-Vallouise by the Col du Sélé (3,283 metres), the first time the pass had been crossed by tourists. Tuckett had planned to call it quits there, but the sapphire-blue sky of Vallouise gave him pause for thought: thus the party headed *back* to the Barre des Écrins and installed a bivouac under a huge rock on the edge of the Glacier Blanc (known as the Tuckett shelter, at an altitude of 2,438 metres). Clouds and fog on the morning of 16 July altered plans once again, and Tuckett led his party to a pass, the Col du Glacier Blanc (3,286 metres). The three men raced that same day all the way to Bourg-d'Oisans.

One month later – 26 August 1862 – the Croz brothers, Michel and Jean-Baptiste, ventured high up the Glacier Blanc with two Englishmen, William Mathews and T.G. Bonney. They got as far as the Lory gap.

But it was another failed attempt for Michel Croz, who had been sure of victory on reaching the bergschrund, shouting, 'Oh, you wretched Écrins, soon you'll meet your death!'

His travellers viewed the snowy rocks of the Barre des Écrins with a different eye. They decided to call it a day. Bonney later regretted that it did not occur to them to climb the Dôme de Neige des Écrins, a 4,000-metre summit almost as easy as the Gran Paradiso, but overshadowed by the much higher Barre des Écrins.

Tuckett published an account of his exploration in the *Alpine Journal* in December 1863. His detailed report ran to forty pages and highlighted the 'wretched Écrins', henceforth creating a new target for the Alpine Club, where the account was read carefully.

Starting in 1863, Tuckett, not yet thirty years old, turned his attention to the eastern Alps. His knowledge of German facilitated his remarkable exploratory journeys. Coolidge rightly credits Tuckett with the first ascent of Königspitze (3,851 metres, on 3 August 1864) three weeks ahead of Stefan Steinberger (24 August 1864). His ascent of Monte Civetta (3,220 metres) with the Andereggs in 1867 was the first for a tourist – a local hunter, Piovanel, had preceded them in 1860 on the heels of a chamois.

At age forty Tuckett was still a great ex-centrist. Coolidge mentioned a campaign of 1874 that began in Appenzell, eastern Switzerland and continued, following an ascent of the Tour Ronde in the Mont Blanc chain, by a high road that included the Ruitor (3,486 metres), Mont Pourri and Rochemelon (3,538 metres), the latter a great pilgrimage mount between Bessans and Suse. There Tuckett was met by a lightning bolt that greatly frightened him.

Tuckett also travelled beyond the Alps a good deal: Greece, the United States, Corsica, Norway, Spain, Morocco (a most unusual destination at the time), Algeria, Tunisia, Egypt and Turkey, and even Australia and New Zealand (1899).

During that trip to the antipodes, Tuckett married a woman from New Zealand. He wedded late in life, at the age of sixty-two.

Tuckett enjoyed long sea voyages, still possible at modest expense in those happy times before air travel shrank distances and spaces.

Tuckett visited Japan with his wife the year he died, 1913, after a two-month cruise from England. His age when gazing upon Mount Fuji perhaps gave him the pause for thought – just as it had beneath the sapphire-blue sky of Ville-Vallouise.

A.W. MOORE

Keeping up the Pace,
20 June–27 July 1864

The Matterhorn seen from the village of Zermatt.

THE BRITONS OF THE ALPINE CLUB had a penchant for wild ruggedness and authenticity. The issue of mountaineering techniques and facilities arose almost immediately after the golden age. During a club meeting on 17 December 1875 one of the most well-known pioneers, A.W. Moore, expressed regret that major peaks such as the Matterhorn were being cheapened by mechanical aids (cables, ropes and rope ladders) and the increase in huts. Moore did not only want to remove all the chains, he thought the shelters should be demolished. Some members of the Alpine Club shared his feelings, which reflected the club's high standards and, more broadly, the philosophy of mountaineering. There could be no adventure without adventure's risk and sweat (both hot or cold). And if people didn't like that, then they should simply head somewhere else – to play tennis or build sand castles on a beach in Brittany. No one, neither God nor the Devil, was forcing anyone to climb the Matterhorn or Mont Blanc. It was entirely to Moore's credit to have raised this issue of artificial aids so early, and to have raised it cogently. Logically, huts should not be excluded from the list of debatable comforts that contradict the aspirations of Alpine travel.

Adolphus Warburton Moore.

Born in 1841, Adolphus Warburton Moore made his first trip to the Alps in 1860, the same year as Whymper. He was nineteen when he reached the top of Petersgat (3,202 metres), a snowy belvedere above Kandersteg. Five years later he would be the inspiration behind the greatest exploit of the golden age, namely the ascent of the Brenva spur on the Italian slope of Mont Blanc, accomplished on 15 July 1865, the day after the Matterhorn was conquered. Obviously, the Brenva party remained unaware of the disaster that had occurred there. Moore was just twenty-four when he climbed the Brenva, while his friend Whymper on the Matterhorn was twenty-five.

It is important to give the age of mountaineers if one wishes to put oneself in their place, to understand and compare the boldness of their feats – and sometimes their sudden decline in boldness. In 1864 Moore carried out a campaign of five weeks, between 20 June and 28 July, across the main chains of the French and Swiss Alps (Écrins, Mont Blanc, Valais, Oberland). He conducted this vast 'ex-centrist' trip with the thirty-nine-year-old Christian Almer as his guide at every point and on every ascent. The campaign was one of the greatest of the golden age, performed by a team of inveterate walkers and terrible 'wanters' (*vouleurs*) of Alpine summits. Usually only the first days of the south-to-north campaign are recounted, highlighted by the ascent of the Barre des Écrins (25 June 1864), the great virgin summit that reigned over the Dauphiné and had sparked desire ever since Tuckett's and Mathews' attempts in 1862.

Yet it is the overall venture, the series of ascents and transitions between two peaks that must be kept in mind in order to appreciate the pace maintained by a young Victorian Englishman and a shaggy guide when they marched side by side in the silence of sustained effort, slope after slope. In the mountains, effort is usually rewarded by yet another effort. It is the variety and ease of this additional effort that lend it a sense of pleasure and reward. The delight of going from rotten snow to decent snow is more easily explained to a fox encountered along the way than to a chap sprawled on the beach or a sofa of his five-star hotel. Moore's closest friend, Horace Walker, did not participate in all the stages of the 1864 trip, any more than Whymper or Michel Croz did. Moore kept a log of those weeks, a journal that ran to 300 pages of well-written prose. Keeping such a detailed journal while on a forced march was an exploit in itself. In 1868 he had a few copies printed for friends. Titled *The Alps in 1864,* it was only published in book form after his early death – even for the times – in 1887 at age forty-six from complications of typhoid fever on a body exhausted by his work in the India Office. Indeed, Moore laboured at the summit of the great British Empire, having begun his career aged seventeen with the East India Company of which his father was a director. Moore became private secretary to Lord Randolph Churchill (father of the famous Winston) at the India Office, then moved to the Treasury, then back to the India Office where he died on the job – the perfect Victorian, with a Victorian's sense of duty. In his obituary of Moore, Walker – who accompanied him on both the Écrins and the Brenva spur – claimed that overwork was 'the only subject on which I found him unreasonable'. Paradoxically, Moore, who helped build and administer the greatest empire the modern world has known, wished that the High Alps retain their atmosphere of a primitive forest. Yet it was a paradox in appearance only, covering an insistence on authenticity.

The most original aspects of Moore's mountaineering life were his two winter expeditions. He was practically the first mountaineer to attempt such an exploit. On the night of 23–24 December 1866, his party effected a combined traverse of the Finsteraarjoch (3,283 metres) and the Strahlegg (3,351 metres) after a late start

A.W. Moore (second row, seated right) with the Walker family.

Almer's leap on the western ridge of the Barre des Écrins.

(3 p.m.) from Grindelwald, where the entire village came out to see them off. On the Finsteraarjoch at 1 a.m. Moore could read his pencilled notes by the moonlight with no difficulty. There was not a breath of wind.

In December of the following year he travelled from Saint-Michel-de-Maurienne to La Grave via Valloire and the Col du Goléon (2,880 metres) in the company of two chamois hunters. Later, this passionate pilgrim returned to the site of his 1864 campaign and crossed the Col de la Lauze (3,504 metres) and the high pass known as the Brèche de la Meije (3,300 metres) in snow that was fortunately hard, for he did not have snowshoes.

According to David Freshfield, '*The Alps in 1864* [is] perhaps the most authentic, exact and vivid record of what climbing was to early explorers of the High Alps.' Despite such praise, no French publisher has found it fit to translate his journal, or to compare Moore's account with Whymper's, notably concerning the ascent of the Écrins. According to Whymper, during the descent Almer leapt across an otherwise unbridgeable gap in the Écrins' west ridge. When the rock on which he landed tottered, Almer had to clutch another one just in time. This passage in *Scrambles* is accompanied by a highly evocative illustration by Whymper himself. Apparently Moore was looking somewhere else at that moment, for his own account makes no mention either of the gap or of the leap that nearly carried the entire party to kingdom come, making Whymper's heart thump. Both versions, however, record the leap across a crevasse on the Pilatte glacier – which turned into a nightmare for the Frenchman Reynaud, who fell into the abyss with a thump. Moore and Whymper also mentioned the disappearance of cigars between La Grave and La Bérarde. The man unfortunately entrusted with the mission of carrying them smoked them all *en route.* He later proved that he merited his nickname of 'the biggest liar in Dauphiné' by first inventing a tale of theft and then claiming that he did not smoke.

Whymper always considered the Barre des Écrins to be the most difficult of his first ascents. During an eight-hour ordeal, the 180-metre-high triangle at the summit nearly defeated the two guides' combined range of skills on snow, ice and rock. Descent seemed impossible: the ice-coated, unstable rocks appeared too risky to everyone. They finally chose the west ridge, led by Almer, whom Whymper quotes as saying, 'The good God has brought us up, and he will take us down in safety.'

The ridge plunged downward, narrowing to a very exposed blade. At one point, Almer straddled the razor's edge, legs on either side, as Moore watched, much amused by the gestures and comments exchanged by the two guides in a mish-mash of poor German and allegedly groaning French. Freshfield pointed out that Moore's journal displayed an autobiographical frankness, hence probably reflected greater truth than Whymper's *Scrambles,* a memoir aimed at the general public. Moore had harsh words for the people of the Dauphiné region, from La Grave to Ville-Vallouise: out-and-out swindlers and braggarts all, bar-room patriots and insolent drunks whose verbose wives jabbered in dialect. Noise, filth, confusion and the refrain of a song bellowed to the glory of Napoleon are all that Moore recalled of an inn at Ville-Vallouise recommended by locals to the party on its return from the Barre des Écrins.

Moore suffered from poor vision, claimed Freshfield, who accompanied him for weeks during their 1868 voyage to the Caucasus with Freshfield's trusty Chamonix guide, François Devouassoud. Freshfield described Moore as an assiduous, rather than brilliant, climber, due to his short-sightedness. Early mountaineers were very concerned by this kind of handicap, which at the time could be remedied only by pince-nez. Tuckett, that ex-centrist

The Écrins, drawn by Whymper.

who made immoderately long trips, was very myopic, which Coolidge mentioned in his posthumous tribute. The Austrian Emil Zsigmondy[12] cited – and criticised – the example of Hermann von Barth (1845–1876), the pioneering mountaineer of Austria's Karwendel, who ventured alone even though he was very short-sighted and wore a pince-nez. A seriously short-sighted person had two options in the mountains: remove his pince-nez, and risk the dangers of poor vision on irregular terrain, or keep the pince-nez and put up with the drawbacks. For example, Emil's brother, Otto Zsigmondy, climbed with pince-nez; one day, a rock dislodged by the rope while they were climbing hit him right on the nose and broke his pince-nez. This unlucky blow was fortunately remedied by a replacement pince-nez. But the lenses would mist up in the rain, in the snow, in the fog. As Zsigmondy pointed out, 'The lenses often become clouded, and since a tourist cannot be constantly taking out his handkerchief to wipe them, he leaves them that way, and no longer sees clearly. This negligence can indeed be the cause of serious risks.'

The death of young Henri Cordier (1856–1877) at Le Plaret in the Oisans greatly moved members of the Alpine Club, especially those elders who shared his condition, Moore and Tuckett. They, too, suffered from poor vision, and readily admitted the hypothesis of the account of the accident published in the *Alpine Journal.* Cordier was the best French mountaineer of the day and often roped up with members of the Alpine Club. He was killed towards the end of an outing, after the rope had been put away, right before his guides' very eyes: a snowbridge over a stream collapsed. According to the *Alpine Journal,* Cordier was glissading down the soft snow and did not see the stream and bridge ahead, due to his poor sight. His guide shouted, but too late. That guide was a

---

12. Emil Zsigmondy, *Les dangers dans la montagne* (Paris: Fieschbacher, 1186).

well-respected, highly reputable man of the golden age, a hero who had accompanied Moore on the Brenva in 1865: Jakob Anderegg from Meiringen, cousin of Melchior Anderegg. It would be Jakob's last season, for he died in the spring of the following year, 1878, aged fifty-one, allegedly plagued by remorse at the thought of young Cordier and the warning shout he should have given earlier.

Moore, a topographer at heart – praised by John Ball for the accuracy and detail of his descriptions – claimed that one did not know a mountain range until one had climbed up and down every valley in that chain. A map had to be drawn up with a telescope, a chronometer, a notebook and a pair of compasses formed by one's own two legs.

On Monday 20 June 1864, the sky harboured a spring-like sun, barely filtered by a few clouds. Around 3 p.m., five men left Saint-Michel-de-Maurienne by the road for Mont Cenis. Their ice axes made tongues wag at the tavern on the main street. Two of them were guides, unable to communicate to each other on being introduced, since they spoke different languages: Michel Croz and Christian Almer. Three were youthful travellers, as pale as their monarch the queen: Moore, Whymper and Walker (the eldest, at twenty-six). At the Col du Télégraphe they made their first halt. Moore took stock under the walls of a chapel, comparing the two maps – French and Sardinian – to the view from the pass. All eyes turned toward a peak in line with the hollow of Valloire, a gem that overlooked the Col du Galibier: Croz immediately recognised the tall, triangular summit as the Barre des Écrins. Shortly afterward, in Valloire, they bought some bread, cheese, wine and eggs which they boiled hard (to Moore's impatience, as time was getting on). That was the men's usual fare during those weeks, not forgetting tobacco in the form a peaceful pipe or cigar, plus the milk, hot or cold, they requested on the Alpine pastures they came across.

Their first night was spent in the hay of a draughty barn in the hamlet of Commandrault. Their hostess admitted them to the barn on condition that they make no light. The adventure began at 3 a.m., in the barely attenuated darkness, when Almer's voice awakened Moore – day was dawning. It would be the longest day of the year, the summer solstice.

In his journal, Moore summed up that summer's campaign:

June 18, 19, 20. London to St-Michel and Valloire.
June 21. Col des Aiguilles d'Arves to La Saussaz.
June 22. Aiguille de la Saussaz to La Grave.
June 23. Brèche de la Meije (first crossing) to La Bérarde.
June 24, 25. Les Écrins (first ascent).
June 26. Val d'Entraigues.
June 27. Col de la Pilatte (first crossing).
June 28. La Bérarde to Bourg-d'Oisans and the Lautaret.
June 29. Col du Galibier to St-Michel.
June 30. Col des Encombres to Bourg-Saint-Maurice.
July 1. Col du Bonhomme to the Pavillon Bellevue.
July 2. Over Mont-Blanc to Chamonix (with Almer only).
July 3 and 4. At Chamonix.
July 5. To Lognan with Whymper and Reilly, Almer, Croz and Baguette.
July 6. Col du Chardonnet to Orsières, Martigny and Sion.
July 7. Sion to the Moiry Glacier.
July 8. Attempt on the Grand Cornier (with Almer and Martin), descent to Evolena.
July 9. At Evolena (Morshead and Perren joined the party).
July 10. To Bricolla.
July 11. Bricolla by the Col d'Herens to Zermatt (in 6¾ hours walking).
July 12. Rimpfischhorn (with Mr and Miss Walker, and Morshead).
July 13. Attempt on the Dom (from and to Zermatt (with Morshead).
July 14. Zermatt to Randa.

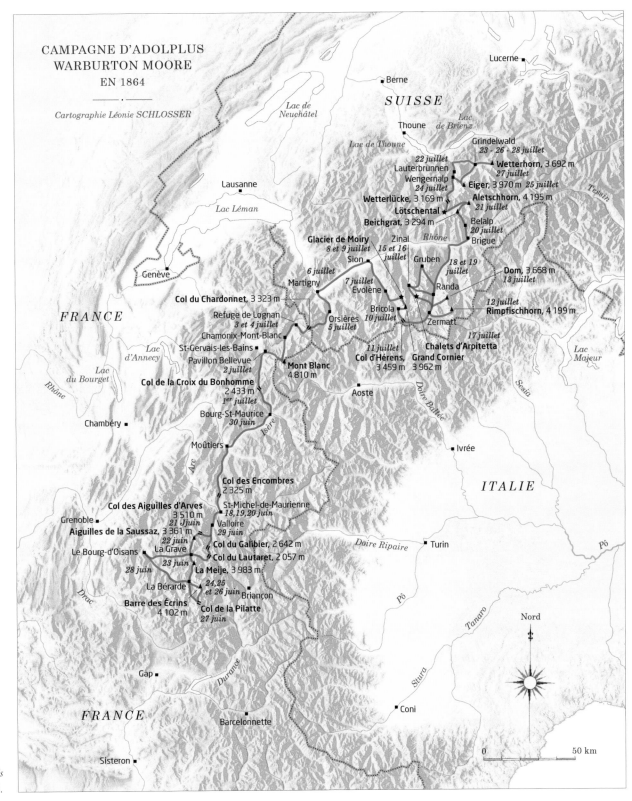

CAMPAGNE D'ADOLPLUS
WARBURTON MOORE
EN 1864

Cartographie Léonie SCHLOSSER

SUISSE

Lucerne

Berne

Lac de Neuchâtel

Lac de Brienz

Thoune

Lac de Thoune

Grindelwald
23 - 26 - 28 juillet

22 juillet
Lauterbrunnen **Wetterhorn**, 3 692 m
Wengernalp *27 juillet*
24 juillet **Eiger**, 3 970 m *25 juillet*
Wetterlücke, 3 169 m **Aletschhorn**, 4 195 m
Lötschental ★ *21 juillet*
Beichgrat, 3 294 m Belalp
20 juillet
Brigue

Lausanne

Lac Léman

Glacier de Moiry Zinal *Rhône*
8 et 9 juillet *15 et 16*
juillet
Sion **Dom**, 3 668 m
6 juillet Gruben *18 et 19* *13 juillet*
Genève *7 juillet* *juillet*
Martigny Evolène Randa

Col du Chardonnet, 3 323 m *12 juillet*
Rimpfischhorn, 4 199 m
Refuge de Lognan Orsières Bricola
3 et 4 juillet *5 juillet* *10 juillet* Zermatt

FRANCE Chamonix-Mont-Blanc *17 juillet*
St-Gervais-les-Bains **Chalets d'Arpitetta**
Pavillon Bellevue *11 juillet* **Grand Cornier**
2 juillet **Mont Blanc** **Col d'Hérens**, 3 962 m
Lac 4 810 m 3 459 m
d'Annecy

Lac
du Bourget Aoste

Col de la Croix du Bonhomme
2 433 m *Doire Baltée*
1er juillet

Bourg-St-Maurice
30 juin ITALIE

Chambéry Moûtiers Ivrée

Col des Encombres
2 325 m

Col des Aiguilles d'Arves St-Michel-de-Maurienne
3 510 m *18,19,20 juin*
Grenoble *21 Jjuin* Valloire *Doire Ripaire*
Aiguilles de la Saussaz, 3 361 m *29 juin* Turin
22 juin **Col du Galibier**, 2 642 m
Le Bourg-d'Oisans La Grave *Pô*
23 juin **Col du Lautaret**, 2 057 m
28 juin **La Meije**, 3 983 m
La Bérarde *24,25*
et 26 juin Briançon
Barre des Écrins
4 102 m **Col de la Pilatte**
27 juin

Drac

Gap

Nord

Coni

Barcelonnette 0   50 km

FRANCE

Sisteron

*A map of Moore's
summer campaign, 1864.*

The Belalp chalet, photo by Luchsinger.

The village of Zermatt in summer.

July 15. Randa over the Biesjoch to Gruben (with Morshead and Gaskell).
July 16. To Zinal (with Almer only).
July 17. Zinal to the Arpitetta Chalets (Whymper and Croz joined party).
July 18. Moming Pass to Zermatt (first crossing).
July 19. Zermatt to Bel Alp.
July 20. At Bel Alp.
July 21. Ascent of Aletschorn and, by the Beich Grat, to the Lötschental (with Almer and Eggel).
July 22. Wetterlücke to Lauterbrunnen (first crossing) and Grindelwald.
July 23. At Grindelwald.
July 24. To the Wengern Alp.
July 25. Ascent of Eiger (with Mr and Miss Walker, Horace Walker and C. Wigram).
July 26. To Grindelwald.
July 27. Over the Wetterhorn and back to Grindelwald, via Rosenlaui and the Scheidegg (a twenty-hour expedition, with Walker, Almer and Boss).
July 28 to 30. Grindelwald to London.

To appreciate the pace maintained by these pioneers, one need merely focus on three legs of this Alpine journey. Those three legs were made by the reduced party of Moore and Almer between Bourg-Saint-Maurice and the summit of Mont Blanc. On 29 June, having returned to Saint-Michel-de-Maurienne via the Col du Galibier following their nine-day campaign in the Oisans, the five men celebrated their victory over the Écrins with champagne. Whymper was still sleeping off his champagne at 2.30 a.m. when the wake-up call came, so he was not yet up when departure time arrived, even though postponed by half a hour. A disappointed and ill-humoured Croz watched the three others prepare to leave. Moore, Almer and Walker made it to Moûtiers, in the Tarentaise range, via the valley and pass of Encombres, that same day – ten hours of walking. Late that afternoon they set off in the carriage for Bourg-Saint-Maurice without either Croz or Whymper, who arrived too late to get seats. The next day, absent Walker – who had set off on mule for the Petit-Saint-Bernard pass on his way to a rendezvous in Aosta with his father and sister, Moore and Almer tramped along the path to Les Chapieux, drenched by torrential rains that only ceased at dawn. Almer suggested they not bother to wait for Croz and Whymper, with whom they were supposed to climb Mont Blanc in a single day (a challenge thrown down in the euphoria of the Écrins champagne). Yet two men alone among the crevasses of Mont Blanc seemed a heresy. Prudence strictly ruled out such an attempt not only in Chamonix but also in Grindelwald, Almer's home village. Had they been two shaggy locals, just maybe; but a traveller with the guide, who was always in the lead on a glacier? Moore was worried:

Christian Almer.

> I was perfectly sure that that, in the event of my slipping through into [a crevasse], he would be able to stand the jerk and pull me out, yet I felt that, with every exertion and care on my part, I could not be confident of my ability to do the same by him should he meet with a similar misfortune, which, as leader, was of course extremely probable. 'Oh', said he, 'I do not fall very easily into a crevasse'; and wound up with *'es muss gehen!'*

The two men arrived at Pavillon Bellevue (1,780 metres) at 6 p.m., after ten and a half hours of actual walking time from Bourg-Saint-Maurice. There they supped. Almer muttered only two words on glancing at the Aiguille du Goûter: *'Etwas schnee!'* (Some snow.) As Whymper said, 'Almer is a quiet man at all times. When climbing he is taciturn – and this is one of his great merits.'

Mont Blanc had not yet been climbed that year, it being early in the season, neither via the Aiguille du Goûter nor via Grands Mulets. So there would be no foot trails on the way up, nor on the way down. There would be all the snow and ice flow of the early season.

At twenty minutes past midnight, Almer knocked on Moore's door. '*Nicht ganz gut!*' (Not at all good.)

The valley was overcast with clouds, but a few stars overhead complicated the picture. Moore got up to take a look, but didn't know what to think. Battendier, the local man hired to lead them through the darkness with a lantern to the foot of the Aiguille du Goûter, was convinced, like everyone else at the inn, that the day would be fine. Almer – grumbling that 'one cannot say for certain' – and Moore decided to go back to bed for half an hour.

Thirty minutes later, Almer woke Moore: a starry sky – the weather would be wonderful. The rascal Battendier got lost when seeking the path for Mont Lachat, and cost them a precious half hour. Another setback occurred in the scree of Mont Lachat. Hindered by his poor eyesight, Moore slipped on a strip of ice and fell hard on his hip. His hip would remain sore for several days. It took them four hours of effort to climb the 800-metre slope of the Aiguille du Goûter alone, as Almer ploughed slowly through fresh snow and cut steps on the ice-covered rock.

They paused for refreshment at 10 a.m., not yet at the top of the Dôme du Goûter, swept by a north wind. After swallowing buttered bread and wetting his whistle with red wine, Almer perked up.

'*Wir müssen auf den mont Blanc gehen!*' (We shall make Mont Blanc!)

Moore hadn't thought the Arête des Bosses would prove so long. They only reached the summit of Mont Blanc at 3 p.m., faces etched by the wind and by twelve hours of solid climbing from Bellevue.

Anyone who has climbed Mont Blanc – and heavens knows many people have, taking the cog railway to the Nid d'Aigle (2,396 metres) and then sleeping at the Goûter hut (3,817 metres) – will appreciate the pace of those pioneers: 3,000 metres of altitude climbed in soft snow after having left Bourg-Saint-Maurice on foot the night before, and Saint-Michel-de-Maurienne the night before that. While descending the snow-blown northern ridge, Moore, despite his weariness, cast his topographer's eye on the terrain. At the Mur de la Côte – the party having veered to the Italian side due to a large crevasse – he noted an incline of snow in the middle of the slope: that would be the exit ramp of his future exploit, the Brenva spur.

That same evening, a moonless night blinded their path through a wood above Chamonix. At 11.30 p.m. they curled up on tree roots and shivered until a faint glow in the sky put them back on their feet around 3 a.m.

They rested in Chamonix for the next two days, leaving again with Whymper, Croz, the geographer and cartographer Anthony Adams-Reilly and his guide François Couttet (1828–1890), who was highly popular in the Chamonix valley and was known as 'Baguette'. Since 1862, Baguette had been lodging English travellers in part of his chalet. According to one of his guests, the French artist Gabriel Loppé, Baguette had 'a true instinct for glaciers', in other words a stylish skill for finding his way across glaciers with a margin of error that was acceptable to his travelling companions. After an attempt on the Aiguille d'Argentière, the two parties split up at the Col du Chardonnet (3,323 metres). Adams-Reilly had been drawing up a map of Mont Blanc since 1863. Moore and Almer headed down to Orsières in Valais, engaging in further battle: they failed on the Grand Cornier, succeeded on the Rimpfischhorn, failed on the Dom. Meanwhile, Adams-Reilly and Whymper carried out a lightning campaign on virgin passes and peaks in the Mont Blanc chain, choosing their targets for topographical reasons:
  – Col du Triolet (3,703 metres, 8 July)
  – Mont Dolent (3,823 metres, 9 July)

François Couttet, nicknamed 'Baguette'.

Every day two or three dozen French, Swiss and Italian guides would chat and smoke their pipes while sitting on a low wall in front of the Monte Rosa hotel.

– Aiguille de Tré-la-Tête (3,930 metres, 12 July)
– Aiguille d'Argentière (3,901 metres, 15 July).

Moore had to congratulate Whymper when they met again in Zinal – what a haul in just a few days! 'Mont Dolent is one of the most beautiful snow-peaks I ever saw,' wrote Moore in his journal. At Zinal, Moore hoped to find a route between Zinal and Zermatt that was shorter than the two known passes. On General Dufour's Swiss map, a low point seemed to lie between the Zinalrothorn and the Schallinhorn. The party that had scaled the Écrins, minus Walker, came together again: Croz, Almer, Moore and Whymper. They had a terrible fright on the Moming pass – an insistent, un-ending fright – on an ice slope that required hours of step-cutting right beneath a row of seracs, which suddenly collapsed a few min-utes after they went by. Whymper and Moore parted once again at Zermatt after a night in the Monte Rosa Hotel. Every day two or three-dozen French, Swiss and Italian guides would chat and smoke their pipes while sitting on a low wall in front of the hotel. The Monte Rosa Hotel, run by Alexandre Seiler – Grandpa Seiler – served as headquarters for Alpine travellers. It was a luxury hotel for those accustomed to sleeping on the high pastures of Valais in beds of old straw and dirty sheepskins.

On 19 July, Moore set out for Belalp and the Oberland. Moore's pace had accelerated further, and his confidence was so strong that he went ahead of Almer and Bohren (the 'glacier wolf') among the rocks of the Eiger, guiding the guides in a variant of the route. Between 21 and 27 July, the Aletschorn, the Eiger and the Wet-terhorn (in a non-stop, twenty-hour stretch, without bivouac) proved – if such proof were necessary – that Moore could match Whymper's stride and endurance.

The stage was set for the campaign of 1865. The hunting season was about to open – the game would be virgin summits.

Alexandre Seiler with his family, 1890.

CHAPTER XIX

THE YEAR 1865

The summit of the Aiguille Verte, colour lithograph (English school, nineteenth century). 'A glorious day.'

CHRISTIAN ALMER'S QUIP JUST BENEATH THE SUMMIT of the Aiguille Verte on 29 June 1865 was typical of a hunter raising his rifle:

'Ah, Aiguille Verte, now you are well and truly dead!'

Michel Croz uttered almost the same words at the foot of the triangle of the Écrins in August 1862, before the ice on the rocks halted him.

'Oh, you wretched Écrins, soon you'll meet your death!'

The guides of the golden age naturally spoke the language of shaggy chamois hunters. They hunted the prey of high altitudes – the flesh, bones and horns of mountains. Ascending an unclimbed summit meant slaying it.

The year 1865 was one of slaughter. In an historical overview of the conquest of the Alps, Coolidge drew up a chronological list, in 1913, of all first ascents from 1358 (Rochemelon, in the upper Maurienne) to 1907 (the Dames Anglaises peak in the Mont Blanc chain). In 1854, the year Wills climbed the Wetterhorn, the charts lists victories over only eight virgin summits, all more or less minor. Nor was the coming boom detectable the following

Monte Rosa is the second highest Alpine chain, after Mont Blanc.

year, 1855, when the list of prey sank to three – two of which, true enough, were significant catches: Dufourspitze (4,634 metres) on Monte Rosa, the highest peak in the Alps after Mont Blanc, and Mont Blanc du Tacul (4,248 metres), the broad shoulder of Mont Blanc climbed by Hudson's party without a guide through the perils of fog.

In the mountains, weather shapes the adventure from start to finish. The sky is the first sign to be scrutinised, and the sky's word is law. The wonderful summer of 1859 might have proved a bumper year during that decade of the golden age. The English had a perfect expression for a fine, windless day, one that was cloud-free, flawless, timeless – 'a glorious day'. The sun would shine in a divinely blue sky. A walker would shed years as well as pounds from the energy imparted by radiant sunshine. That was the era of Nietzsche's strolls around the lakes of Engadin, of sudden inspirations at the foot of a mountain, of candle lit climbs among the 'indescribable beauty' of the peaks.

It might be recalled that in August 1858 it was the glorious weather that prompted Tyndall to risk the glaciers alone, in order to get to the top of Monte Rosa: 'The unspeakable beauty of the morning filled me with a longing to see the world from the top of Monte Rosa.' I feel that sentence is crucial to an understanding of the most profound, most authentic spirit of mountaineering. Moore's journal is dotted with the expression, 'a glorious day'. According to Tuckett, the summer of 1859 was one long succession of glorious days. An equally glorious haul of summits might therefore have been expected. But mountaineering still lacked the inspiration and boldness of the younger generation, the fleet-footed climbers like Moore and Whymper.

The list of prey in 1859 was thus limited to nine kills. It nevertheless included a few fine, tall summits always visible in the sky of their respective ranges: the Aletschhorn (4,195 metres) in the Oberland, the Grivola (3,969 metres) in the Gran Paradiso chain, and the Grand Combin (4,314 metres) in the Valais all represented major advances in Alpine exploration, the explicit goal of the members of the Alpine club.

The summer of 1860 was dreadful. Tuckett recorded his dismay for posterity. Seven virgin summits nevertheless fell to the movement that year, all climbed by Englishmen. The ascent of the Grande Casse (3,852 metres) by William Mathews and Michel Croz on 8 August 1860 was a double victory: the first ascent of a fine summit and a first incursion into the western, Graian Alps, practically *terra incognita*. Other decent game included the Gran Paradiso (4,061 metres), already legendary for its ibex and for being the highest point in a chain that constituted the border between France and Italy once Savoy was annexed to France.

The turning point in the race for wonderful – or wretched – summits came in 1861. The pioneers' ice axes bought down a major haul of serious game, including Monte Viso (3,841 metres), Mont Pourri (3,779 metres), the Weisshorn (4,505 metres) and the Lyskamm (4,527 metres). The thrust and enthusiasm of the little band of shaggy locals and gentlemen travellers would never flag again. In 1862 what Whymper called the 'irresistible attractions' of the Dent Blanche (4,357 metres) on travellers crossing the Col d'Hérens finally yielded to the tenacity of English climbers, who began extending their hunting grounds to the central Alps (Monte Disgrazia, 3,678 metres).

In 1865, a third ascent of the Dent Blanche by Whymper and his guides (Croz, Almer, Biener) was a constant battle with the wind. As Whymper recalled in a footnote in his *Scrambles Amongst the Alps*: 'The ascent of the Dent Blanche is the hardest that I have made. [But] there was nothing upon it so difficult as the last 500 feet of

Whymper's party makes the third ascent of the Dent Blanche.

The Dent Blanche with the Grand Cornier in the foreground, by Johann Martin Steiger.

the Pointe des Écrins.' Imagine the effect of that note upon readers' minds – the Écrins would long retain its reputation for great difficulty due to those few lines. Whymper still broke into a sweat at the thought of Almer's leap!

After 1862, the good years came hard and fast: 1863, 1864, 1865. Coolidge drew up his list of victories with the earnestness and application of a midshipman at the battle of Trafalgar.[13] Although born a Yankee in New York, Coolidge included himself among English mountaineers, and never failed to indicate with an asterisk all those peaks first conquered by his 'compatriots'. One of the major conquests of 1863 was the Dent d'Hérens (4,172 metres) in the Valais by a party of four travellers and three guides. Melchior Anderegg uttered expressed caution and modesty with respect to the nearby Matterhorn:

'*Es geht, aber … ich gehe nicht.*' (It'll work … but *I* won't.)

It remained to be seen how it could be made to work.

Twenty virgin summits fell in 1863, thirty-two in 1864, and forty-three in the year 1865. The Englishmen were active from one end of the Alps to the other, in almost every lofty chain, meeting competition in Valais, Engadin and Oberland from top-notch Swiss travellers such as Jakob Weilenmann, Joseph A. Specht, and Edmund von Fellenberg. On the Matterhorn itself they had to compete with the people of Valtournenche, spurred by the Club Alpino Italiano. The English claimed the lion's share of this list of prey, climbing twenty-two virgin summits including the Matterhorn, which had fought off nineteen attempts in the previous nine years.

The year 1865 was memorable not only for the Matterhorn and a record number of first ascents. Some mountaineers were beginning to cast a hunter's eye at virgin slopes of conquered peaks.

---

13. The list drawn up by the mountaineer and writer W.A.B. Coolidge is reproduced in an appendix on page 365.

Coolidge's list therefore overlooks one of the two major accomplishments of 1865, namely the ascent of Mont Blanc by a significant new route, the Brenva spur. It similarly ignores a whole series of first ascents that reflect the same need to expand the playground. When first ascents by *new routes* are added to the list, the number of victories in 1865 includes sixty-five climbs by a horde of mountaineers whose names have often been forgotten.[14] The Matterhorn swept everything else away in the *danse macabre* of comments on the tragedy that occurred there. History is Matterhorn-mad, remembering only the names of Matterhorn and Whymper for the year 1865.

The second ascent of the Matterhorn, on 17 July 1865 by Jean-Antoine Carrel and Jean-Baptiste, was the first up a new route, via the Lion ridge. The Aiguille Verte, a 'weathervane' summit over Chamonix (as the Wetterhorn is above Grindelwald), fell to Christian Almer's ice axe on 29 June 1865; that same summer, however, two other parties reached the top by two different routes, one via the Moine ridge (5 July 1865) the other by the Grande Rocheuse spur (17 September 1865).

Behind these first ascents by new routes lay the curiosity expressed by the likes of Moore upon descending Mont Blanc in 1864, when he noticed the Brenva incline. That same year, on returning from the Rothorn, Melchior Anderegg had fun enumerating eleven potential routes up the virgin summit of the Grand Cornier. Some routes are born from a spirit of rivalry, from the cheeky competition that naturally arises between independent parties heading toward the same summit. A spirit of rivalry – or perhaps a point of honour. Christian Almer, who was expected to climb the Matterhorn with this companions Croz and Whymper,

---

14. That list, drawn up by professional guide Claude Marin, is appended to this volume, page 375.

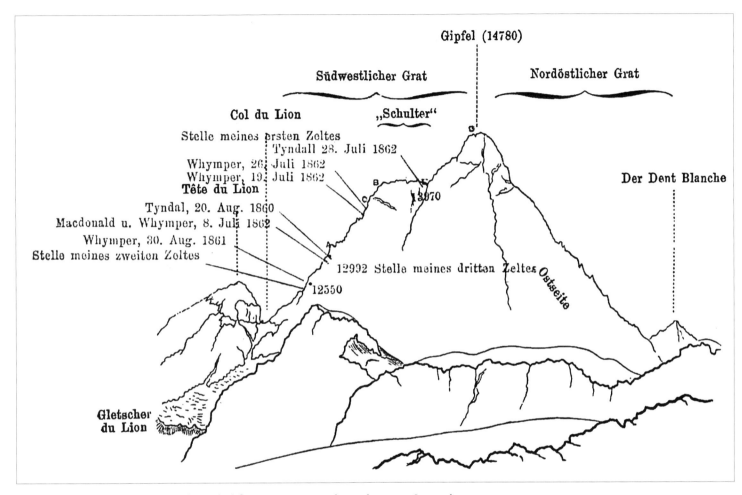

The Italian face of the Matterhorn with, on the left, a commentary on the south-west, or Lion, ridge.

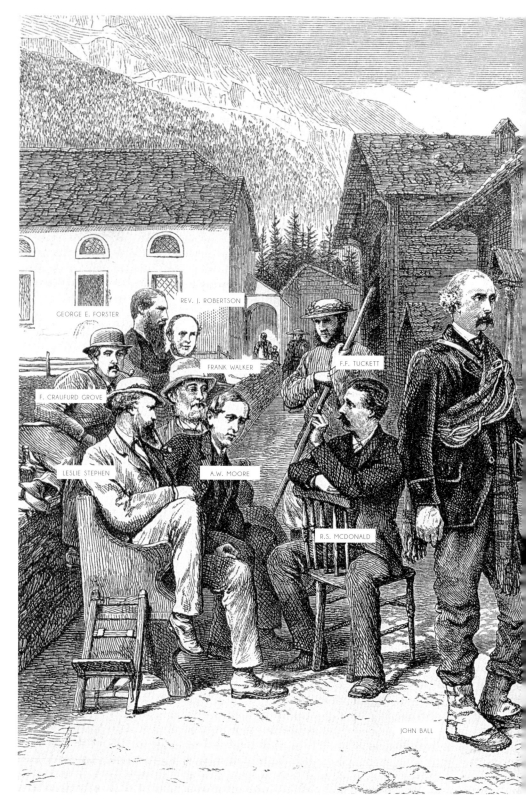

The cream of the Alpine Club and a few of their guides in front of Alexandre Seiler's Monte Rosa Hotel in Zermatt. Drawing by Whymper, 1864.

The Tête du Lion on the side of the Matterhorn.

inaugurated four new routes in his home mountains with Christian Lauener (brother of 'giant' Ulrich Lauener). The first was on the Lauterbrunnen Breithorn (31 July). Almer was pipped at the post by Edmund von Fellenberg's party, which arrived at the summit ten minutes before him but willingly shared their champagne with the loser of the race, who was the swiftest of Oberland guides. In fact, the new route was a shortcut devised by Almer on the hop in an attempt to overtake von Fellenberg's party, whose fresh footprints he had encountered on the glacier. The party organised by von Fellenberg (a Swiss who, weighing 100 kilograms, was unusually hefty in a usually slim crowd), included four guides. Almer recognised their silhouettes, faces, voices and even tools, as all being from Grindelwald.

The Matterhorn disaster probably made Almer more circumspect but did not slow his activity. In the month of August 1865 he opened four new routes (the Silberhorn and Guggi routes on the Jungfrau, the north spur of the Silberhorn, and the Wetterhorn via Gleckstein). Shortly afterward, he made the first ascent of the tall Nesthorn peak in the Oberland. Thanks to his reputation, Almer was in frequent demand and thus never out of work. He was busy throughout the summer whenever weather permitted. It was on 18 September 1865 that he scaled the Nesthorn (3,824 metres) with his son and future great guide, Ulrich Almer, and two members of the Alpine Club, Alexander Mortimer and H.B. George (1838–1910).

George specialised in the Oberland, and was the first editor of the *Alpine Journal*. There, in 1863, he summed up the conquests already made, even as he identified the last citadel: 'While even if all other objects of interest in Switzerland should be exhausted, the Matterhorn remains (who shall say for how long?) unconquered and apparently invincible.'

Melchior Anderegg.

In 1864 no one made an attempt on the Matterhorn – not even Whymper or Jean-Antoine Carrel, the 'Bersagliere' and first to attack the summit the Italians called La Becca.

In 1865, Moore toured the Engadin valley with his long-time friend, Horace Walker, and a single guide, Jakob Anderegg. On 28 June the party made the first ascent of Piz Roseg (3,937 metres). It was a dynamic trio: Moore claimed that Anderegg was as strong as horse. It was the thirty-six-year-old Anderegg's second season, which continued on 6 July with the summit of the Obergabelhorn (4,063 metres) with Moore and Walker. The trio was joined on 9 July by Jakob's cousin Melchior Anderegg for the Pigne d'Arolla (3,796 metres) a virgin snow-peak in the Valais – easy but with a fine view.

Moore never climbed the Matterhorn. Perhaps he shared the opinion of Melchior Anderegg and Christian Almer: there were plenty of virgin peaks to climb in the Alps, why become besotted with the Matterhorn as Whymper was? Whymper had just made an attempt on 21 June 1865. His party of five men included Almer, as well as the hunchback from Breuil, Luc Meynet. At about 3,400 metres on the Breuil side, beneath the Furggen escarpment, huge blocks crashed into the couloir of show and ricocheted hellishly, sending fragments of rock toward the party. The guides, who were dining a few dozen metres below Whymper – who had set out to reconnoitre – dropped the leg of mutton and flask of wine in their hectic race for shelter beneath some rocks. Following this warning shot, Almer buried his face in his hands and Croz shouted up to Whymper, who had begun to climb once more:

'Come down, come down! It is useless!'

Whymper then suggested crossing over to the Zermatt side via the Furggjoch (3,271 metres) – they would try their luck on the east slope of the Matterhorn. On reaching the pass they discovered they could not cross it due to shrinkage of the glacier, which left a small but steep wall of rock. Almer asked Whymper sharply:

'Why don't you try to go up a mountain that *can* be ascended?'

He was echoed by Biener, who said, 'It is impossible.'

Croz had a prior commitment, hence had to be back in Chamonix on 27 June. He suggested they head to the Mont Blanc range, where there was plenty of fruit for the picking.

For Whymper, this was the first twist in the Matterhorn tale – the defection of his best guides and a forced change of destination. He bent to their will, while noting Croz's arrogance during that sharp exchange between them on the Furggjoch. The party grew sombre, as did the ridge amidst the cloud of a local squall – snow began to fall.

Another reason for pulling up stakes.

The Zermatt glacier, by Jean-Antoine Linck.

EDWARD WHYMPER

A Keen 'Wanter'

The Matterhorn men.
Top (L–R): old Taugwalder,
Hudson and Hadow.
Bottom (L–R): Croz,
Douglas, Whymper and
young Taugwalder.

IT IS WORTH RECALLING THAT WHYMPER'S CAMPAIGNS were Napoleonic in their swift, constant movement from one range or valley to another, via summits to be conquered, summits for observing a peak targeted for future conquest, transitional passes (both known and unknown) and connecting valleys. Whymper's legs tirelessly supported his bold moves. He made forced marches between highly demanding climbs. Whymper wasn't the only extraordinary hiker of his day – just take Moore. One day, Whymper discussed walking with a friend, another pioneer:

> I remember speaking about pedestrianism to a well known mountaineer some years ago and venturing to remark that a man who averaged thirty miles a day might be considered a good walker. 'A fair walker,' he said, 'a *fair* walker.' 'What then would you consider good walking?'
> 'Well,' he replied, 'I will tell you. Sometime back a friend and I agreed to go to Switzerland, but a short time afterwards he wrote to say he ought to let me know that a young and delicate lad was going with him who would not be equal to great things, in fact, he would not be able to do more than fifty miles a day!'

'What became of the young and delicate lad?'
'He lives.'
'And who was your extraordinary friend?'
'Charles Hudson.'

 Like Moore and Almer, Charles Hudson – who climbed Mont Blanc without guides and accompanied Whymper on the fatal ascent of the Matterhorn – was an exceptional walker. Once he covered the entire route between Saint-Gervais and Geneva and back again in less than twenty-four hours, a distance of 132 kilometres.

 Whymper's campaign in the summer of 1865 reflects not just an obsession with the Matterhorn but also the capacities of a climbing party in the golden age. It began in the valley of Lauterbrunnen with a failure to reach the summit of Ebneflujoch (13 June) despite nineteen hours of effort. There followed a transitional march (14 and 15 June) to Zinal (1,675 metres) via Petersgrat, the valley of Tourtemagne (Turtmann) and the Col de la Forcletta (2,874 metres). On 16 June, his party – Croz, Almer, Biener, Whymper – made the first ascent of the Grand Cornier (3,961 metres), having left Zinal at 2 a.m. That same evening, after the ascent, the remains of a burnt-out hut at Bricola (2,400 metres) sheltered the weary Whymper and Almer, while their companions, who were thirsty for milk, slept in a pasture hamlet further down. On 17 June, the four men's feet and hands tingled from a return trip to the top of the Dent Blanche (4,357 metres) in an icy, biting wind – seventeen hours of actual walking.

 The next day (18 June), Biener did not return to Bricola until 2.30 p.m., having wished to attend mass at Evolène (1,346 metres), two or three hours walk away. The party then left for the Col d'Hérens. The mist so thickened at the Hérens pass itself (3,462 metres) that the men travelled in circles. They beat a retreat, disappointed and annoyed with Biener, who was scolded by Croz.

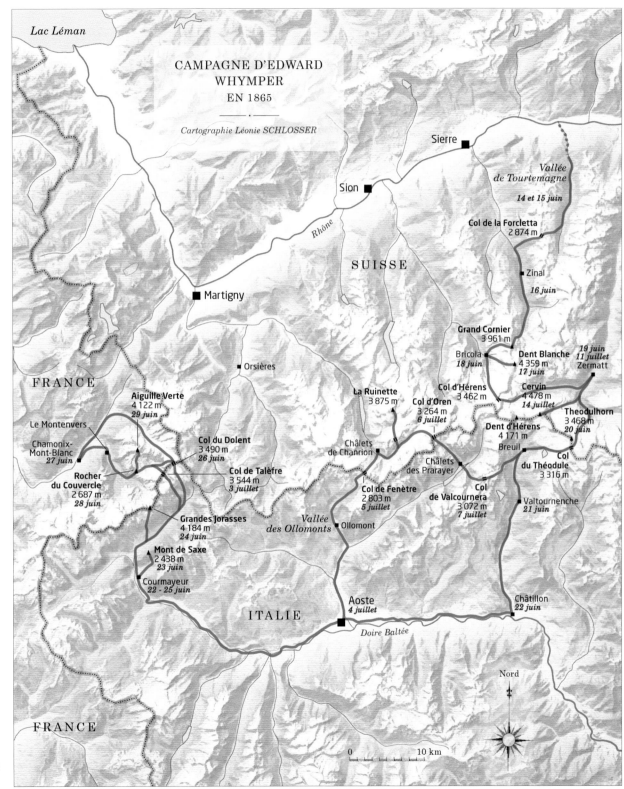

Lac Léman

Sierre

Sion

*Vallée
de Tourtemagne*

14 et 15 juin

Col de la Forcletta
2 874 m

Zinal

16 juin

Martigny

SUISSE

Rhône

Orsières

Grand Cornier
3 961 m

Bricola   **Dent Blanche**

*19 juin
11 juillet*

Zermatt

18 juin   ▲ 4 359 m

17 juin

FRANCE

Col d'Hérens
3 462 m

Cervin
4 478 m

14 juillet

Aiguille Verte
4 122 m

29 juin

La Ruinette
3 875 m

Col d'Oren
3 264 m

6 juillet

Theodulhorn
3 468 m

20 juin

Le Montenvers

Dent d'Hérens
4 171 m

Chamonix-
Mont-Blanc

27 juin

Col du Dolent
3 490 m

26 juin

Châlets
de Chanrion

Breuil   **Col
du Théodule**
3 316 m

**Rocher
du Couvercle**
2 687 m

28 juin

Col de Talèfre
3 544 m

3 juillet

Châlets
des Prarayer

**Col
de Valcournera**
3 072 m

7 juillet

Col de Fenètre
2 803 m

5 juillet

Valtournenche

21 juin

Grandes Jorasses
4 184 m

24 juin

*Vallée
des Ollomonts*

Ollomont

▲ **Mont de Saxe**
2 438 m

23 juin

Courmayeur

22 - 25 juin

Aoste

4 juillet

Châtillon

22 juin

ITALIE

Doire Baltée

Nord

FRANCE

0   10 km

*Map of Whymper's
1865 campaign.*

*The Grandes Jorasses
by E.T. Compton.*

On 19 June the party enthusiastically joined the table at the Monte Rosa Hotel, run by Alexandre ('Grandpa') Seiler ever since he bought the Lauber inn during the Forbes years. Seiler was a godsend to mountaineers, and his hotel became a well-known gathering spot, thanks to Whymper's tales and engravings. The party took just six and a half hours to reach Zermatt (1,600 metres) from Bricola via the Col d'Hérens.

When crossing the Theodul pass (3,316 metres) on 20 June, the party scampered up the Theodulhorn (3,468 metres). Whymper wanted to study the Matterhorn before attacking its Italian slope the next day via a new route of his own devising. They spent the night at Breuil (2,000 metres).

On 21 June, the guides were beaten back by heavy fire from the Matterhorn. The night was spent in the village of Valtournenche (1,640 metres).

On 22 June the party headed down to Châtillon (550 metres), then climbed to Courmayeur (1,200 metres).

On 23 June the men climbed Mont de la Saxe (2,438 metres) to study the Grandes Jorasses, the ascent of which would serve as a vantage point for studying the Aiguille Verte.

On 24 June they made the first ascent of the Grandes Jorasses (the peak now known as Pointe Whymper, 4,184 metres), starting from and returning to Courmayeur. On the way down the party slipped in the snow and tumbled down a good portion of the slope, Croz managing to halt the fall just metres from a crevasse thanks to a terrific blow of his axe.

The men rested on 25 June.

At forty minutes past midnight on 26 June the party left Courmayeur and reached Chamonix at ten that evening after crossing the Col du Dolent (3,490 metres). The French slope of the Col du Dolent had been hard with ice along its 300 metres of steep

The narrow summit ridge of the Aiguille Verte rises above the Whymper couloir.

slope. The guides spent seven hours cutting steps. Whymper's diary reads: 'Chamonix at 10.05 p.m., where I ordered a St Peray and then a champagne and then a beer, and under the combined effect leant back in my chair and slept till daybreak when I got into bed. Actual walking time, 18 hours 30 minutes. Halts, 2 hours 55 minutes. Total time, 21 hours 25 minutes.'

Once at Chamonix, Croz regretfully parted from Whymper, for he had another engagement. Whymper's target was the Aiguille Verte (4,122 metres), the most famous needle in Croz's native valley – it must have broken the guide's heart to leave.

On 28 June, Whymper's party – now composed of Almer, Biener and a porter from Chamonix – slept in a tent sheltering beneath a large rock at the Couvercle (2,687 metres). They settled scores with the Aiguille Verte the next day (29 June) after briefly hesitating between a gully of snow and the rocks along the shoulder. In general, guides preferred gullies to shoulders, and snow to rocks. On arriving just beneath the summit, Almer, whom Whymper appreciated for his silence, shouted, 'Ah, Aiguille Verte, now you are well and truly dead!'

They reached the summit at 10.15 a.m. The descent was tricky and difficult in wind-whipped snow. Finding the soft snow slippery, they descended slowly. Too slowly. Below, on the rock of the Couvercle, the porter was convinced that the Aiguille Verte had got the better of his employers. He began folding the tent after consuming a feast intended for four: mutton, bread, cheese, wine, eggs, sausage. The glutton consumed it all. The party came across him while he was still digesting, and punished him with a hectic descent to Chamonix at a pace that made the wretch sweat out the fat he had feasted upon.

On reaching Chamonix the three men were received like heroes. Then one man, Zacharie Cachat, came forth from the group of guides and harangued them with the eloquence and spite of one-too-many drinks at the nearby inn. The party of strangers was poaching summits throughout the range, offending all Chamoniards. Just think: the Englishman hadn't hired a single guide from Chamonix! What's more, they were liars. 'Where were their proofs [of ascent]? Where was the flag upon the summit?' A challenge to repeat the climb ensued: 'Take three of us with you, and we will bet you 2,000 francs to 1,000 that you won't make the ascent!'

Whymper declined the wager, leaving it to his compatriots, T.S. Kennedy and Charles Hudson. He headed at once to Montenvers (2 July). At that time the Col du Géant was the only known direct passage between Chamonix and Courmayeur. But Whymper reached Courmayeur at 5 p.m. on 3 July after a ten-hour crossing of the Col de Talèfre (3,544 metres) with its glaciers on both slopes. On 4 July Whymper was in Aosta, at the inn run by Jean Tairraz. His summer campaign had specific goals, all of which he had achieved – except the Matterhorn. On 5 July the party reached the chalets of Chanrion ('a foul spot', wrote Whymper) via Val d'Ollomont and the Col de la Fenêtre (2,803 metres). The next day (6 July) the party made the first ascent of the Ruinette (3,875 metres) then pushed on as far as the Chalets of Prarayer (2,025 metres) via the Col des Portons, the Otemma glacier, and the Col d'Oren (3,264 metres) – yet another Napoleonic-style forced march: two mountain ranges were crossed *after* ascending the Ruinette.

On 7 July the party crossed the Col de Valcournera (3,066 metres). As soon as they reached Breuil, the three men's minds all turned to the Matterhorn. But in different ways. 'Anything but the Matterhorn, dear sir,' said Almer, '*anything* but the Matterhorn.'

Whymper released both Oberland guides and went to look for Jean-Antoine Carrel. The weather began to turn. Carrel prevaricated.

On the morning of 11 July, Whymper leapt to his telescope on learning that a party of guides was already making its way up the

Mᵗ. Cervin
4505 m.

D.ᵗ d'Hérens
4180 m.

Ober Gabelhorn
4073 m.

The Matterhorn (or Cervin).
On the left is the steady curve of the
Hörnli ridge, a giant natural staircase.

Lord Francis Douglas.

Matterhorn. Carrel had tricked Whymper – he was a member of a party hired by Italian engineer Felice Giordano.

Whymper resorted to tobacco to calm himself. He then ran into a young Briton who had just crossed the Theodul pass with a guide from Zermatt, young Peter Taugwalder (the twenty-two-year-old son of 'old' Peter Taugwalder, aged forty-five). The Briton was Lord Francis Douglas, freshly and proudly returning from the second ascent of the Obergabelhorn on 6 July. His was the first ascent from the Zinal side, and his guides had been old Peter Taugwalder and Joseph Viennin.

Born in 1847 into a family of the old Scottish aristocracy, Lord Francis Douglas was the brother of the Marquis of Queensberry and was an experienced traveller despite his youthful age of eighteen. He provided Whymper with encouraging news: 'Old Peter had lately been beyond the Hörnli, and had reported that he thought an ascent of the Matterhorn was possible upon that side.' Douglas unhesitatingly accepted Whymper's suggestion of a joint attack on the Matterhorn before the Italians managed to plant their flag on it. They headed back to Zermatt, where they intended to recruit old Peter.

On arriving at the Monte Rosa Hotel in Zermatt on 12 July, Whymper immediately recognised a guide sitting on the low wall opposite the hotel. It was Michel Croz. The Chamonix guide had just been to the top of Mont Blanc with Charles Hudson and D.R. Hadow, an ascent made at a brisk pace. Now they, too, were targeting the Matterhorn. Hudson defended the young Hadow, all of nineteen years old, claiming that he would be able to deal with the difficulties of the Matterhorn even though his experience was limited to the normal routes up Mont Buet and Mont Blanc. 'I consider he is a sufficiently good man to go with us,' Hudson told Whymper.

That evening, around the table at the Monte Rosa Hotel, it was decided that the two parties would combine their efforts, and that they would all attack the summit via the Hörnli ridge.

The joint party lacked cohesion – it was a random coalition, cooked up overnight. And it was too numerous for a terrain where the followers risked being bombarded by rocks unleashed by the leaders. In fact, that was the main cause of the ensuing disaster: the party numbered seven men, whereas a normal team ranged from three to five. This long procession took 170 metres of rope belonging to Whymper: sixty metres of Manila hemp, fifty metres of a stouter, stronger rope, and sixty metres of a lighter rope to be used to equip certain passages. Hudson had a metallic rope that was much too heavy, so was not even examined or offered to Whymper – fortunately, as it turned out, for Whymper and the Taugwalders. Indeed, metallic rope would not have snapped like the lighter one later did, and thus there would have been seven deaths instead of four, plus the mystery of a fall unwitnessed by anyone except the heavens over the Matterhorn.

The Hörnli ridge was to be Whymper's final thrust, following eight unsuccessful attempts from the Italian side.

Meanwhile, Carrel's assault, commissioned by Giordano in the name of the Club Alpino Italiano, was underway. That assault was carried out with a ladder and steel pegs to be driven into the rock of a thirty-metre-high crag, thereby equipping it with climbing aids. Giordano's plans were ambitious and wide-ranging – he anticipated a ten-day effort. In the end, it lasted four days and four nights (10 to 14 July). Carrel was making his seventh attempt, but this time he had an official mission: to claim victory for Italy. *Avanti Bersagliere!*

Back in Zermatt, no one knew how far the Bersagliere's party had got. Whymper and the others enjoyed the rush of confidence that goes with last-minute preparations. All summer Hudson had been thinking that the Hörnli ridge would provide the final word.

Es geht!

Douglas Robert Hadow.

THE MATTERHORN

Mr Whymper's White Trousers

Edward Whymper and his guides leave Courmayeur for an ascent of Mont Blanc, 3 August 1893.

AT DAWN THE HORIZON UNFOLDED AROUND THE PLATFORM and scree of the bivouac at 3,350 metres. The sky was clear, cloudless, promising – a glorious day. Whymper, Douglas and the two Taugwalders, father and son, slept in the tent, while the others preferred to sleep under the stars wrapped in their blankets. Shortly after setting off with the first light of day, the party rounded a rock step and finally got a look at the Hörnli ridge. As Whymper described it, 'The whole of this great slope was now revealed, rising for 3,000 feet like a huge natural staircase.' Any obstacles on the ridge could be skirted by ledges or passages on the eastern flank. They climbed for hundreds of metres with no one asking to be roped up. Croz and young Taugwalder had reconnoitred a good part of the route the previous afternoon; watched from the tent where Whymper was sketching, the two men appeared to race up the rocks.

On returning from their reconnaissance, Croz confirmed the impression of ease:

'Not a difficulty, not a single difficulty! We could have gone to the summit and returned today easily!'

The Hörnli ridge is one of the finest examples of illusionism in the history of mountaineering. Such optical illusions vanish once you get close enough to them. The Hörnli ridge was obviously a boulevard as far as the Épaule (Shoulder), but above that shoulder, the spiky head of the Matterhorn had fooled both minds and spyglasses. Even Bennen had been mistaken – had he attacked the Matterhorn by the Hörnli ridge, the 'Garibaldi of guides' would have reached the summit with Tyndall as early as 1862.

Bennen died in February 1864. Six months later, Tyndall, already shaken by Bennen's death, had a close call with an avalanche on the Morteratsch. Neither man – savvy guide, great scholar – ever suspected what a simple reconnoitre would have shown them. Whymper, too, was fooled. Again and again. He made eight attempts from the Breuil side. And now, on his ninth attempt, he found himself on the Hörnli ridge almost by chance rather than choice, leading the way in alternation with Hudson.

At 9.55 a.m. – Whymper's accounts are precisely timed – the party rested for fifty minutes beneath the head of the Matterhorn, at an altitude of 4,270 metres. The head of the Matterhorn is the tip of the pyramid, 'which, from the Riffelberg or from Zermatt, seems perpendicular or overhanging'. Here the eastern face was no longer feasible. The party made its way up the snow on the edge of ridge for a short stretch, then by common accord the leaders decided to attack the snowy rocks on the northern side. This required a nearly horizontal traverse of 120 metres starting from the Épaule, which offered a striking view of both slopes. The party roped up. 'Now,' said Croz as he led off, 'now for something altogether different.' Yet these rocks seemed less steep to Whymper than those on the Écrins. It was a slope that would not have been difficult had it been dry, but snow had accumulated in the pockets between the rocks, themselves sometimes covered with a thin film of ice. The party crossed the north face much further than is usually done today. Croz led the way slowly and steadily, for young Hadow required regular assistance. The traverse was followed by a vertical ascent of some twenty metres, then a long and difficult detour around a corner of red rock. There they found themselves back on the snowy ridge, which flattened a few dozen metres further on – the last doubts melted away. Unroping themselves, Croz and Whymper raced up the crowning rubble. 'At 1.40 p.m. the world was at our feet, and the Matterhorn was conquered. Hurrah! Not a footstep could be seen.'

What is striking about Whymper's account is the ease, the obviousness, the mastery of every step of this ascent: a steady pace (until the race to the summit), a clear route, good coordination. The only fear – a steadily growing one – was that the shaggy natives from Italy had beaten them to it. The summit of the Matterhorn is a roughly level ridge some 100 metres long. Suddenly seized by doubt, Whymper walked along with his eyes down, scanning the snow for footprints. On reaching the southern end, he leaned over and immediately shouted:

'Croz! Croz! Come here!'

'Where are they, Monsieur?'

'There, don't you see them, down there?'

'Ah, the *coquins* [rascals], they are low down.'

Carrel's party was struggling near Tyndall Peak, apparently motionless when seen from that distance and steeply plunging angle. Whymper and Croz yelled until they were hoarse to make the Italians realise they had lost. But had they heard?

'Croz, we *must* make them hear us; they *shall* hear us!'

Whymper hurled a rock into the void and instructed Croz to do the same. They used their sticks to prize away huge blocks. The Italian slope rumbled and smoked under a torrent of stones.

'Croz! Croz! Come here!'

This time, the rascals' eyes and ears certainly opened. Carrel recognised 'Mr Whymper's white trousers' on the summit. The poor native; he had made seven assaults since 1857, three of them alongside Whymper. And he had abandoned the Englishman in favour of Giordano and a claim of glory for Italy. His desertion to the Italian king's troops had cost him dearly.

Having returned to the northern end of the ledge, where the others were piling rocks into a cairn, Croz drove a tent pole into the ground. One of the guides had taken it along that morning despite Whymper's 'protest that it was tempting Providence', having been foiled on so many previous attempts. The tent pole was now used for the flag which they planted that very day. Croz pulled off his Savoyard peasant's blue smock and affixed it to the pole. Although it made a poor flag, the smock was seen all around, at Zermatt, at the Riffel, at Valtournenche and at Breuil. The people of Breuil assumed that their four natives had achieved success, until the men returned the next day. Giordano even dispatched two victory messages to Quintino Sella, the founder of the Club Alpino Italiano. The disheartened guides had to confess humiliating defeat: 'It is true, we saw them ourselves – they hurled stones at us!'

In a little known account, Canon Georges Carrel reported the version of the Bersagliere's three companions, outraged by an overly late start on the morning of 14 July, which allegedly cost them the victory. Their *ex post facto* outrage seems a little convenient, and supplied them with a reason for refusing to make a second attempt despite Giordano's urging. 'On 14 July 1865,' wrote the canon, 'instead of leaving the tent early, they only set out at 6 a.m., thus it was noon when they arrived at the shoulder where Mr Tyndall had halted on 28 July 1862.' Two of the guides wanted to turn around, while the Bersagliere and the fourth guide wanted to continue. The Bersagliere settled the matter: 'All, or none.' So the four men

The mountaineers scaling the final few metres of the Matterhorn in 1865, as depicted by Gustave Doré.

The second ascent of the Matterhorn was a true exploit, an exceptional piece of climbing led by Jean-Antoine Carrel, that shaggy, thirty-six-year-old native with pick-axe head and deep-set eyes.

were already heading back to their tent when Whymper's cannon-ade reached them. It seemed that everyone in the party was slug-gish that day, for one reason or another – the native 'tortoise' saw no reason for haste. Giordano had given them ten days to complete their mission. Meanwhile, that 'hare' Whymper was nowhere to be seen.

At the summit, Whymper made some sketches and scanned the full horizon, embracing all the Alps in his victor's gaze. The air was unusually clear, with that extraordinary clarity which often precedes bad weather. There was no cloud or haze to north, east, south or west of the Matterhorn. Everything was perfectly still in that indescribable beauty mentioned by Tyndall.

Three days later, on 17 July 1865, Jean-Antoine Carrel and Jean-Baptiste Bich spent only twenty minutes on the summit, just enough time to erect a cairn on the western knoll and attach a red handkerchief, taking back a few rocks marked by lightning. From a technical standpoint, their ascent via the Lion ridge was a tour de force, requiring acrobatic moves on the rock and awkward traverses of gullies of snow exposed to rockfall. As Abbé Amé Gorret put it, 'I don't like those traverses above a void, I prefer climbing.' Although from a distance it appears easier than the north-east (Hörnli) ridge, the south-east (Lion) ridge is a distinctly more difficult and complex route.

For that second Italian assault, all the other guides from Breu-il having ignored Giordano's patriotic arguments, Jean-Antoine Carrel recruited Gorret and two men employed at the local inn, Bich (or Bic, known as 'Bardolet') and Jean-Auguste Meynat. Gorret took up his cherished alpenstock and removed his cassock, donning a hunter's garb in the chapel of Breuil, stuffing the ends of his trousers in stockings in order to walk more easily. Later that autumn Gorret published his story of that second ascent of the

The Hörnli ridge, with the line of the route.

Abbé Amé Gorret, a Matterhornmaniac.

Matterhorn – the first via the Lion ridge – in a local newspaper. His lively, impulsive account of the climb (including two nights in a tent), written in the picturesque, local French language, should always be read alongside Whymper's book.

The first ascent of the Matterhorn was not an exploit. It was a tragedy. The second, however, was a true exploit, an exceptional piece of climbing led by Jean-Antoine Carrel, that shaggy, thirty-six-year-old native with pick-axe head and deep-set eyes. The first difficult passage was dubbed the *ciarfou* (chimney) because they had to climb like chimney-sweeps, 'using elbows, knees, feet and hands.' High above, past the Enjambée (4,249 metres, that deep, narrow cleft that had thwarted Bennen in 1862), the party reached the Col Félicité below the head of the Matterhorn, then traversed the Tiefenmatten slope (via the now-named Carrel gallery) to reach the Zmutt ridge. The final stretch of rock was suddenly barred to them by a precipitous gully six or seven metres deep. For lack of a piton, the priest sacrificed himself for the sake of the mission: he lowered Carrel and Bich into the gully on a rope. 'Placing my heels on the edge, back resting against the rock, arms clutched to my chest, I lowered two of my companions, one after the other. The third wished to remain with me, I was pleased.' A few minutes later, Carrel and Bich climbed up the gully and scrambled toward the summit on easy rocks. Gorret had to remain at the cleft in order to haul them back up. Astride a ridge that he had spurred with his heels like a horse, the abbé urged them onward with his eyes.

In 1869, Whymper still wondered how Carrel, whom he considered 'the most expert cragsman [he] had seen,' had managed it. Ten years later the two men hitched up again, as in the old days above Breuil, on a magnificent campaign of first ascents in Ecuador (including Chimborazo).

In 1882, aged fifty-two, Carrel made the first winter ascent of the Matterhorn with Vittorio Sella. The 'Bersagliere' died on 24 August 1890 of cold and exhaustion on a lower ridge of the Matterhorn (the Grande Tour), having safely led his party back down in a storm. All his life Carrel clung to his manner as a taciturn, shaggy native. When, in 1869, Whymper asked Carrel about the difficulty of that first ascent of the Lion ridge, the Bersagliere calmly replied:

'Man cannot do anything much more difficult than that!'

CHAPTER XXII

THE MATTERHORN

Taugwalder's Rope

The void of the north face of the Matterhorn between the legs of a climber using the fixed rope on the Hörnli ridge.

WHYMPER REMAINED ON THE SUMMIT OF THE MATTERHORN for an hour – 'One crowded hour of glorious life.' All around Whymper were the peaks of mountaineering's birthplace, the trophies of the golden age: First came the Dent Blanche, hoary and grand; the Gabelhorn and pointed Rothorn; and then the peerless Weisshorn: the towering Mischalbelhörner, flanked by the Allalinhorn, Strahlhorn, and Rimpfischhorn; then Monte Rosa – with its many spitzes – the Lyskamm and the Breithorn. Behind were the Bernese Oberland, governed by the Finsteraarhorn; the Simplon and St Gothard groups; the Disgrazia and the Orteler … The Viso – one hundred miles away – seemed close up on us … Then came my first love – the Pelvoux; the Ecrins and the Meije; the clusters of the Graians; and lastly, in the west, gorgeous in the full sunlight, rose the monarch of all – Mont Blanc.

One hour of celebration, windless, beneath the flag of victory, from peak to peak. As the party prepared to descend, someone realised that they had not left their names in a bottle. Whymper fulfilled that task as the others headed off, Croz in the lead.

Debate will never end over the order of the climbers during the descent of the Matterhorn. The order had been agreed by Whymper and Hudson, the latter wanting to remain immediately behind Hadow. Hadow was the weakest link, the novice who had to be watched and assisted during the ascent, and all the more so during the descent, which is always trickiest. Croz led the way, followed, in order, by Hadow, Hudson, Douglas, old Taugwalder, Whymper and young Taugwalder. Initially they were roped in two teams, then, at the request of Douglas around 3 p.m., Whymper and young Taugwalder tied on to old Taugwalder, who was already tied to the first four with a rope of his choosing. What length of rope was left between each member of the party? Barely four or five metres. At the moment of the accident, Croz, Hadow and Hudson were very close to one another, the rope slack. The exact site has been located some eighty metres below the summit. Whymper did not see the start of the fall, for a mass of rock partly hid Croz and Hadow from his view. He did, however, hear the startled shout given by Croz – the last shout given by his dear friend Croz.

The tragedy of the Matterhorn was one of tragic overconfidence. Hudson should never have expressed confidence in young Hadow, that year's rookie, a novice who had only climbed Mont Buet and Mont Blanc days earlier, an easy ascent in snow even at the time, thus in no way comparable to the inaccessible peak of the Matterhorn, that target of the best climbers of the day. What was going through the mind of the thirty-seven-year-old Hudson, a battle-hardened climber with the experience and discernment of a great guide? Undue confidence, probably. When one exudes optimism and self-confidence, one tends to overestimate the

The Matterhorn
disaster, depicted by
Gustave Doré.

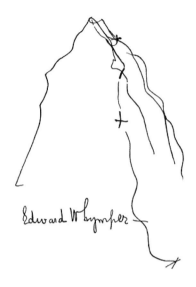

The broken rope.

abilities of others. 'Remember to remain wary,' was the maxim of Prosper Mérimée, a French writer of the day (and friend of Empress Eugénie). That maxim has universal application.

Hadow was a great walker, but a poor climber, and he was wearing shoes whose soles were poorly nailed. Croz laid down his ice axe as he turned to place young Hadow's feet in the steps he had just cut. According to Whymper, if Croz had still had his axe in hand, he could have halted the fall instantly. But just then Hadow slipped, his feet flying into the small of Croz's back. The startled guide went over, falling along with Hadow. Hudson, caught off guard, had no outcrop of rock on which to cling to brake the full weight of two bodies falling simultaneously. He and Lord Francis were swept off their feet. According to Whymper, 'All this was the work of a moment. Immediately we heard Croz's exclamation, old Peter and I planted ourselves as firmly as the rocks would permit: the rope was taut between us, and the jerk came upon us as on one man. We held; but the rope broke midway between Taugwalder and Lord Francis Douglas.'

In the next few seconds Whymper watched as his four companions slid downward on their backs, arms spread to clutch at passing rock but hurled over the edge, one by one, into the 1,000-metre drop of the north face.

The Zermatt guides lost their nerve after the accident. In a blind panic, old Peter wailed, 'Chamonix! Oh, what will Chamonix say?'

Young Peter just sobbed, 'We are lost! We are lost!'

It was half an hour before Whymper, tied between the two, could move. When the three men finally stood together, Whymper examined the rope that had snapped. '[I] found, to my surprise — indeed, to my horror — that it was the weakest of the three ropes. It was not brought, and should not have been employed, for the purpose for which it was used. It was old rope, and, compared with the other, feeble. It was intended as a reserve, in case we had to leave much rope behind, attached to rocks.' The rope had clearly broken in mid-air.

In a state of shock, unnerved by fear, the two guides were unable to lend assistance to Whymper during the next two hours of descent. Father and son were both pathetic during the climb down to the shoulder, entirely led by Whymper, who tied the rope to rocks to secure the descent. The two guides only came to their senses once they reached the shoulder. All three men leaned over the ridge and gave great cries toward the north face. No reply came back.

Unless the apparition that occurred shortly after was a response. At 6.30 p.m. high in the sky over the Lyskamm there suddenly appeared a huge arch of mist, a colourless arch with two motionless crosses, opposite the sun shining at the backs of the three dumbfounded men. The two guides considered it a sign from heaven; Whymper viewed it as a mysterious atmospheric phenomenon, initially thinking it was a mirage involving their own shadows. It has been suggested that the effect was a Brocken spectre.

On 18 July of that year Abbé Gorret saw a magnificent Brocken spectre while descending the Matterhorn after a night of hail. 'It was clear in Switzerland; we saw ourselves in the middle of a circle of rainbow colours; this mirage formed a ring around us, in the middle of which we could see our shadows.' But the crosses seen on 14 July by the survivors did not move when they did.

Still later during the descent, Whymper became quietly, intensely angry with the Taugwalders. Young Peter went up to Whymper and asked him to write in the register of the Monte Rosa Hotel that they had climbed the Matterhorn but had not been paid. The youth claimed that it would bring in more business at Zermatt the following year.

The vision of the crosses.

Peter Taugwalder

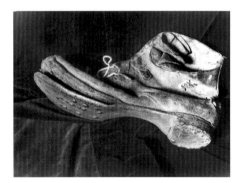

Lord Francis Douglas's boot.

After spending the night – six hours – on a wretched slab of stone, the party reached Zermatt the next morning. Grandpa Seiler greeted Whymper at the door of the hotel, and asked him what was the matter. 'The Taugwalders and I have returned.' Seiler needed no more, and burst into tears.

That same day, a Saturday, the bodies were spotted at the foot of the Matterhorn by a party of twenty men who climbed the surrounding heights with spyglasses. Since Zermatt guides were strictly prohibited from working on Sunday, Whymper organised a party in the Monte Rosa Hotel. The eight-man party which set out at 2 a.m. on Sunday morning, 16 July, contained no Zermatt guides, but was composed of Hudson's best friend, Reverend Joseph McCormick, and two guides from Chamonix, Frédéric Payot and Jean Tairraz, the latter the owner of the inn in Aosta where Croz often stayed. The shattered bodies were discovered around 8.30 a.m. on a small plateau of the Zmutt glacier, in the same order as they had fallen from above, except that there was no trace of Lord Francis Douglas apart from a boot, a belt and a pair of gloves. His body was never found.

As soon as he learned of the four men's deaths, Tyndall hastened to Zermatt and briefly considered descending the entire north face with ropes. In Zermatt guides and neighbours were already insinuating that old Taugwalder might have cut the rope. Government authorities in Valais ordered an inquest into the circumstances of the tragedy. On 21 July 1865, in the Matterhorn Hotel in Zermatt itself, an investigating panel of five magistrates proceeded to question 'Mr Whymper, tourist,' and Peter Taugwalder senior. Taugwalder was questioned a second time in the same hotel on 23 July.

Question 27: 'Who tied you to Lord Douglas?'

Reply (Taugwalder): 'I myself.'

Question 28: 'Why was a different rope used between Lord Douglas and yourself?'

Reply: 'Because the first rope was not long enough for me to tie on to it.'

Question 29: 'Was the rope between Lord Douglas and yourself sufficiently strong, in your opinion?'

Reply: 'If I had found that the rope between Lord Douglas and myself was not strong enough, I would have been very careful not to use it to tie myself to Lord Douglas, not wanting to put him, any more than myself, in danger. Had I found the rope too weak, I would have said as much before the ascent of the Matterhorn and would have rejected it.'

The inquest dismissed the case without charges.

Incriminated by popular opinion, however, old Taugwalder had to leave Zermatt for several months, and later immigrated to the United States. The minutes of the inquest were only published fifty-five years after the accident.

The catastrophe on the Matterhorn – variously recounted in all the newspapers of Europe, discussed among all classes of society from the beggars in Savoy to Her Majesty Queen Victoria of Great Britain – became one of the most famous disasters of the nineteenth century.

In his 1871 memoirs, Whymper exonerated old Peter Taugwalder from all charges of cutting the rope with his axe, yet made defamatory suppositions concerning the guide who was said to have gone mad – or at any rate strange and unable to work – after the accident:

> In regard to this infamous charge [of cutting the rope], I say that he *could* not do so at the moment of the slip, and that the end of the rope in my possession shows that he did not do so beforehand. There remains, however,

The report of the Matterhorn disaster.

Edward Whymper.

the suspicious fact that the rope which broke was the thinnest and weakest one we had. It is suspicious, because it is unlikely that any of the four men in front would have selected an old and weak rope when there was abundance of new, and much stronger, rope to spare; and, on the other hand, because if Taugwalder thought that an accident was likely to happen, it was to his interest to have the weaker rope where it was placed.

Here Whymper was settling scores with the guides whose behaviour he had despised. He never wanted to see young Peter again. The latter reascended the Matterhorn twenty-five times, and died aged eighty shortly after midnight on 10 March 1923 after smoking three pipes on his deathbed. 'Ten minutes before he died,' said his daughter, 'he was still smoking his pipe.'

Whymper, as fond of tobacco as many of his guides, smoked all his life. He carefully filled his pipe with the strongest tobacco, which he dried and chopped very fine. Whymper died alone in a hotel room in Chamonix. His solitude was deliberate. Having suffered a first stroke on 13 September 1911, the former celebrity locked himself in his room. Neither doctor, priest, minister nor friend – not a soul – was admitted to the bedside of mountaineering's first great hero.

Edward Whymper gave up the ghost at some unknown hour on 16 September 1911.

CHAPTER XXIII

THE BRENVA SPUR

Brenva was what Chamonix guides called 'the back of Mont Blanc'. It was the name of the mountain's Italian slope.

BRENVA WAS WHAT CHAMONIX GUIDES called 'the back of Mont Blanc'. It was the name of the mountain's Italian slope, directly above Courmayeur, a face some 1,400 metres high from the bergschrund. It was a face of snow, ice and granite with more or less rocky ribs interrupted by rows of seracs. Much steeper than the French side of Mont Blanc, the Brenva slope was striking when viewed from afar, and more striking still when viewed close up. French climber Lucien Devies said that the Brenva slope produced 'a unique impression of vastness and altitude'. The spur of rock on the Brenva, which divides the face into two cirques, diminishes in the higher part into broad slopes of snow and seracs that vary greatly from year to year.

There is now a Moore route, and the crescent of snow that serves as a pass between the two cirques is known as Col Moore — A.W. Moore was the brains behind that route.

But the key man during the moment of truth was Jakob Anderegg. The right man in the right place, it was Anderegg who hoisted the party on to the slope of no return.

What a feat! It was the greatest exploit of the golden age, yet remains the least well known to the general public, that ignorant

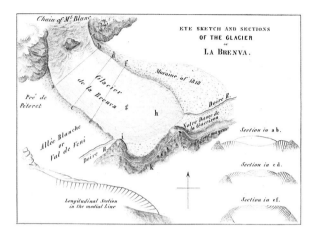

F.D. Forbes' sketch of the Brenva glacier, 1843.

The Brenva glacier drawn by Töpffer.

vulture who has feasted on the corpses of the Matterhorn for these past 150 years. In the fancy hotels of Zermatt people still debate the difficulties of the Matterhorn, an ascent that presents no difficulty whatsoever. The Matterhorn's Hörnli ridge is a boulevard that was swiftly equipped with huts.

On the Brenva slope, in contrast, rows of seracs and cornices overhang the wall for almost its entire two-kilometre width, resulting in major avalanches and snowslides of all kinds. The Brenva will not become civilised until the day that date palms grow in Courmayeur. Serious mountaineering begins where certainty ends – it is a question of pushing to the limit, of threats and surprises, of the unpredictability of a glacier that constantly changes in mass and appearance, of the state of crevasses, snow bridges, bergschrunds and seracs. It is the glaciers, which have shrunk substantially since 1865, which create the beauty and wildness of the Brenva slope.

'*Ein schöner Eisfall!*' gasped Melchior Anderegg, breath taken away by the sight of the 'magnificent icefall' on the Brenva glacier. The Oberland guide was familiar with some of the largest glaciers in Europe but had never seen such a cascade of ice. When, five years later to the day (15 July 1870), Reverend Coolidge made the second ascent of this slope, he had to hire three shaggy Oberland natives, the indefatigable Christian Almer, Almer's son Ulrich and Christian Gertsch. For the moment there were five men aiming for the summit behind Jakob Anderegg and his ice axe: guide Melchior Anderegg, Moore, Horace Walker, Walker's father Francis and G.S. Mathews.

A route like the Brenva spur long seemed impossible without professional guides, without their skills and knowledge of ice and snow. Thirty years would pass before the first party ascended the slope without guides. It was a party of three Englishmen including the famous Albert Mummery, who advocated 'fair means' when climbing, and who was very proud to finally equal the likes of Jakob and Melchior Anderegg. 'In Jakob,' wrote Moore when comparing his two guides on the Brenva spur, 'the virtue of prudence is conspicuous chiefly by its absence.' Melchior, in contrast, when faced with an uncertain passage, was not always as forthright as legend would have it – *Es geht, aber ich geht nicht* (It'll work, but I won't) – and refused (like most guides, according to Moore) to take responsibility for a decision unless it had been discussed.

As recounted earlier, a guide like Bennen left the decision up to Tyndall, who then left it up to Bennen. A guide captained the party but was hired and paid by a gentleman to whom he owed respect. Melchior Anderegg, when in doubt, would consult the men of his party with Olympian serenity, with a calm as natural and above suspicion as his prudence – prudence must not lead to suspicions of cowardice, for then it is no longer prudence. The Middle Ages rightly placed prudence among the cardinal virtues alongside justice, fortitude and temperance.

Melchior was prudence itself. Had he been leading the way, he would have hesitated before the key obstacle of a knife-edged stretch of ice: suddenly and sharply the ridge narrowed to a blade of ice several dozen metres long, with abrupt drops on both sides. A ridge of pure, hard ice. Melchior's doubt would obviously have influenced the decision in the direction of hesitation and retreat. Jakob, however, did not hesitate for an instant before the unexpected obstacle. Ice axe in hand, he sliced off the top of the ridge and advanced at the head of the five men who uttered not a word. The travellers were concentrating on placing their feet with care – they were not wearing crampons – and using their hands. Each guide had an ice axe, each traveller an alpenstock. Willy-nilly, Melchior followed his cousin Jakob along this horizontal ridge exposed to the dizzying heights of the Brenva. *Es muss gehen!* He had to get on with it. According to Moore, it was 'the narrowest and

Melchior Anderegg, photographed in 1894.

most formidable ice arête I ever saw, which extended almost on a level for an uncomfortably long distance.'

As early as 1863 Moore thought he had perceived a route up this huge slope. One day, studying the Brenva face from the heights above Courmayeur, Moore held a war council with his three guides, who passed the telescope from hand to hand. With his usual calm, Melchior Anderegg called the idea *eine miserable Dummheit,* 'a wretched piece of folly.'

Peter Perren from Zermatt was of the same opinion. Christian Almer declined to pronounce himself one way or other. Moore appreciated Anderegg's judgment and prudence, so no attempt was made. But the idea wouldn't go away. In July 1864, when descending Mont Blanc with Almer, their path down the Mur de la Côte was blocked by a crevasse. Skirting it to the right, on the Italian side, Moore noticed a long, relatively gentle incline of snow that could serve as the exit to a route, leading to what would later be named the Col de la Brenva (4,303 metres).

On 12 July 1865, Moore, Horace Walker and their guide Jakob Anderegg enjoyed a drink at Bertolini's Hotel, a hospitable inn in Courmayeur, after a wearying, and summitless, reconnaissance mission up Valgrisenche. It was only the second season for Anderegg, who took up the trade at age thirty-six and was all the more eager to do battle, serving as sole guide to two travellers whereas the reverse ratio – two guides per traveller – was usually recommended. The trio had notched up one victory after another in the preceding weeks, from the first traverse of the Tödi and the Rheinwaldhorn to the first ascents of Piz Roseg and the Obergabelhorn, the second crossing of the Sesiajoch, the first crossings of the Bertol and Breney passes in Valais, and the first ascent of the Pigne d'Arolla.

The next day, 13 July, the trio welcomed Jakob's cousin Melchior and the latter's two clients, Francis Walker (Horace's fifty-six year old

Horace Walker and A.W. Moore (centre), two of the mountaineers who climbed the Brenva spur in July 1865.

A sketch of the Italian, or Brenva, face, showing Col Moore.

father) and George Mathews. That afternoon the six men strolled up a little path above Courmayeur and sat down in the grass opposite the Brenva slope. Moore studied the spur of rock and became convinced that it would lead to the broad incline of snow he had noticed the year before. The spur should provide shelter from falling seracs. His friends from the Alpine Club agreed to go for it. Jakob, too, enthusiastically backed Moore. Only Melchior stuck to his earlier opinion – 'a folly' – but made no formal objection to an attempt.

At roughly 3 p.m. on 14 July, after a four-hour hike from Courmayeur, the party (joined by two porters who would remain at the bivouac), lounged on a patch of grass not far from the Brenva glacier. At that very moment, on the Matterhorn, Michel Croz gave the startled shout that curdled the blood of his friend Whymper. The Brenva party carried on and finally bivouacked a little higher up. At 2.50 a.m., in the dark, they set out again behind Melchior Anderegg, whose admirable wisdom led them across the glacier's crevasses as dawn broke, up to the first buttresses of the ridge. The party advanced quickly and climbed well. At 7.20 a.m., after four hours of progress, they paused at the pass now known as Col Moore. Jakob took the lead from his cousin Melchior, followed by the elder Walker, Horace Walker, Mathews, Melchior and, finally, Moore. They advanced up the side and then the edge of the ridge toward a peak that hid what came next. On reaching what they thought was the peak, they discovered the incredible blade of ice between two sheer drops. Here it is worth quoting Moore at length:

> 'On most arêtes, however narrow the actual crest may be, it is generally possible to get a certain amount of support by driving the pole into the slope below on either side. But this was not the case here. We were on the top of a wall, the ice on the right falling vertically (I use the word advisedly), and on the left nearly so. On neither side was it possible

to obtain the slightest hold with the alpenstock. I believe, also, that an arête of pure ice is more often encountered in description than in reality. But here, for once, we had the genuine article – blue ice, without a speck of snow on it. The space for walking was, at first, about the breadth of the top of an ordinary wall, in which Jakob cut holes for the feet. Being last in the line, I could see little of what was coming until I was close upon it, and was, therefore, considerably startled on seeing the men in front suddenly abandon the upright position, which, in spite of the insecurity of the steps, and difficulty of preserving the balance, had been hitherto maintained, and sit down à *cheval*. The ridge had narrowed to a knife edge, and for a few yards it was utterly impossible to advance in any other way.'

As the men in the lead began to stand again, Moore began to do likewise, but remained seated at Melchior's insistence, working himself along with his hand. Moore speculated, 'with an odd feeling of amusement', about what would happen if one of his companions slipped into the abyss on either side. 'Regular steps could no longer be cut, but Jakob, as he went along, simply sliced off the top of the ridge.' Once the ridge widened somewhat, the party rested for a good ten minutes. A steep slope of snow rose steadily above the six men, now perched at 3,900 metres.

At 9.40 a.m. they headed up the steep slope with no visible exit, shut off by a mass of seracs that had to be got round one way or another. Two hours later, slowed by fresh snow on the ice, the party ran up against the seracs and discovered they could not be skirted. The situation was critical. Retreating was unthinkable. To the left were the seracs, to the right – toward the Col de la Brenva, at roughly the same level as the party was – lay a more or

The narrowest and most formidable ice arête I ever saw, which extended almost on a level for an uncomfortably long distance.

less descending traverse that looked impossible. With the same calm he had displayed on the crevassed glacier at dawn, Melchior angled across the steep, icy slope of the seracs, leading the party through them to the mouth of a crevasse choked with debris. But its upper edge 'was about fifteen feet' above them. It looked like it might prove impossible, but in the party's final exploit Melchior made it to the upper lip thanks to 'vigorous pushes *a tergo* [from behind].' After hauling up the two Walkers by rope, Melchior turned to reconnoitre and gave a great shout on seeing the gentle slope of snow. It was the way out of their trap, that terminal slope noticed by Moore the year before. They reached the summit at 3.10 p.m., and Chamonix at 10.30 that night. It was a masterstroke: twenty-one hours of climbing up a totally unknown slope. In terms of scope, commitment and difficulty this ascent constituted the high point of the golden age of mountaineering. The Brenva route is the great leap before which some mountaineers still hesitate today, 150 years after that historic date of 15 July 1865. Today's mountaineers not only have crampons on their feet, but ice screws on their harness, two ice axes, a hut just an hour from Col Moore, a lift to the Col du Géant, three huts on the way back down Mont Blanc, a trodden path, vitamin-enriched provisions, reliable weather forecasts, updated route descriptions, a mobile telephone within reach, maps, GPS, altimeter and headlamp – not to mention a fleet of rescue helicopters in both Courmayeur and Chamonix.

Seen from today's perspective, the commitment of those pioneers on the Brenva wall seems almost mythological. It was just yesterday, yet so long ago – the ice age of camp fires whose coals had to be stirred at 1 a.m. to heat the mixture of coffee and hot wine that Moore found so difficult to digest. Col Moore (3,500 metres), that crescent of snow between two cirques, remains today the epicentre of true mountaineering. •

APPENDICES

Major Alpine Firsts since 1358 and in 1865

The summit of Mont Blanc, by F. and G. Charnaux.

This list of first ascents made in the Alps since 1358 was compiled by W.A.B. Coolidge in his book *The Alps in Nature and History*, published by Librairie Payot et Cie in 1913.

N.B. — Unless stated otherwise, the first ascents as per this list relate to the highest summit of the mountain in question. First ascents having taken place in the same year are not listed by chronological order, but following the topographical plan, from west to east.

1358
Rochemelon

1492
Mont Aiguille

c.1654
Karwendelspitze, west peak

By 1694
Mont Thabor

By 1707
Piz Beverin

Between 1716–1742
Scesaplana

1744
Titlis

c.1762
Ankogel

1770
Buet

1778
Terglou (Triglav)

1779
Mont Vélan

1782
Scopi

1784
Aiguille du Goûter
Dent du Midi

1786
Mont Blanc

1788
Hangendgletscherhorn
Grande Dent de Morcles
Stockgron

1789
Pizzo Bianco
Rothorn da Gressoney
Rheinwaldhorn

Between 1792–1797
Uri Rothstock

c.1792
Blaues Gletscherhorn

1792
Theodulhorn
Klein Matterhorn
Oberalpstock

1793
Piz Urlaun

By 1799
Gross Wiesbachhorn

1800
Gross Glockner

1801
Punta Giordani
Piz Aul
Piz Scharboden

1802
Piz Terri

1804
Ortler

1806
Güferhorn

c.1810
Aiguille de la Grande Sassière

1811
Jungfrau

Between 1811–1818
Rizlihorn

1812
Finsteraarhorn

1813
Zermatt Breithorn

By 1817
Mettenberg

By 1819
Rochebrune

1819
Vincent Pyramid

1820
Zumsteinspitze, Monte Rosa
Zugspitze

1822
Roche d'Ambin
Ludwigshöhe

1823
Grand Rubren
Monte Emilius
Bristenstock

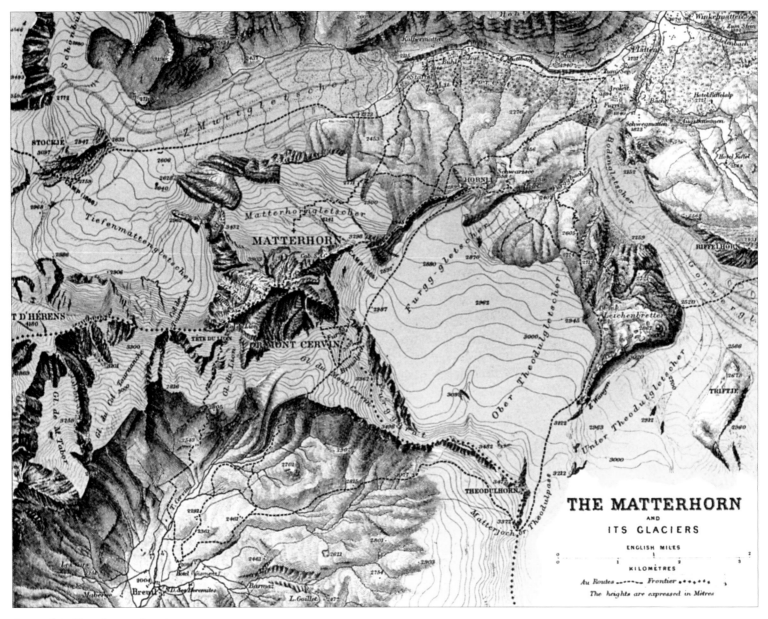

A map of the Matterhorn and its glaciers.

1824
Tödi

1825
Hafnereck

By 1827
Hocharn

**Between
1828–1835**
Mont Pelvoux,
Pic de la Pyramide
Pizzo Tambo

1829
Torrenthorn

1830
Schalfkogel

1831
Kleine Windgälle

1832
Monte Clapier
Becca di Nona
Hausstock
Dachstein

1833
Strahlkogel

1834
Altels
Similaun

1835
Sasseneire
Oldenhorn
Piz Palü, lower peak

Pizzo Porcellizzo
Piz d'Agnelli
Piz Linard

1836
Mont Tinibras
Rognosa di Sestrière
Gstellihorn
Mädelegabel
Fernerkogel

1839
Aiguilles d'Arves,
central peak

By 1840
Galenstock

1840
Mattwaldhorn
Schrankogel

1841
Sustenhorn
Ewigschneehorn
Düssistock
Gross Venediger

1842
Tersiva
Cime de l'Est,
Dents du Midi
Stockhorn,
Col d'Hérens
Signalkuppe,
Monte Rosa
Riffelhorn
Gross Lauteraarhorn
Gross Scheerhorn
Vorab

1843
Wildhorn
Gross Löffler

1844
Rosenhorn,
Wetterhorn
Hasle Jungfrau,
Wetterhorn
Wasenhorn
Johannisberg

1845
Mittelhorn,
Wetterhorn
Hoch Ducan

1846
Piz Surlej
Piz Aguagliouls
Piz d'Esan
Piz Languard
Piz Lischana
Piz Kesch, lower peak
Weisskugel
Gross Mörchner

1847
Schrammacher

1848
Mont Pelvoux,
highest peak
Grenzgipfel,
Monte Rosa
Ulrichshorn
Stockhorn,
Gornergrat
Gross Windgällen,
lower peak
Piz Quattervals

Wildspitze,
lower peak

1849
Tête Blanche
Krone
Piz Mundin

1850
Diablerets
Piz Bernina
Il Capütschin
Piz Tschierva
Piz Corvatsch
Piz Misaun

1851
Combin de
Corbassière

1852
Hohe Wilde
Schwarzenstein
Hochschober

1853
Glarner Tödi
Glockthurm

1854
Ostspitze, Monte
Rosa
Strahlhorn
Rossbodenhorn
Cima di Jazzi
Gross Rinderhorn
Monte Vioz
Hochgall
Monte Peralba

1855
Mont Blanc du Tacul

Dufourspitze,
Monte Rosa
Weissmies

1856
Aiguille du Midi
Mont Avril
Mettelhorn
Allalinhorn
Laquinhorn
Wildstrubel, west
peak

1857
Pointe Garin
Punta Lavina
Ciamarella
Bessanese, lower peak
Croce Rossa
Levanna, east peak
Pointe de Graffeneire
Tête du Lion
Mönch
Klein Schreckhorn
Trugberg, lower peak
Wildstrubel, central
peak
Piz da la Margna
Piz Calderas
Monte Pelmo

1858
Testa del Rutor
Punta Bianca, Grivola
Dômes de Miage
Tour Sallière
Dom des Mischabel
Nadelhorn
Eiger
Piz Morteratsch
Muttler
Hinterer Brochkogel

1859
Grivola
Grand Combin
Rimpfischhorn
Aletschhorn
Bietschhorn
Monte Leone
Piz Julier
Piz Tremoggia
Pizzo Stella
Pizzo della Duana
Rainerhorn
Hochalmspitze

By 1860
Levanna, west peak

1860
Gran Paradiso
Grande Casse
Signal du Mont Iseran
Château des Dames
Alphubel
Blümlisalphorn
Oberaarhorn

1861
Monte Viso
Aiguille and Dôme
de Polset
Doravidi Sud
Mont Pourri
Dôme de la Sache
Mont Gelé
Weisshorn
Nordendspitze,
Monte Rosa
Castor
Lyskamm
Gross Schreckhorn
Gwächtenhorn
Piz Segnes

Pizzo Gallegione
Piz Grisch
Fluchthorn
Wildspitze

1862
Pointe de Charbonnel
Dent Blanche
Besso
Täschhorn
Gross Fiescherhorn
Weisse Frau
Gross Doldenhorn
Monte Disgrazia

1863
Grandes Rousses,
north peak
Dent Parrachée
Granta Parey
Dent d'Hérens
Diablons
Parrotspitze, Monte
Rosa
Balfrin
Silberhorn
Schlossberg
Basodino
Helsenhorn
Bifertenstock
Claridenstock
Selbsanft
Piz Zupo
Piz Roseg, lower peak
Piz Cambrena
Zuckerhütl
Antelao
Tofana, central peak

1864
Cima dei Gelas
Barre des Écrins

Punta Rossa, Grivola
Grande Motte
Aiguille d'Argentière
Aiguille de Tré-la-tête
Aiguille du Tour
Mont Dolent
Zinal Rothhorn
Bouquetin
Punta di Fontanella
Pollux
Balmhorn
Fleckistock
Berglistock
Studerhorn
Gross Wannehorn
Ochsenhorn
Ofenhorn
Vogelberg
Gross Ruchen
Piz Sol
Monte Sissone
Piz Kesch, highest
peak
Hoher Riffler
Königspitze
Monte Cevedale
Monte Venerocolo
Presanella
Adamello
Marmolada
Sorapiss

By 1865
Brunnegghorn

1865
Tsanteleina
Petit Mont Bassac
Aiguille Verte
Grandes Jorasses,
lower peak
Aiguille de Bionnassay
Aiguille du

Chardonnet
Matterhorn
Obergabelhorn
Grand Cornier
Wellenkuppe
Triftthorn
Pigne d'Arolla
Mont Blanc de Seilon
Ruinette
Pointe de la Rosa
Blanche
Gross Grünhorn
Lauterbrunnen
Breithorn
Tschingelhorn
Stücklistock
Gross Nesthorn
Dammastock
Piz Medel
Ringelspitz
Piz Roseg, highest
peak
Piz Umbrail
Piz Pisoc
Crast' Agüzza
Piz d'Aela
Gross Piz Buin
Silvrettahorn
Punta San Matteo
Pizzo Tresero
Monte Cevedale,
highest peak
Finailspitze
Hochvernagtspitze
Ruderhofspitze
Wilder Freiger
Carè Alto
Cima Tosa
Mösele
Hochfeiler
Monte Cristallo
Monte Cogliano

1866
Albaron
Monveso di Forzo
Aiguille de
l'Eboulement
Bec d'Epicoun
Pointe d'Otemma
Mont Fort
Bec de Luseney
Tête de Valpelline
Klein Wannehorn
Wellhorn
Blindenhorn
Cima di Castello
Piz Cengalo
Pizzo del Teo
Pizzo Scalino
Corno di Campo
Corno di Dosdè
Corno di Lago
Spalmo
Piz Platta
Tinzenhorn
Piz Vadret, lower peak
Verstanklahorn
Gross Litzner
Monte Zebrù
Tuckettspitze
Punta Taviela
Monte Rosole
Dreiherrnspitze
Ruthnerhorn

1867
Torre del Gran San
Pietro
Tresenta
Punta Furà
Tour Ronde
Mont Collon
Evêque
Mont Pleureur
Jägerhorn

Gletscherhorn
Gross Spannort
Campo Tencia
Bündtner Tödi
Mürtschenstock
Cima di Piazzi
Piz Badile
Cima di Rosso
Piz Michel
Piz Vadret, highest peak
Hintere Rotspitze
Palon de la Mare
Hintere Schwärze
Olperer
Monte Civetta

1868
Grandes Jorasses, highest peak
Aiguille de la Za
Grosshorn
Ebnefluh
Dreieckhorn
Krönte
Tschingelhörner
Bellavista
Piz Palù, highest peak

1869
Piccolo Paradiso
Pointe de Ronce
Hohberghorn
Morgenhorn
Gspaltenhorn
Schienhorn
Breitlauihorn
Pizzo Rotondo
Piz d'Argient
Surettahorn
Piz Fliana
Gross Seehorn

Parseierspitze
Thurwieserspitze
Sonklarspitze
Watzespitze
Langkofel
Grosse Zinne (Cima Grande)
Cima di Ball
Cima di Fradusta
Dreischusterspitze

1870
Meije, central peak
Ailefroide
Pointe de Zinal
Südlendspitze
Trugberg, central peak
Drusenfluh
Weisseespitze
Wilder Pfaff
Pizzo di Presolana
Cimone della Pala
Rosetta
Piz Popena
Hohe Gaisl (or Croda Rossa)

1871
Monte Stella
Punta Sommeiller
Monte Ciusalet
Cima di Charforon
Aiguille du Plan
Aiguille du Moine
Mont Mallet
Dent des Bouquetins
Dent Perroc
Pointe de Mountet
Portjengrat
Rothorn, Fusshörner
Trugberg, highest peak

Piz Lucendro
Piz Blas
Sandgipfel
Porphyr
Cima di Brenta
Gross Geiger
Simonyspitze

1872
Aiguille de Leschaux
Combin de Valsorey
Aiguilles Rouges d'Arolla
Agassizhorn
Unterbächhorn
Scheuchzerhorn
Grunerhorn
Wildstrubel, highest peak
Zapporthorn
Trafoier Eiswand
Thurnerkamp
Wildgall
Gross Rother Knopf
Glocknerwand
Cima di Vezzana
Kesselkogel, Rosengarten
Marmarole, lower peak

1873
Grande Ruine
Râteau
Sommet des Rouies
Roche Faurio
Montagne des Agneaux
Mont Herbetet
Bessanese, highest peak
Punta d'Arnas

Aiguille de Rochefort
Schallihorn
Schwarzhorn, Monte Rosa
Gross Wendenstock
Gross Greiner
Daberspitze

1874
Grandes Rousses, south peak
Pic de la Grave
Mont Thuria
Punta di Ceresole
Roccia Viva
Bec de l'Invergnan
Aiguille de Blaitière
Aiguille de Triolet
Aiguille des Maisons-Blanches
Monte delle Loccie
Patteriol
Zwölferkogel
Rosengartenspitze

1875
Aiguille de Scolette
Dents d'Ambin
Rognosa d'Etache
Roche de la Muzelle
Punta di Gay
Becca di Montandeyné
Levanna, central peak
Becca della Tribolazione
Balmenhorn, Monte Rosa
Gross Lohner
Cima Viola
Sass Maor

1876
Bric Bouchet
Roche Taillante
Aiguille du Plat
Aiguille des Arcas
Tête de l'Êtret
Dôme de Chasseforêt
Pointe des Sengies
Tour Noir
Grande Fourche
Petites Jorasses
Les Droites
Les Courtes
Mont Brulé
Fusshorn
Gross Engelhorn
Klein Spannort
Gross Windgälle, highest peak
Pizzo Bianco, Bernina
Pizzo del Ferro
Recastello

1877
Bric Froid
Meije, highest peak
Pic d'Olan
Pic Sans Nom
Grande Sagne
Pic Coolidge
Cime de Clot-Châtel
Sirac
Plaret
Pic des Aupillons
Roche du Grand Galibier
Dôme de l'Arpont
Pointe de la Sana
Ondezana
Grand Nomenon
Mont Blanc de Courmayeur

John Ball described the Matterhorn (in the distance, left) as a peak that is 'chief of them all ... [a] stupendous obelisk whose form defies the boldest speculations of the geologist.'

371

Aiguille Noire
de Péteret
Monte di Scersen
Küchelspitze
Jôf di Montasio

1878
Cima di Nasta
Brec de Chambeyron
Pointe de la Font-
Sancte
Pic du Thabor
Les Bans
Meije, east peak
Pic Gaspard
Pointe du Vallon des
Etages
Pic des Arcas
Aiguille du Soreiller
Aiguilles d'Arves,
south peak
Aiguilles d'Arves,
north peak
Aiguille du Péclet
Pointe de la Galise
Grande Aiguille
Rousse
Roc du Mulinet (or
Cima Martellot)
Mont Maudit
Grand Dru
Aiguille des Glaciers
Mittaghorn
Elferkogel
Sass Rigais (or
Geislerspitzen)
Croda da Lago,
highest peak
Sasso Vernale
Pala di San Martino
Kellerwand

1879
Punta dell'Argentera
Monte Matto
Aiguille de
Chambeyron
Pointe Haute de Mary
Tête des Toillies
Pavé
Pic du Says
Pic de Verdonne
Pic Bonvoisin
Tête de Lauranoure
Punta di Forzo
Grand Sertz
Aiguille de Talèfre
Petit Dru
Pointe de Bricolla
Sonnighorn
Pizzo di Dosdé
Zsigmondyspitze
Vordere Zinne
Vernel
Cima di Canali

1880
Becca du Lac
Pointe du Chatelard
Aiguille des Grands
Charmoz
Aiguille du Tacul
Geisshorn
Cima d'Ambies
Fussstein
Grohmannspitze
Grosse Furquetta
Cinque Torri
Innerkoflerthurm

1881
Pointe des Henvières
Panestrel
Pic du Pelvat

Visolotto
Aiguille de Jean
Rostan
Fifre
Grande Arolla
Becca di Monciair
Aiguille du Grépon
Dôme de Rochefort
Tour Saint-Martin
Siedel Rothhorn
Pizzo di Scais
Vajoletthurm
Kleine Zinne (Cima
Piccola)
Sasso di Mur

1882
Rocca Bernauda
Levannetta
Aiguille du Géant
Calotte de Rochefort
Pointe de Mourti
Tschigelochtighorn
Tiefenstock
Banhorn
Piz Prievlusa
Pizzo Torrone
Dosson di Genova
Torre di Brenta
Dirupi di Larsec

1883
Tête de Moyse (or
Monte Oronaye)
Aiguille de la Varappe,
highest peak of the
Aiguilles Dorées
Les Périades
Sattelhorn
Lentahorn
Pizzo Terre
Piz Bacone

Piz Schumbraida
Monte Cornacchia
Monte del Ferro
Croda Grande

1884
Punta Gastaldi
Pointe Rénod
Pointe de l'Echelle
Pointe de Piatou
Punta Francesetti
Cima Monfret
Punta della Gura
Bieshorn
Klein Bietschhorn
Schönbühlhorn
Galmi
Wendenhorn
Fünffingerspitze
Pizzo dei Piani
Piz Timun
Stammerspitz
Kuchenspitze
Crozzon di Brenta
Croda da Lago, lower
peak

1885
Punta Bonneval
Grivoletta
Punta Budden
Testa della
Tribolazione
Aiguille Blanche
de Péteret
Grand Darreï
Pointe des Genevois
Gross Hohwänghorn
Gross Nässihorn
Kamm
Wasenhorn
Piz d'Albana

Campanile di Brenta
Grasleitenspitze,
central peak

By 1886
Cherbadung

1886
Pic du Clapier du
Peyron
Monte Nero
Dents de Bertol
Ober Mominghorn
Hühnerstock
Olmenhorn
Thieralplistock
Dreiländerspitz
Cima della Madonna

1887
Tête de Vautisse
Pic Bourcet
Pic des Prés les Fonds
Cime du Grand
Sauvage
Mont Savoyat
Pointe de la Glière
Cime d'Oin
Aiguille Verte
de Valsorey
Stecknadelhorn
Ankenbälli
Kingspitze,
Engelhörner
Fermeda Thurm

By 1888
Punta Nera, Grivola

1888
Roc Péou
Becca di Noaschetta
Tête de Valnontey

Cresta Gastaldi
Aiguille de
la Neuvaz
Aiguilles Rouges
du Dolent
Bächlistock
Sciora di Dentro
Thorwache

1889
Pic du Ribon
Pointe de la Goletta
Cime de Quart
Dessus
Punta del Broglio
Pointe des Pattes
des Chamois
Becca di Suessa
Punta Crevasse
Aiguille de l'Allée
Blanche
Grande Luis
Gletschhorn
Fluchthorn,
central peak
Busazza
Grasleitenspitze,
west peak

1890
Pic des Souffles,
lower peak
Rocher de Pierre
Pointe
Petit Darreï
Klein Schienhorn
Monte di Zocca
Fluchthorn, north peak
Fünffingerspitze
Marmarole

1891
Aiguille Noire,

Rochilles
Pointe des Cerces
Pic des Souffles,
highest peak
Dent des Rosses
Moine
Ritord
Hinter Sustenhorn
Pierre Cabotz
Pizzo di Pesciora
Hüllehorn
Cima di Cantone
Cima del Largo
Piz Plavna Dadaint

1892
Punta del Tuf
Becca d'Arbiera
Pointe des Grandes
Murailles
Distelhorn
Güschihorn
Wittenwasserstock
Neufelgiühorn
Punta Mottiscia
Gross Schienhorn
Pizzo Columbé
Corbet
Cima dei Cogni
Cima di Balniscio
Cima di Vazzeda
Punta Rasica
Sciora di Fuori
Pizzi Gemelli
Pioda di Sciora
Zahnspitz

1893
Dent du Requin
Aiguille Forbes
Lonzahorn
Alperschellihorn

Weisshorn
Piz Murtaröl
Piz Tavrü
Piz Laschadurella
Piz Zuort
Piz San Jon
Ago di Sciora
Piz d'Arblatsch
Piz Forbisch

1894
Combin de Zessetta
Punta del Dragone
Cima di Livournea
Pizzas d'Annarosa
Cima di Saoseo
Piz Por

1895
Cima della Maledia
Aiguille de Toule
Monte Valnera
Corno di Capra
Monte Saliente
Delagothurm

1896
Steinlauenenhorn
Kranzberg
Piz del Diavel
Cime di Redasco
Sasso di Conca
Piz Pisoc, south peak
1897
Tour d'Arpisson
Aiguille d'Entrèves
Hugihorn
Corno Sinigaglia

1898
Simmelistock

1899
Guglia di Brenta

1900
Kastensteinhörner

1901
Picco Luigi Amedeo
Grüneckhorn
Scheidegg Wetterhorn
Pizzo di Sena

1902
Piz Grass

1903
Klein Nässihorn

1904
Klein Lauteraarhorn

1905
Aiguille de Pélens
Aelplistock

1906
Mont Brouillard

1907
Dames Anglaises

John Ruskin's watercolour drawing of the Matterhorn seen from the north-east, 1849.

This list of sixty-five first ascents in the Alps in 1865 was compiled by Claude Marin, a professional mountain guide and project coordinator in Chamonix for the celebrations of the 150th anniversary of the golden age of mountaineering.

Names followed by (1) are first ascents of a summit, while those followed by (2) are first ascents of a new route. Country codes: A = Austria, CH = Switzerland, F = France, GB = Great Britain, I = Italy.

	DATE	SUMMIT	AMATEUR MOUNTAINEERS	GUIDES
1	28 May	Piz Pisoc(1) – 3,173m (Val Mustair – Grisons- CH)	Marug (CH)	Alexandre Flury (CH)
2	/	Cima Libera(1) – 3,418m (Stubaï – Tyrol – A/I)	F. Leis (A)	Two guides
3	/	Cima di Campo(1) – 3,416m (Zillertal – Tyrol – A/I)	Johann Kirchler (A)	/
4	/	Wilde Leck(1) – 3,361m South face (Stubaï – Tyrol – A)	Zachäus Grüner (A)	/
5	9 June	Piz Medel(1) – 3,210m (Alpes d'Adulla – Grisons – CH)	Madame Deplaci (CH) Madame Strori (CH)	Baptiste Monn (CH)
6	16 June	Grand Cornier(1) – 3,969m East ridge (Valais – CH)	Edward Whymper (GB)	Michel Croz (F) – Christian Almer (CH) Franz Biner (CH)
7	16 June	Grande Mèsule(1) – 3,478m (Zillertal – Tyrol – A/I)	Douglas W. Freshfield (GB) Francis Fox Tuckett (GB) J.H. Fox (GB)	François Devouassoud (F) Peter Michel (CH)
8	24 June	Langtaufere Spitze(1) – 3,529m (Stubai – Tyrol – A/I)	Douglas W. Freshfield (GB) Francis Fox Tuckett (GB) Joseph H. Fox (GB)	François Devouassoud (F) Peter Michel (CH)
9	24 June	Grandes-Jorasses(1) – 4,184m South face - Pointe Whymper (Mont-Blanc)	Edward Whymper (GB)	Michel Croz (F) Christian Almer (CH) Franz Biner (CH)
10	28 June	Col du Dolent(1) – 3,490m East face (Mont-Blanc)	Edward Whymper (GB)	Michel Croz (F) Christian Almer (CH) Franz Biner (CH)

11	28 June	Piz Roseg[1] – 3,937m North-west ridge (Bernina – CH)	Adolphus W. Moore (GB) Horace Walker (GB)	Jakob Anderegg (CH)
12	28 June	Pizzo Tresero[1] – 3,594m South face (Ortler – I)	Francis Fox Tuckett (GB) J.H. Backhouse (GB) J.H. Fox (GB) D.W. Freshfield (GB)	François Devouassoud (F) Peter Michel (CH)
13	28 June	Punta San Matteo[1] – 3,678m West face, south-west ridge (Ortler – I)	Francis Fox Tuckett (GB) John H. Backhouse (GB) J.H. Fox (GB) D.W. Freshfield (GB)	François Devouassoud (F) Peter Michel (CH)
14	29 June	Aiguille Verte[1] – 4,121m East couloir (Mont-Blanc – F)	Edward Whymper (GB)	Christian Almer (CH) Franz Biner (CH)
15	July	Unter-Gabelhorn[1] – 3,392m South-east ridge (Valais – CH)	Francis Douglas (GB)	Peter Inäbnit (CH) Peter Taugwalder (CH)
16	1 July	Wellenkuppe[1] – 3,903m (Valais – CH)	Francis Douglas (GB)	Peter Taugwalder (CH) Peter Inäbnit (CH)
17	5 July	Trifthorn[1] – 3,728m South-west ridge (Valais – CH)	Francis Douglas (GB)	Petert Taugwalder (CH) Peter Inäbnit (CH)
18	5 July	Aiguille Verte[2] – 4,121m Moine ridge (Mont-Blanc – F)	G.C. Hodgkinson (GB) C. Hudson (GB) T.S. Kennedy (GB)	Michel Croz (F) Michel A. Ducroz (F) Peter Perren (CH)
19	6 July	La Ruinette[1] – 3,875m South-west ridge (Valais – CH)	Edward Whymper (GB)	Christian Almer (CH) Franz Biner (CH)
20	6 July	Obergabelhorn[1] – 4,063m North-east ridge (Zermatt side) (Valais – CH)	Adolphus W. Moore (GB) Horace Walker (GB)	Jakob Anderegg (CH)
21	7 July	Obergabelhorn[2] – 4,063m North-west ridge (Valais – CH)	Francis Douglas (GB)	Peter Taugwalder (CH) Josef Vianin (CH)
22	9 July	Pigne d'Arolla[1] – 3,790m East face (Zinal side) (Valais – CH)	Adolphus W. Moore (GB) Horace Walker (GB)	Jakob Anderegg (CH) Melchior Anderegg (CH)
23	11 July	Piz Umbrail[1] – 3,033m South face (Ortler – I)	Johann Wilhelm Coaz (CH)	/

24	14 July	Matterhorn[1] – 4,482m North-east ridge (du Hörnli) (Valais – CH)	E. Whymper (GB) C. Hudson (GB) – F. Douglas (GB) Douglas R. Hadow (GB)	Michel Croz (F) Peter Taugwalder (CH) Peter Taugwalder Jnr. (CH)
25	14 July	Piz Buin[1] – 3,312m North face and north-west ridge (Silvretta – CH)	Joseph A. Specht (A) J.J. Weilenmann (CH)	Jakob Pfitscher (A) Franz Pöll (A)
26	15 July	Brenva Spur[2] – 4,809m South-east face (Mont-Blanc – F/I)	George S. Mathews (GB) Adolphus W. Moore (GB) F. and H. Walker (GB)	Jakob Anderegg (CH) Melchior Anderegg (CH)
27	17 July	Crast' Agüzza[1] – 3,854m West ridge (Bernina – CH)	J.A. Specht (A) J.J. Weilenmann (CH)	Jakob Pfitscher (A) Franz Pöll (A)
28	17 July	Matterhorn[2] – 4,482 m South-west ridge (Lion) (Val d'Aosta – I)	/	Jean-Antoine Carrel (I) Jean-Baptiste Bich (I)
29	17 July	Piz Ela[1] – 3,338m (Alpes d'Albula – Grisons – CH)	/	Alexandre Flury (CH) Peter and Georg Jenny (CH)
30	20 July	Cima Tosa[1] – 3,173m (Brenta – Dolomites – South Tyrol – I)	Giuseppe Loss (I) and five companions	/
31	24 July	Gran Pilastro[1] – 3,510m (Zillertal – Tyrol – A/I)	Paul Grohmann (A) Peter Fuchs (A)	Georg Samer (A)
32	28 July	Pizzo Tresero[1] – 3,594m Southwest ridge (Ortler – I)	Mansell (GB) Sowerby (GB) Thompson (GB)	/
33	28 July	Aiguille de Bionnassay[1] – 4,052m North-west face (Mont-Blanc – F/I)	E.N. Buxton (GB) F. Crauford-Grove (GB) R.S. MacDonald (GB)	Jean-Pierre Cachat (F) Michel Payot (F)
34	31 July	Lauterbrunnen Breithorn[1] – 3,779m West ridge (Oberland – CH)	E. von Fellenberg (CH) James John Hornby (GB) T.T Philpott (CH)	Peter Michel – Peter Egger Johan Bischoff – Peter Inäbnit Christian Almer – Christian Lauener
35	July	Ortler[2] – 3,902m North ridge 'Tabaretta' (Ortler chain – I)	Edmund Mojsisovics (A)	Johann Pinggera (A)
36	6 August	Jungfrau[2] – 4,158m Silberhorn route (Oberland – CH)	James John Hornby (GB) T.T. Philpott (GB)	Christian Almer – Ulrich Almer (CH) Christian Lauener – Johan Bischoff (CH)
37	7 August	Grünhorn[1] – 4,043m West face (Oberland – CH)	E. von Fellenberg (CH)	Peter Michel (CH) Peter Egger (CH) Peter Inäbnit (CH)

38	8 August	Caré Alto[1] – 3,463m North-west face (Adamello chain – Trentino – I)	Sedley T. Taylor (GB) Hugh F. Montgomery (GB)	/
39	9 August	Punta Beltovo di Dentro[1] – 3,325m (Ortler – I)	Edmund Mojsisovics (A)	Sebastian Janiger (A)
40	9 August	Brenta Alta[1] – 2,960m (Dolomites – I)	John Ball (GB) William E. Forster (GB)	Matteo Nicolussi (A)
41	10 August	Silberhorn[2] – 3,695m North spur (Oberland – CH)	James John Hornby (GB) T.T. Philpott (CH)	Christian Almer – Ulrich Almer Christian Lauener (CH) Johann Bischof (CH)
42	22 August	Silvrettahorn[1] – 3,244m (Silvretta – Voralberg/Grisons – A/I)	Jules Jacot (CH)	Christian Jegen Peter Schlegel
43	23 August	Cima di Solda[1] – 3,387m (Ortler chain – A/I)	Julius von Payer (A)	Veit Reinstadler (A)
44	25 August	Wetterhorn [2] – 3,692m via the Gleckstein (Oberland – CH)	/	Christian Almer (CH) and five companions
45	26 August	Cima di Campo[1] – 3,469m South-east peak, east ridge (Zillertal – Tyrol – A/I)	Oster Joseph Mazzag (A)	/
46	27 August	Tofana di Dentro[1] – 3,237m (Ampezzo Dolomites – I)	J.A. Specht (A) J.J. Weilenmann (CH)	Angelo Dimai (A)
47	28 August	Cima Vertana[1] – 3,545m South face, south-west ridge (Ortler chain – I)	Julius von Payer (A)	Johann Pinggera (A) Veit Reinstalder
48	29 August	Jungfrau[2] – 4,158m Guggi route Wengernjungfrau, 4,060m (Oberland – CH)	Hereford B. George (GB) George Young (GB)	Christian Almer (CH) Johann Baumann (CH) Ulrich Almer (CH)
49	4 September	Ortler [2] – 3,902m North-south traverse (Ortler chain – I)	Julius von Payer (A)	Johann Pinggera (A)
50	6 September	Tschingelhorn[1] – 3562m South couloir (Oberland – CH)	Heinrich Feuz (CH) W.H. Hawker (GB)	Christian Lauener (CH) Ulrich Lauener (CH)
51	7 September	La Ruinette[1] – 3,875m South-east ridge (Valais – CH)	J.J. Weilenmann (CH)	Jean-Maurice Rossoz (CH)

52	7 September	Monte Cevedale[1] – 3,769m North-west face (Ortler – I)	Julius von Payer (A) Joseph Reinstadler (CH)	Johann Pinggera (A)
53	8 September	Finailspitze[1] – 3,514m (Ötztal – Tyrol – A)	Franz Senn (A)	Cyprian Granbichler (A) Peter Paul Gstrein (A)
54	9 September	Hochvernagtspitze[1] – 3,539m South face (Ötztal – Tyrol – A)	Franz Senn (A)	Cyprian Granbichler (A) E. Neurauter (A)
55	10 September	Rosablanche[1] – 3,336m South ridge (Valais – CH)	J.J. Weilenmann (CH)	Maurice-Justin Fellay (CH)
56	11 September	Mont-Blanc de Cheilon[1] – 3,858m West ridge (Valais – CH)	J.J. Weilenmann (CH)	Maurice-Justin Fellay (CH)
57	14 September	Monte Cristallo[1] – 3,221m South-east face (Ampezzo Dolomites – I)	Paul Grohmann (A)	Angelo Dimai (A) Santo Siorpaes (A)
58	17 September	Aiguille Verte[2] – 4,121m Grande-Rocheuse spur (Mont-Blanc – F)	R. Fowler (GB)	Michel A. Ducroz (F) Michel Balmat (F)
59	18 September	Nesthorn[1] – 3,820m (Valais – CH)	Hereford B. George (GB) H. Mortimer (GB)	Christian Almer (CH) Ulrich Almer (CH)
60	19 September	Brunegghorn[2] – 3,833m South-west ridge (Valais – CH)	G.F. Cobb (GB) W.D. Rawlins (GB) R.B. Townsend (GB)	François Devouassoud (F) Antoine Clément (F)
61	20 September	Le Chardonnet[1] – 3,824m West face, west ridge (Mont-Blanc – F)	R. Fowler (GB)	Michel A. Ducroz (F) Michel Balmat (F)
62	30 September	Mont Coglians[1] – 2,780m (Carnic Alps – Frioul – A/I)	Paul Grohmann (A)	U. Sottocorona A) Franz Hofer (A)
63	October	Kreuzspitze[1] – 3,455m North ridge (Ötztal – Tyrol- A)	Franz Senn (A)	Cyprian Granbichler
64	/	Tournelon Blanc – 3,702m South-west ridge (Valais – CH)	/	Joseph Gillioz (CH)
65	/	Pic Russell[1] – 3,206m (Pyrenees – F)	Henry Russell (F)	/

We started in delightful weather. Had Flinker and Blotter on my rope, but they, constan'ly in agony of suspense about Maud and Muriel, quite ignored me. So I tugged the rope as a gentle reminder

Being dreadful duffers, they couldn't stop themselves, and dragged me down too. But for my guide Otto, who is perfectly sweet, we might still be rolling

After this I gave them a lecture on love-making on glaciers, and left them, intending to complete my climbing, as I began, alone with my Otto

I thought I would break it to the others gen'., so asked them all to a quiet little dinner, and introduced Otto. They were rather upset

I intend to marry dear Otto. I have asked him this morning on the top of the biggest thing we've done.

And left hurriedly, much disturbed, because now that I have Otto there will be less for Maud and Muriel

THE HISTORY OF A MOUNTAIN SCRAMBLE, EXTRACTED FROM THE DIARY OF MRS. "GENERAL" PUTTIE

DRAWN BY REGINALD CLEAVER

An excerpt from the diary of Mrs "General" Puttie," published in The Graphic.

BIBLIOGRAPHY I

Arve, Stéphen d', *Histoire du Mont-Blanc et de la vallée de Chamonix* (Paris: Librairie Delagrave, 1878).

Beraldi, Henri, *Cent ans aux Pyrénées* (Pau: MonHélios, 2011).

Brockedon, William, *Journals of Excursion in the Alps* (London: James Duncan, 1833).

Casella, Georges, *L'alpinisme* (Geneva: Slatkine, 1980).

Chaubet, Daniel, *Histoire de la compagnie des guides de Chamonix* (Montmélian: Fontaine de Siloé, 1996).

Chevrillon, André, *Nouvelles études anglaises* (Paris: Hachette, 1910).

Clark, Ronald, *The Victorian Mountaineers* (London: B.T. Batsford, 1953).

Cook, E.T. and Alexander Wedderburn, eds., *The Works of John Ruskin*, vol. 13. (London: George Allen, 1905).

Coolidge, W.A.B., *The Alps in Nature and History* (London: Methuan, 1908).

— *Josias Simler et les origines de l'alpinisme* (Grenoble: Allier Frères, 1904).

Cunningham, C.D. and William de Wiveleslie Abney, *The Pioneers of the Alps* (Boston: Estes and Lauriat, 1888).

Devin, Georges. 'Ascensions de la Jungfrau, du Cervin et de la Barre des Écrins', *Annuaire du Club Alpin Français 1874* (Paris: Hachette, 1875).

Dumas, Alexandre, *Travels in Switzerland*, trans. R.W. Plummer and A. Craig Bell. (London: Peter Owen, 1958).

Durier, Charles, *Le Mont Blanc* (Montmélian: La Fontaine de Siloé, 2000).

Engel, Claire Éliane, *A History of Mountaineering in the Alps* (London: Allen & Unwin, 1950).

Forbes, James David, *Travels through the Alps*, foreword by W.A.B. Coolidge (London: Adam & Charles Black, 1900).

Frey, Pierre A. and Lise Grenier, eds. *Viollet-le-Duc et la montagne* (Grenoble: Glénat, 1993).

Frison-Roche, Roger and Sylvain Jouty, *A History of Mountain Climbing*, trans. Deke Dusinberre (New York: Flammarion, 1996).

Gaillard, Émile, *L'Aiguille de Bionnassay* (Chambéry: Dardel, 1929).

Gattlen, Anton and Giorgio and Lauria Aliprandi, *Das Matterhorn im Bild* (Visp: Rotten Verlag, 1979).

Gautier, Théophile, *Les vacances du lundi* (Seyssel: Champ Vallon, 1994).

Gos, Charles, *Alpinisme anecdotique* (Paris/Neuchatel: Victor Attinger, 1934).

—— *L'hôtel des Neuchâtelois* (Lausanne: Payot, 1928).

—— *Le Cervin*, vols 1 and 2 (Paris/Neuchatel: Victor Attinger, 1948).

—— *Propos d'un alpiniste* (Lausanne: Payot, 1922).

—— *Tragédies alpestres* (Lausanne: Payot, 1940).

Grellet, Pierre, *La Suisse des diligences* (Lausanne: Marguerat, 1947).

Helard, André, *John Ruskin et les Cathédrales de la terre* (Chamonix: Guérin, 2005).

Hudson, Charles, and E.S. Kennedy. *Where There's a Will, There's a Way: An Ascent of Mont Blanc* (2nd edn, London: Longman, Brown, Green & Longmans, 1856).

Irving, R.L.G., *The Romance of Mountaineering* (New York: Dutton, 1935).

Isselin, Henri, *La Barre des écrins* (Paris: Arthaud, 1954).

—— *Les Aiguilles de Chamonix* (Paris: Arthaud, 1961).

Javelle, Émile, *Souvenirs d'un alpiniste* (Paris: Payot, 1929).

Jouty, Sylvain and Hubert Odier, *Dictionnaire de la montagne* (Paris: Arthaud, 1999).

Jouty, Sylvain, *Les mots de la montagne* (Paris: Belin, 2006).

Keenlyside, Francis, Peaks and Pioneers: *The Story of Mountaineering* (London: Elek, 1975).

Kurz, Marcel, *Alpinisme hivernal* (Paris: Payot, 1925).

Maggetti, Daniel, ed., *Töpffer* (Geneva: Skira, 1996).

Modica, Gilles, *Alpinisme: La saga des inventions* (Les Houches: Les Editions du Mont-Blanc, 2013).

—— *Le roman des premières: Alpinistes français, 1871–1914* (Grenoble: Volopress, 2009).

—— *Les grandes premières du Mont-Blanc* (Chamonix: Guérin, 2011).

Moore, A.W., *The Alps in 1864* (Edinburgh: Douglas, 1902).

Payot, Jules, *Les Alpes éducatrices: mon Chamonix* (Chamonix: Payot, 1933).

Payot, Venance, *Herbier des Alpes* (Paris: Editions de l'Amateur, 2006).

Perret, Jacques, *Guide des livres sur la montagne et l'alpinisme*, 2 vols. (Grenoble: Belledonne, 1997).

—— *Regards sur les Alpes* (Les Houches: Les Editions du Mont-Blanc, 2011).

Ramond de Carbonnières, Louis, *Voyages au Mont-Perdu et dans la partie adjacente des Hautes-Pyrénées* (Geneva: Slatkine, 1978).

Rébuffat, Gaston, *Le Cervin, cime exemplaire* (Paris: Hachette, 1965).

Rey, Guido, *Le Mont Cervin* (Lausanne: Spes, 1922).

Russell, Henry, *Souvenirs d'un montagnard* (Pau: Vignancour, 1888).

Samivel and S. Norande, *Montagne paradis ou le rêve romantique* (Paris: Arthaud, 1988).

Saussure, Horace Bénédict de, *Premières ascensions au Mont-Blanc* (Paris: La Découverte, 1999).

Schrader, Franz, 'À quoi tient la beauté des montagnes?' *Annuaire du Club Alpin Français* (Paris: Club Alpin Français, 1898).

Segogne, Henry de and Jean Couzy, eds., *Alpinistes célèbres* (Paris: Lucien Mazenod, 1956).

Smythe, F.S., *Edward Whymper* (London: Hodder & Stoughton, 1940).

Stephen, Leslie, *The Playground of Europe* (1st edn, London: Longmans, Green & Co., 1871).

Taine, Hippolyte, *Notes on England*, trans. W.F. Rae (London: Strahan & Co., 1872).

Töpffer, Rodolphe, *Nouveaux voyages en zigzag* (Paris: Victor Lecou, 1854).

Tschudi, Friedrich von, *Sketches of Nature in the Alps* (London: Longman, Brown, Green, Longmans & Roberts, 1862).

Tyndall, John, *Hours of Exercise in the Alps* (New York: D. Appleton, 1873).

—— *The Glaciers of the Alps* (London: J.M. Dent, 1906).

Viollet-le-duc, Eugène, 'Hygiène du voyageur dans les contrées alpestres' *Annuaire du Club Alpin Français* (Paris: G. Chamerot, 1878).

Whymper, Edward, *Chamonix and the Range of Mont Blanc: A Guide* (London, John Murray, 1896).

—— *Scrambles Amongst the Alps in the Years 1860–69* (London: John Murray, 1871).

Wills, Alfred, *Wanderings among the High Alps* (London: Richard Bentley, 1856).

Zsigmondy, Emil, *Les dangers dans la montagne* (Paris: Fischbacher, 1886).

Zurcher, Frédéric and Elié Margollé, *Les ascensions célèbres* (Paris: Hachette, 1867).

—— *Les glaciers* (Paris: Hachette, 1868).

REVIEWS AND JOURNALS

Peaks, Passes and Glaciers (2 editions; early journal of the Alpine Club)

Alpine Journal

Annuaire du Club Alpin Français

Grande Encyclopédie de la Montagne

Colonel Clive Puttie, with his two dear girls, 3, and and Muriel, suggested a little mountain-climbing to brace us all up. Mr. Blinker (Bengal Army) and Mr. Blotter (Indian Civil), who also wanted bracing up, joined us. I noticed that they were better at once on seeing Maud and Muriel. However, with Clive very much in command, we arrive safely at our Mountains Hotel

The idea was that I should be tucked up and stowed away by the stove while the rest went climbing

So I decide on an expedition by myself. I engaged a lovely guide, and climbed hard all day

The next week I spent in procuring suitable climbing rig, and, feeling very smart, decided to astonish the young ones

I caught them napping, or just awakening, at Alpine Club Hut, and certainly astonished them

THE HISTORY OF A MOUNTAIN SCRAMBLE, EXTRACTED FROM THE DIARY OF MRS. "GENERAL" PUTTIE

DRAWN BY REGINALD CLEAVER

An excerpt 'from the diary of Mrs "General" Puttie,' published in The Graphic.

The original language or spelling has been retained in the titles, subtitles and texts of some of the works illustrated here in digital form.

INTRODUCTION
9: Alpine Club.

CHAPTER I: EARLY ASCENTS
16: Markus Pernhart (1824–1871), oil on canvas, 300 x 400, 1857, Landesmuseum, Carinthia – 18: DR – 19: Johann Martin Steiger (1829–1899), watercolour, 85 x 243 – 20: F.J. Hugi (1796–1855), *Naturhistorische Alpenreise*, 1830, Linda Hall Library – 21t: Unknown artist, oil painting, 530 x 400, Rhaetian Museum, Chur – 21b: Johann Ludwig Bleuler (1792–1850), watercolour, 1818, Rhaetian Museum, Chur – 22t: B. Hacquet (1739–1815), engraving, 1782, State Archives, Carinthia – 22b: Julius Beck (1825–19..), *19 phot. des montagnes des cantons de Berne du Valais, et du Tyrol*, 1891, BNF – 23t: Markus Pernhart (1824–1871), oil on canvas, 576 x 682, 1850, Neue Galerie Graz – 23b: DR – 24: Edward Whymper (1840–1911), portrait of Horace Benedict de Saussure, after the picture by St. Ours, wood engraving – 25: Eugène Rambert (1830-1886), *Les Alpes suisses*, 1866, Joël Cherbuliez publisher – 27: DR – 28: Josef Kriehuber (1800–1876), lithograph, 1848, Private collection – 29t: Nicolas Pérignon (1726–1782), *Tableaux topographiques, pittoresques, physiques, historiques, moraux, politiques, littéraires de la Suisse*, Viatimages/Bibliothèque Cantonale et Universitaire de Lausanne – 29b: Leopold Kupelwieser (1796–1862), oil on canvas, 1828, Neue Galerie Graz – 30: Mrs Aubrey Le Blond (1860–1934), *True Tales of Mountain Adventure, for Non-Climbers Young and Old*, 1903, New York – 31t: Ludwig von Welden (1780–1853) and Joseph Zumstein, *Le mont Rose: Une esquisse topographique et historique naturelle*, 1824, Viatimages/Bibliothèque Cantonale et Universitaire de Lausanne – 31b: DR – 32t: Unknown photographer, 1870 – 32b: John Ruskin (1819–1900), *Study of Jungfrau*, watercolour, 235 x 180, Ruskin Library, Lancaster – 33: Unknown photographer, *Über Eis und Schnee*, 1896 – 34: Unknown artist, *Terra Grischuna* – 35: Alpine Club.

CHAPTER II: JAMES D. FORBES AND ALBERT SMITH
38: James D. Forbes (1809–1868) and WAB Coolidge (1850–1926), *Travels trough the Alps*, London, Adam and Charles Black, 1900, 572 pp., 235 x 180 – 41: Mathias Gabriel (1784–1846), *Les pierres sur le glacier de l'Aar, Voyage pittoresque de l'Oberland Bernois*, 1822, Viatimages/Bibliothèque Nationale Suisse, Gugelmann (petits-maîtres suisses) – 42t&b, 46, 51: James-David Forbes (1809–1868), *Travels through the Alps of Savoy and other parts of the Pennine Chain*, lithograph, 200 x 140, 1843, Viatimages/Bibliothèque de Genève – 43t: John Watson Gordon (1788–1864), oil on canvas, 140 x 110, 1860/1861, The Royal Society of Edinburgh – 43b: DR – 44–45: J.J. MacGregor, *The Arrival at the Summit: The Ascent of Mont Blanc by Albert Smith*, colour lithograph, 1855 – 47t: engraving, *The Illustrated London News*, 1853, Look & Learn/Illustrated Papers Collection/Bridgeman Images – 47b: *The Illustrated London News*, 25 December 1852, engraving, Look & Learn/Peter Jackson Collection/Bridgeman Images – 48, 49: Albert Smith, Alpine Club.

CHAPTER III: THE WETTERHORN

54: Charles-Henri Contencin (1898–1955), oil on canvas, 500 x 610 – 56: engraving, London, 1882, Universal Images Group/Getty Images – 57: DR – 59: engraving, Swiss school, nineteenth century, Look & Learn/Bridgeman Images – 60t: William de Wiveleslie Abney (1843–1920), photoengraving, The British Library – 60b: William Henry Lartlett (1809–1854), *La Suisse pittoresque*, engraving, 175 x 120, 1836 – 61: C.D Cunningham and William de Wiveleslie Abney (1843–1920), *The Pioneers of the Alps*, 1888 – 62: Unknown artist, Henri Chapu Album -8- Folio 21, drawing on verso, Musée d'Orsay, Paris, currently in the Louvre/RMN-Grand Palais (Musée d'Orsay)/Thierry Ollivier.

CHAPTER IV: CHAMONIX GUIDES

66: Alpine Club – 68,69: DR – 70: Bisson frères, Savoie 44, *Ascension du mont Blanc*, albumen paper print, 394 x 230, 1863 – 71t, 72: All rights reserved – 71b: Alpine Club – 72–73: C.D. Cunningham and William de Wiveleslie Abney (1843–1920), *The Pioneers of the Alps*, 1888.

CHAPTER V: CHAMOIS HUNTERS

76: Grenier, France, nineteenth century, De Agostini Picture Library/G. Dagli Orti/Bridgeman Images – 78: E. Edwards, 1865, Alpine Club – 79: Ridiger, *Chamois sur les hauteurs*, burin engraving, 540 x 440, Paul Payot Collection/Conseil Général de la Haute-Savoie – 81: chromolithograph, English school, nineteenth century, Look & Learn/Bridgeman Images – 82: R. Taner, Suisse, eighteenth century, De Agostini Picture Library/G. Dagli Orti/Bridgeman Images – 84: Carl Haag (1820–1915), engraving, 1851, Exhibition of the Society of Painters in Water Colours, Liszt Collection/Bridgeman Images – 85t: Johann Baptist Zwecker (1814–1876), Look & Learn/Bridgeman Images – 85b: 1862, French school, nineteenth century, Liszt Collection/Bridgeman Images – 86: illustration taken from *La Suisse pittoresque et ses environs*, 1835, Viatimages/Bibliothèque Cantonale et Universitaire de Lausanne – 87: Louis-Albert-Ghislain Bacler d'Albe (1761–1824), *Souvenirs pittoresques du Général Bacler d'Albe*, lithograph, 1818, Viatimages/Bibliothèque Nationale Suisse – 88: colour engraving, German school, nineteenth century, Purix Verlag Volker Christen/Bridgeman Images.

CHAPTER VI: ONE GUIDE TO ANOTHER

92: Martin Barry (1802–1855), *Ascent to the Summit of Mont Blanc in 1834*, colour lithograph, 1836, Viatimages/Bibliothèque de Genève – 94: Jakob Samuel Weibel (1771–1846), *Joseph Couttet*, watercolour and gouache, 180 x 233, written in the centre of the lower margin: *Couttet Joseph guide âgé de 55 ans*, 1847, Paul Payot Collection / Conseil Général de la Haute-Savoie – 95: John Ruskin (1819–1900), Ruskin Library, Lancaster – 96: I.D.G. Glennie, *Mont Blanc and Glacier de Bionnassai from the Col de Voza*, lithograph, 230 x 320, Paul Payot Collection/Conseil Général de la Haute-Savoie – 97t: Charles Hudson (1828–1865) and E.S. Kennedy (1817–1898), *An Ascent of Mont Blanc by a New Route and without Guides*, 248 x 294, London, 1856 – 97b: John MacGregor (1825–1892), The Summit of Mont Blanc, intaglio engraving, aquatint, colour, watercolour highlights, gum arabic, 1853, Musée Alpin, Chamonix – 98: Edward Whymper (1840–1911), *A Brief History of British Mountaineering*, Colin Wells, 2001 – 99: facsimile, *Narrative of an Ascent to the Summit of Mont Blanc on the 8th and 9th August*, 1827, published in 1828, Viatimages/Bibliothèque de Genève – 100: DR – 101: Auguste-Xavier Leprince (1799–1826), *Vue de Susten (Canton d'Uri) en Suisse*,

1824, Musée du Louvre, Paris, RMN-Grand Palais (Musée du Louvre)/Hervé Lewandowski – 102: W. Pitschner, *Crevasses*, 1860, Paul Payot Collection/Conseil Général de la Haute-Savoie – 103: William Beverley, *Au Sommet du Mont Blanc*, taken from *The Story of Mont Blanc*, Albert Smith, London, 1853, Amis du Vieux Chamonix.

CHAPTER VII: CHARLES HUDSON
106: DR –108: *Voyages dans les Alpes*, 1779–1796, engraving, 170 x 210, Viatimages/Bibliothèque de Genève – 109: *Der Monte-Rosa*, engraving, folding sheet, 1824, Viatimages/Bibliothèque Cantonale et Universitaire de Lausanne – 110, 111: T.D.H. Browne, *Ten Scenes in the Last Ascent of Mont Blanc*, colour lithographs, 1853, Paul Payot Collection/Conseil Général de la Haute-Savoie – 113: Gabriel Loppé (1825–1913), artist; Champod, lithographer; Joseph Perrin, publisher in Chambéry, *Traversée du glacier sous les Grands Mulets: Chemin de Chamonix au Mont-Blanc*, black and white lithograph, 295 x 208, 1855, Musée Alpin, Chamonix – 115: engraving, English school, 1891, Liszt Collection/Bridgeman Images – 117: Edmund Thomas Coleman (1824–1892), *Scenes from the Snow-Fields*, colour lithograph, 225 x 355, 1859, Paul Payot Collection/Conseil général de la Haute-Savoie – 118: Jean-Antoine Linck (1766–1843), *L'aiguille verte, le Dru et le glacier des Bois au clair de lune*, drawings in black chalk, stump, white chalk and watercolour highlights on brown paper, 267 x 330, signed lower right in black ink, Paul Payot Collection/Conseil Général de la Haute-Savoie.

CHAPTER VIII: THE ALPINE CLUB
122, 124: Alpine Club – 126: Henry Atkins, *Halte sur le Sommet du Mont-Blanc*, lithograph, 1837 – 127t: Mairie de Loucrup – 128b: Domenico Morelli, *Ritratto di Quintino Sella* (1827–1884), Museo Nazionale del Risorgimento Italiano di Torino – 129t: Leicester Literary and Philosophical Society – 130: Louis-Oscar Roty (1846–1911), sculpture, single-sided plaque, bronze, RMN-Grand Palais (Musée d'Orsay)/Stéphane Maréchalle – 131: John Ball, Natural History Museum, London/Bridgeman Images – 132t&b: Alpine Club – 133: Lyskamm, 1870, Émile Gos Collection, Médiathèque Valais–Martigny.

CHAPTER IX: JOHN BALL AND JOHN RUSKIN
136: John Ruskin (1819–1900), *Modern Painters*, vol. IV, Chapter 13, 1856 – 138: Alpine Club – 139: Ben Lomond, 1874, engraving, Hulton Archive/Getty Images – 141: John Everett Millais (1829–1896), oil on canvas, 1853–1854, Ashmolean Museum, Oxford – 142: DR – 143: John Ruskin (1819–1900), lithograph from *The Works of John Ruskin*, 181 x 104, London, 1903–1912, Viatimages/Bibliothèque de Genève – 144: John Ruskin (1819–1900), *Étude des Aiguilles de Chamonix*, Ruskin Library, Lancaster – 146: Osterreichischer Alpenverein.

CHAPTER X: JOHANN JOSEF BENNEN
150, 155b: Edward Whymper, *Scrambles Amongst the Alps in the Years 1860–69*, engravings published in 1871 – 152: Paul Payot Collection/Conseil Général de la Haute-Savoie – 153: Professor John Tyndall, English photographer, nineteenth century, Look & Learn/Rosenberg Collection/Bridgeman Images – 154, 155t, 156: DR – 157: *Berg – und Gletscherfahrten in den Alpen in den Jahren 1860 bis 1869*, engraving, 100 x 75, 1872, Viatimages/Médiathèque Valais–Martigny – 158: Louis-Joseph Mingret, called José (1880–1969), Le Cervin, oil on wood, first half of 20th century, Musée Alpin, Chamonix.

CHAPTER XI: CONQUERING THE WEISSHORN

162: Eduard Spelterini (1852–1931) – 164: English Photographer, 19th century, black and white photograph, Private Collection/Bridgeman Images – 165t: Edward Theodore Compton (1849–1921), *Weisshorn–Nordgrat vom Bieshorn*, drawing, 1908 – 165b: John Tyndall (1820–1893), The Royal Institution, London/Bridgeman Images – 166: Alpine Club – 167: John Singer Sargent (1856–1925), *Splendid Mountain Watercolours*, drawing, wax crayon on off-white vellum paper, 406 x 276, 1870, Mrs Francis Ormond Collection/The Metropolitan Museum of Art – 168: Edward Theodore Compton (1849–1921), *The Weisshorn seen from the Furgg Glacier above Zermatt*, oil on canvas, signed, 650 x 1003, 1891.

CHAPTER XII: THE RACE TO THE MATTERHORN

172: John Ruskin (1819–1900), *An Alpine Valley: The Matterhorn in the Distance*, Birmingham Museums and Art Gallery, Bridgeman Art Library – 174, 175t&b, 176, 177, 178, 179, 181, 182: Edward Whymper, *Scrambles Amongst the Alps in the Years 1860–69*, engravings published in 1871.

CHAPTER XIII: JOHN TYNDALL

186: Florence E. Haig, *Portrait of John Tyndall* (1820–93), pastel on paper, nineteenth century, The Royal Institution, London / Bridgeman Images – 188: Edward Whymper, *Scrambles Amongst the Alps in the Years 1860–69, Portrait of the Author*, engraving published in 1871 – 189: Portrait of John Tyndall, English school, nineteenth century, charcoal with white highlights on paper, The Royal Institution, London/Bridgeman Images – 190: Anthony Adams-Reilly (1836–1885), *The Chain of Mont Blanc*, published under the Authority of the Alpine Club, London, 410 x 735, 1864, Alpine Club – 192: Alpine Club – 193t: The Royal Society, illustration for *The Graphic*, 20 July 1889, English school, 19th century, Look & Learn/Illustrated Papers Collection/Bridgeman Images – 193b: *Professor Tyndall Lecturing at the Royal Institution*, engraving, 1870, English school, nineteenth century, Look & Learn/Peter Jackson Collection/Bridgeman Images – 195: Jean-Antoine Linck (1766–1843), watercolour on paper, 332 x 450, c. 1799, signed lower right: *fait par Jn. Ante. Linck* – 196: *Professor John Tyndall*, English school, nineteenth century, Look & Learn/Bridgeman Images – 197: The Royal Institution.

CHAPTER XIV: NUTRITION AND HEALTH

200, 202: DR – 205: Unknown photographer, Private collection – 206, 207: All rights reserved – 208: Eugène Fieffe, 1858, Universal History Archive/UIG/Bridgeman Images – 209 : *The Ascent of Mont Peter Botte on Mauritius,* engraving published in *Le Magasin Pittoresque, 1833* – 211: Eugène Viollet-le-Duc (1814–1879), *Le massif du Mont Blanc*, 1160 x 1920, 1876 – 212: engraving, English school, nineteenth century, Look & Learn/Illustrated Papers Collection/Bridgeman Images – 213: engraving, *Connais-toi toi-même*, Camille Gilbert, 1879, Jonas/Kharbine-Tapabor – 214: advert, 1938, Kharbine-Tapabor – 215t&b: DR – 216: *Two Mountaineers*, 1910, Science & Society Picture Library/Getty Images – 218, 219: DR – 220: Johann Jakob Scheuchzer (1672–1733), *Ouresiphoites Helveticus, sive itinera per Helvetiae alpinas regiones*, engraving, 129 x 171, Viatimages/Bibliothèque Cantonale et Universitaire de Lausanne.

CHAPTER XV: EARLY EQUIPMENT AND TECHNIQUES

224: Édouard Pingret (1788–1875), nineteenth century – 226: Josef Kriehuber (1800–1876), *Herrenjäger mit Alpenstock*, watercolour, 175 x 127, Albertina, Vienna – 227: Mountaineer's outfit, Oberbayern, Germany, engraving, nineteenth century – 228t&b, 233t&b, 240, 250t&b: Edward Whymper, *Scrambles Amongst the Alps in the Years 1860–69*, engravings published in 1871 – 229: Marquardt Wocher, *Voyage de Mr de Saussure à la cime du Mont Blanc au mois d'août MDCCVXXXVII* – plate II (detail), Paul Payot Collection/Conseil Général de la Haute-Savoie – 231: C.D. Cunningham, *The Pioneers of the Alps*, 1888 – 232: Alpine Club – 234, 235: black and white glass-plate negative, Émile Gos Collection, Médiathèque Valais–Martigny – 236: Jean-Philippe Linck (1770–1812), *Passage d'une crevasse au glacier des Bossons en descendant des Grands Mullet pour arriver au-dessous du glacier des Pélerins*, watercolour, 446 x 349, handwritten in black ink, upper right: *dessiné le 20 août 1811 en attendant que l'on eût trouvé le passage*, Paul Payot Collection/Conseil Général de la Haute-Savoie – 238: photograph, 1890, Avant-Demain/Kharbine- Tapabor – 239: *Mountaineering Outfit*, engraving, English school, twentieth century, Look & Learn/Bridgeman Images – 241: *A Slip towards the Edge: A Close Call for a Member of the Alpine Club in Switzerland*, illustration, London, 1882, Universal Images Group/Getty Images – 242: Alphonse de Neuville (1835–1885), after an illustration taken from *Le Tour du Monde*, 1872, Kharbine-Tapabor – 243: Club Alpin Français, Grenoble – 245: Unknown photographer, RMN-Grand Palais (Musée d'Orsay) – 246: All rights reserved – 247: John Auldjo, *Sliding Down a Snow Hill*, lithograph, 121 x 164, Paul Payot Collection/ Conseil Général de la Haute-Savoie – 251: advertisement for S.W. Norman Alpine Climbing Boots, English school, nineteenth century, 1911, Private Collection/Bridgeman Images.

CHAPTER XVI: LESLIE STEPHEN
254: George Frederic Watts (1817–1904), *Sir Leslie Stephen*, oil on canvas, 1878, National Portrait Gallery, London/Stefano Baldini/Bridgeman Images – 256: Collection Musée Alpin, Chamonix – 257: Alpine Club – 258: George Charles Beresford (1864–1938), *Portrait of Virginia Woolf*, 1902 – 259: Hills & Saunders, photograph, Club Alpin Français, Grenoble – 260: Julia Margaret Cameron, Bibliothèque Nationale de Paris – 261: All rights reserved – 262: Albert Bierstadt (1830–1902), *The Matterhorn*, oil on paper mounted on cardboard.

CHAPTER XVII: FRANCIS FOX TUCKETT
266: Unknown artist, *Mountaineers*, colour engraving, Private Collection/Bridgeman Images – 268: All rights reserved – 269: All rights reserved – 270: Aimé Civiale (1821–1893), *Les Alpes: au point de vue de la géographie physique et de la géologie*, 1882, Viatimages/Bibliothèque de Genève – 271: Unknown photographer, postcard, IM / Kharbine-Tapabor – 272: Émile Gos Collection/Médiathèque Valais–Martigny – 274: Unknown artist, 1868, Frenchay Museum Archives – 275: Edward Whymper, *Scrambles Amongst the Alps in the Years 1860–69*, engraving published in 1871 – 276t: Unknown photographer, *Popular Science Monthly*, vol. 75, 1909 – 276b: Edward Theodore Compton (1849–1921).

CHAPTER XVIII: A.W. MOORE
280: Adolphe Braun (1812–1877), *View of Zermatt and Mount Cervin, c. 1863–1865*, albumen print from a glass negative (b&w photo), Musée Condé, Chantilly, France/Bridgeman Images – 282, 283: Alpine Club – 284, 285: Edward Whymper, *The Valley of Zermatt and the Matterhorn*, 1897 – 290t: Luchsinger, Rose-Claire Schule Collection/Médiathèque Valais–Martigny – 289: Léonie Schlosser – 290b: DR – 291, 293: C.D. Cunningham and William de Wiveleslie Abney (1843–1920), *The Pioneers of the Alps*, 1888 – 294: Mrs Aubrey Le Blond, *True Tales of Mountain Adventure, for Non-Climbers Young and Old*, 1903, New York – 295: Émile Gos Collection/ Médiathèque Valais–Martigny.

CHAPTER XIX: THE YEAR 1865

298: *The Summit of the Aiguille Verte*, colour lithograph, English school, nineteenth century, Look & Learn/Bridgeman Images – 301, 305, 306: Edward Whymper, *The Valley of Zermatt and the Matterhorn*, 1897 – 302: Johann Martin Steiger (1829–1899), *The Dent Blanche and the Grand Cornier*, watercolour on paper, 102 x 175 – 308: Edward Whymper, Alpine Club – 310: C.D. Cunningham and William de Wiveleslie Abney (1843–1920), *The Pioneers of the Alps*, 1888 – 311: Jean-Antoine Linck (1766–1843), semi-panorama, pencil lithograph, Gugelmann Collection/Swiss National Library.

CHAPTER XX: EDWARD WHYMPER

314, 324, 325: Alpine Club – 317: Léonie Schlosser – 318: Edward Theodore Compton (1849–1921), Alpine Club – 320: All rights reserved – 322: Maison Hospitalière du Grand-Saint-Bernard/Médiathèque Valais–Martigny.

CHAPTER XXI: THE MATTERHORN, WHYMPER'S WHITE TROUSERS

328, 336: Émile Gos Collection/Médiathèque Valais–Martigny – 331: Edward Whymper, *The Valley of Zermatt and the Matterhorn*, 1897 – 333: Gustave Doré (1832–1883), historic depiction of the first ascent of the Matterhorn, 1865 – 334: Archives Barmasse – 335: Mrs Aubrey Le Blond (1860–1934), *True Tales of Mountain Adventure, for Non-Climbers Young and Old*, 1903, New York.

CHAPTER XXII: THE MATTERHORN, TAUGWALDER'S ROPE

340: Carlos Simonetta Collection, Fonds Médiathèque Valais–Martigny – 343: Gustave Doré (1832–1883), *Catastrophe au Mont Cervin; la chute*, gouache and pen and ink, c.1865, Musée d'Orsay, Paris, now in the Louvre – 344, 345: Edward Whymper, *The Valley of Zermatt and the Matterhorn*, 1897 – 346t&b: Émile Gos Collection/Médiathèque Valais–Martigny – 348: Musée de Zermatt.

CHAPTER XXIII: THE BRENVA SPUR

352: All rights reserved – 354t: James-David Forbes (1809–1868), *Travels through the Alps of Savoy and other parts of the Pennine Chain*, colour lithograph, 120 x 90, 1843, Viatimages/Bibliothèque de Genève – 354b: François Jalabert (1740–1798), *Voyages dans les Alpes*, 1779–1796, engraving, folding sheet, 340 x 220, Viatimages/Bibliothèque de Genève – 355: Mrs Aubrey Le Blond (1860–1934), *True Tales of Mountain Adventure, for Non-Climbers Young and Old*, 1903, New York – 357: Alpine Club – 358: Dominique Potard – 360: All rights reserved.

APPENDICES

364: F. and G. Charnaux, *Sommet du mont Blanc*, albumin paper print, 170 x 240, 1886 – 366: Edward Whymper, *The Valley of Zermatt and the Matterhorn*, 1897 – 370: *Mount Cervin*, c.1900 (b&w photo), French photographer, twentieth century, Bibliothèque des Arts Décoratifs, Paris/Archives Charmet/Bridgeman Images – 374: John Ruskin (1819–1900), *The Matterhorn*, from *Modern Painters*, vol. IV, pencil and watercolour on paper, 242 x 337 – 380, 384: Reginald Thomas Cleaver (1870–1954), *The History of a Mountain Scramble*, excerpted from *The Diary of Mrs 'General' Puttie*, colour lithograph, Look & Learn/Illustrated Papers Collection/Bridgeman Images.

THE AUTHOR |

Gilles Modica is an independent journalist who specialises in the history of mountaineering and exploration. He has written six books on the subject as well as numerous articles for *Montagnes* magazine and *Trek* magazine. He was a top-level climber for fifteen years (1975–1990), notably completing six routes on the north face of the Grandes Jorasses (including the second ascent of the MacIntyre-Colton line in 1980), making solo climbs in the Alps and Peru, scaling the big walls of Yosemite, and racking up several first ascents (including the Ginat route on the Droites, and the Modica-Noury gully on Mont Blanc du Tacul). He is a member of France's elite Groupe de Haute Montagne (G.H.M.).

ACKNOWLEDGEMENTS |

Heartfelt thanks go to all individuals and institutions who have helped to produce this book, most especially:
Claude Gardien, editor in chief of *Vertical* magazine; Françoise Redon, Brigitte Saint-Maurice, Claude Marin, Claire Burnet, and Jacques Ulrich (library, Club Alpin Français, Isère).

We are also grateful to the Centre de Documentation de l'École Nationale de Ski et d'Alpinisme de Chamonix, Elsa Claret-Tournier, Martine Colonel and François Viroulet; to the Musée Alpin in Chamonix, especially curatorial assistant Stéphanie Mazuer; and to Susan Hare and Peter Rowland from the Alpine Club's photo collection; and to the collections department of the Conseil Général de la Haute-Savoie for engravings from the Paul Payot Collection; to the cultural department of the city of Chamonix; to Daniela Vaj, scholarly coordinator of the ViaticAlpes project and head of the Viatimages database, as well as to all partner libraries in Switzerland; to the photo department of the Réunion des Musées Nationaux in Paris; to the Bibliothèque Nationale de France; to picture archive agencies Bridgeman Images, Kharbine-Tapabor and Getty Images.

Thanks finally to Jon Barton and John Coefield from Vertebrate Publishing.

VIATIMAGES is an online database developed in collaboration with several Swiss historical libraries. It contains over 3,000 images and offers outstanding documentation on travel – or 'viatic' – imagery related to the Alps, that is to say illustrations of Alpine voyages published from the sixteenth to the early twentieth centuries. The database not only establishes links between these illustrations, but also relates them to descriptive texts, which are made available in screen-readable form. It also provides short biographies of writers, travellers, illustrators, and so on, as well as links to bibliographic entries and digitised books available online. Research can be carried out by field, period, key work, publication author, or illustrator, or by an interactive map of geographical features (mountains, rivers, towns, etc.). VIATIMAGES is not aimed solely at specialists, but also at members of the general public interested in discovering this cultural heritage. The database was compiled at the University of Lausanne in the context of the VIATICALPES project, which explores the history of the travellers' representations of Alpine regions, landscapes, and cultures. The VIATICALPES team has produced various multimedia tools now available on the internet, notably animated video narratives that bring travel images to life. These videos transform the static world of historic pictures into lively stories that are entertaining as well as educational and artistic. The project is currently developing virtual exhibitions and applications for tablets and smartphones. VIATICALPES also contributes to numerous books and publications, thereby seeking to promote interconnections between printed books, the internet, and multimedia.

Claude Reichler and Daniela Vaj

Participating libraries: Bibliothèque Cantonale et Universitaire, Lausanne – Bibliothèque de Genève, Geneva – Bibliothèque Publique et Universitaire, Neuchâtel – Bibliothèque Nationale Suisse, Bern – Burgerbibliothek, Bern – Médiathèque Valais, Sion.
VIATIMAGES : www.unil.ch/viatimages and VIATICALPES : www.unil.ch/viaticalpes

Left: Samuel Birmann, 'A View from Le Jardin', published in *Souvenirs de la vallée de Chamonix* (Basel, 1826). Viatimages/Bibliothèque Nationale Suisse.

ÉDITIONS GUÉRIN
IN THE SAME COLLECTION

www.editionspaulsen.com

150 ans 1865
& l'âge d'or
de l'alpinisme
CHAMONIX MONT-BLANC

THIS BOOK WAS PUBLISHED AS PART OF THE CELEBRATIONS ORGANISED
BY THE CHAMONIX MONT-BLANC VALLEY TO COMMEMORATE THE
150TH ANNIVERSARY OF THE GOLDEN AGE OF MOUNTAINEERING

French Editor – Layout: Stéphanie Thizy
English Editor : John Coefield
Cartographer: Léonie Schlosser – Translator: Deke Dusinberre
Editorial assistant: Katie Burnet

Printed and bound in Italy by
Ermes Graphics, Turin.

Legal deposit : May 2016 – All rights reserved.
ISBN : 978-1-910240-52-6